TIMBER BUILDING TECHNIQUES IN LONDON *c*.900-1400:

AN ARCHAEOLOGICAL STUDY OF WATERFRONT INSTALLATIONS AND RELATED MATERIAL

TIMBER BUILDING TECHNIQUES IN LONDON *c.*900-1400

AN ARCHAEOLOGICAL STUDY OF WATERFRONT INSTALLATIONS AND RELATED MATERIAL

by Gustav Milne
with contributions from Trevor Brigham, Damian Goodburn, and Chrissie Milne, and also from Morag Colquhoun, Jennifer Hillam, Nigel Nayling, Jo Stevenson and Ian Tyers: illustrations by Tracy Wellman

London & Middlesex Archaeological Society
Special Paper 15

Published by the London & Middlesex
Archaeological Society

First published 1992

Series editor: Francis Grew

Typeset by Chrissie Milne
Printed by BAS Printers Limited,
Over Wallop, Hampshire

Design and production: Melissa Denny of
Diptych

The cover photograph shows an earthfast
timber waterfront structure (TX4) on the early
13th-century foreshore. Thames Exchange
excavations 1988, Upper Thames Street,
London.

ISBN 0 903290 41 3

**The Society is grateful to English
Heritage for a grant towards the
publication of this Special Paper**

CONTENTS

ABSTRACT

The embanking of the River Thames in the late Saxon period and the subsequent extensions of the bank throughout the medieval period incorporated a sequence of timber revetments, of which 25 closely-dated examples are described in this report. They range in date from the 10th to the 14th century and were selected from the sequences excavated on four sites, Billingsgate Lorry Park (1982-3), Seal House (1974), Trig Lane (1974-86) and Thames Exchange (1988-9). A late 17th-century revetment from the City of London Boys' School site (1986-7) is also considered. This study examines the structures primarily as examples of medieval timber building practice, rather than as waterfront installations. Although all the revetments were designed to achieve the same end, there were significant differences between the techniques used to construct the early examples and those employed in the later ones. It is argued here that those differences reflect wide-ranging changes in vernacular timber-building practice in general, most notably the transition from earthfast to timber-framed building. Some of the implications of these developments are considered with reference to further examples of well-preserved waterfront carpentry from London. This part of the report had its genesis in a thesis prepared by Gustav Milne for Birkbeck College, University of London in 1985.

In Chapter 5, those conclusions are compared with the study of a range of timbers derived from medieval buildings which once stood in the City. This important assemblage was recovered from the Billingsgate Lorry Park site, where the house timbers were reused in waterfront structures. Once again, the focus is on the development of timber-framed buildings in the medieval period, but this time through the examination of surviving baseplates and in particular the changing form of mortises. This assessment is based upon a dissertation written by Trevor Brigham in 1984 for University College, London.

In Chapter 6, Damian Goodburn presents another approach to the study of changes in medieval timber-building, this time through consideration of the changes in timber-working practice, tools and woodland management. This is related to the changing medieval woodscape. The evidence was derived from examination of a selection of timbers recently excavated from London waterfront sites.

In conclusion, Chapter 7 brings together the evidence presented in the previous chapters. An assessment is then made of the building traditions and types of timber buildings which, it is now suggested, would have been present in medieval London.

PREFACE

For the archaeology of the City of London, 1973 was a crucial year. It saw the publication of that most important survey of the capital's archaeological needs *The Future of London's Past* and witnessed the formation of the professional archaeological unit in the City which had been so powerfully advocated in the report. The progressive closure of the enclosed docks to the east of the City had begun, as the Port of London Authority concentrated its activities at Tilbury, 25 miles downstream of the original focus of the port, the Pool of London. As a consequence, the obsolete warehouses which once accommodated cargoes brought into the port were being demolished: major redevelopment schemes from Blackfriars to the Tower were transforming the London waterfront on both banks. A unique archaeological opportunity therefore presented itself, in which a sequence of remarkably well-preserved Roman, Saxon and medieval harbour sites would be subject to redevelopment in the space of just two decades. Martin Biddle had stressed that the history of the waterfront was critical for all periods of London's history (Biddle *et al* 1973, 4.14) and that 'the archaeology of the waterfront presents remarkable opportunities as well as the requisite of large-scale excavation, its associated research and publication' (Biddle *et al* 1973, 4.43). Guided by these insights and inspired by the work on the Baynard's Castle and Custom House sites (Tatton-Brown 1974; 1975), the newly-formed Department of Urban Archaeology considered waterfront archaeology a priority. As a consequence eight major medieval sites were excavated on the north bank between 1973 and 1990, while ground works on a similar number of developments were monitored (Fig 1). From this it is now known that most of the land between Thames Street and the Thames was reclaimed from the river in a piecemeal fashion from the 10th to the 15th centuries. Fragments of a hundred structures erected during this process have been recorded, together with the remains of medieval buildings and other features.

This work prompted studies on waterfront topography and development (Milne & Milne 1979; Milne 1981), on waterfront buildings (Schofield 1981; Milne & Milne 1981), on waterfront installations (Milne 1979; Milne & Milne 1982; Steedman *et al* forthcoming), on boats (Marsden 1979; Goodburn 1988; Milne & Goodburn 1990) and on the extensive documentary sources related to the riverside area (Dyson 1981; 1987; 1989). Thus considerable advances have been made in our understanding of a wide range of themes. In particular, the broad outline of the chronology of waterfront development is now clear, and a firm dating framework which integrates dendrochronology and artefact studies has been compiled, although research in these areas is continuing.

The results of the first 15 years work have also laid substantial foundations to support a new generation of studies. The waterfront has produced large assemblages of well preserved artefacts, discarded in the refuse thrown behind the riverfront revetments or lost on the foreshore. Studies of this material have begun in which artefacts are considered not in relation to harbourside developments, with which their association is often incidental, but in their own right, relying on the waterfront solely for provenance and preservation. Externally-dated groups of pottery, shoes, knives, and dress fittings have been assessed with profit in this way (Cowgill *et al* 1987; Egan & Pritchard 1991; Grew & de Neergaard 1988; Vince 1985), while an assemblage of reused house timbers recovered from the waterfront is examined in Chapter 5 in this report. But first a selection of the better-preserved timber waterfront structures is examined, not primarily as specimens of harbourside engineering but as a series of structures which encapsulates wide-ranging changes in construction and timber-working techniques. It is hoped that, as a result, light will be thrown on the timber-building traditions of medieval London, on the contemporary woodlands (Rackham 1980), and on the carpenters, tools and techniques used (Munby 1988).

1: INTRODUCTION

Gustav Milne

Medieval timber buildings in London

The student of medieval vernacular timber buildings in London has little direct evidence to draw upon, since so few examples have survived the ravages of fire, the Blitz and urban renewal. Nevertheless, some fragments of the medieval carpenter's craft may still be seen in London, a considerable body of illustrative and documentary material survives, and archaeologists have excavated the desiccated foundations of a series of 9th- to 15th-century structures.

However, a fourth class of evidence has recently been uncovered, the use of which represents potentially the most profitable way in which the major changes in London's timber building traditions may still be studied in detail. This is the ever-increasing corpus of well-preserved riverfront structures excavated on a series of Thames-side sites since 1972. It is suggested that examination of those waterfront revetments, not as harbour installations but as well-dated examples of timber-working practice, reveals much of wider interest. For example, the dates for the introduction into English medieval carpentry of such crucial features as the mortise and tenon joint or of a particular type of saw can be established. In addition, the more gradual development of timber-framed structures incorporating squared posts and baseplates can be traced through earlier traditions using stave work or earthfast building techniques in which timber was used in the round.

But before discussing that material, the three other classes of evidence need to be briefly considered. First, the surviving examples of London's medieval carpentry which have been described by Cecil Hewett include the late 13th-century samson post floor at St Etheldreda's, Ely Place (Hewett 1980, 123-4), a late 14th-century crown-post roof on base-crucks at Barnard's Inn, High Holborn (Hewett 1980, 182; fig 166), scissor-braced transverse roof frames in the Old Hall, Lincoln's Inn (Hewett 1980, 212; fig 190), a 14th-century roof in the first floor hall known as the Guard Room (Hewett 1980, 155; fig 140) and a mid 15th-century floor in Chichell's Tower (Hewett 1980, 195; fig 297), both at Lambeth Palace; and Hugh Herland's masterpiece, the late 14th-century hammer beam roof at Westminster Hall (Hewett 1980, 188; pl VI,VII). None of these items can be dated before 1250, none could be said to be examples of domestic vernacular architecture (Brunskill 1971, 20), and none lie within the City walls, although City carpenters presumably worked on most of the projects.

Secondly, there are the excavated buildings. In contrast with Dublin (Murray 1983) or York (Hall 1982) well-preserved timber buildings rarely survive on London sites: the notable exceptions are confined to a narrow riverside area where a number of pre-Conquest structures were recently recorded on the Thames Exchange, Vintry and Bull Wharf sites. Nevertheless, the decayed traces of walls with timber elements have been recorded on several late Saxon sites (*eg* Grimes 1968; Horsman *et al* 1988) and dwarf stone walls of later medieval date are known (*eg* Milne & Milne 1981). These buildings seem to represent a variety of forms and functions, ranging from sub-surface storage buildings, to outhouses and domestic dwellings. Despite this, any attempt at reconstructing the superstructure of these fragmentary remains would obviously benefit from an assessment of the contemporary building practices gained from other sources. While not decrying the importance of recovering fragmentary building plans, it is clear that a wider study of major changes in timber building practices requires a better degree of preservation than is normally the case on medieval occupation sites in London beyond the waterfront. The systematic recording of seemingly isolated building timbers, discarded or reused on waterlogged sites is of importance in this regard, as the study in Chapter 5 shows.

Thirdly, there is illustrative and documentary material. Panoramic views of the pre-Fire City survive, together with 18th- and 19th-century sketches, engravings and watercolours of medieval

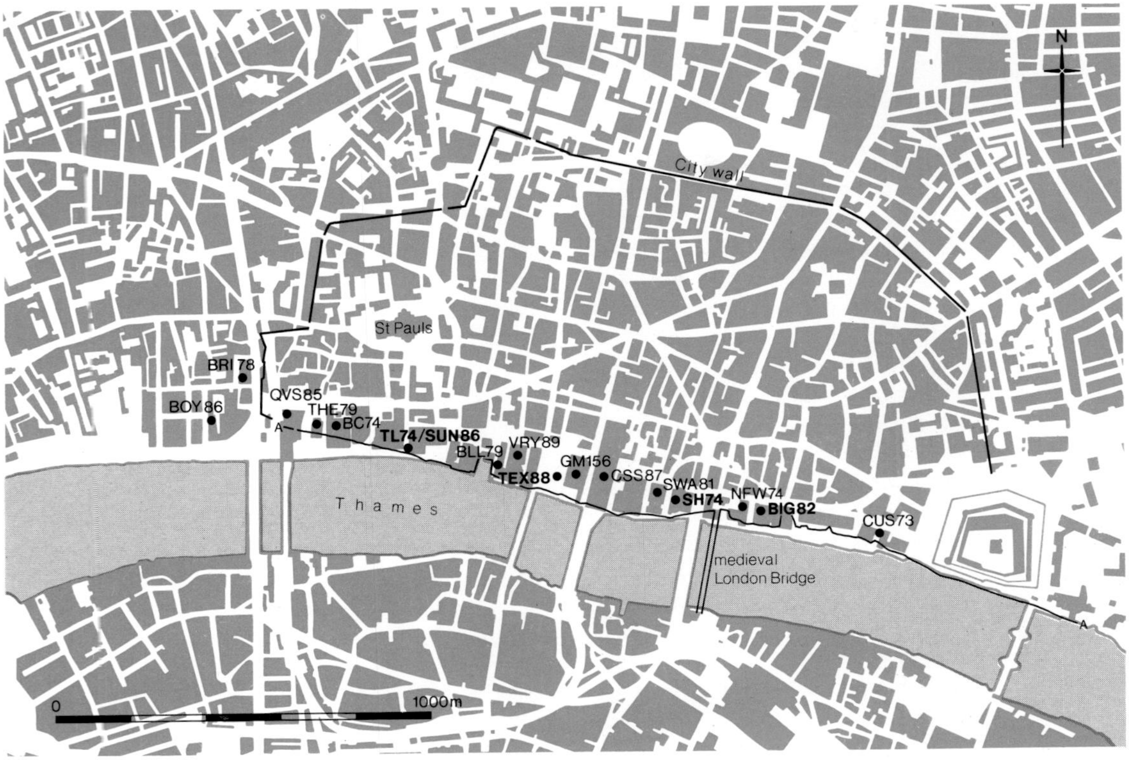

1. Plan of present-day City of London with the line of the medieval wall superimposed upon it, showing the location of main medieval waterfront sites (cf. Fig 2): City of London Boys' School BOY86; *Bridewell* BRI78; *Queen Victoria Street* QVS85; *Mermaid Theatre* THE79; *Baynard's Castle* BC72; *Trig Lane* TL74/ *Sunlight Wharf* SUN86; *Bull Wharf* BLL79; *Vintry* VRY89; *Thames Exchange* TEX88; *Dowgate* GM156; *Cannon Street Station* CSS87; *Swan Lane* SWA81; *Seal House* SH74; *New Fresh Wharf/ St Magnus* NFW74; *Billingsgate Lorry Park* BIG82; *Old Custom House* CUS73. *Alignment of waterfront surveyed in 17th century shown by line marked* A-A. *Scale: 1:20,000.*

buildings, often prepared on the eve of demolition. House plans drawn up in the late 16th and early 17th centuries provide another important source of evidence. The value and problems of studying such material together with the considerable body of documentary evidence for building practice has recently been assessed (Schofield 1984; 1987; 1991). Among the most valuable documents on the subject are the contracts for over sixty buildings erected between 1308 and 1493 in and around the City (Salzman 1952, Appendix B, nos 3, 4, 15B, 16, 21-2, 24, 38, 41-2, 51-2). They include work on shops, houses, halls, wharves, mills, bake- and brew-houses and stable blocks, often giving the cost, time needed for construction, dimensions of the buildings, the number of stories, and occasionally even the scantling of the timbers. They also demonstrate that some carpenters were literate and numerate, while others worked from drawings prepared on parchment (Salzman 1952, 483). It is not known how many carpenters lived in London, but at least 30 are known by name in the 14th century from the surviving documentary sources (Harvey 1987). Out of 107 persons working in the building trades in York in 1381, a total of 52 were engaged in wood-working (Harvey 1975, 152), and a larger figure for London would not be unreasonable. The City carpenters were certainly numerous enough to form a 'Brotherhood of Carpenters' by 1333 (Welch 1912; Alford & Baker 1968). Nevertheless, while much useful information may be ascertained from the 14th century onwards, there is little documentary data and no illustrative material to illuminate the earlier medieval period.

A sequence of vernacular timber structures

Taken together, the evidence reviewed above provides too unrepresentative a data bank, in terms of date and character, for an intensive study of the sort proposed. If the history of the development of London's timber buildings is to be understood, what is clearly required is the discovery of a series of vernacular structures dating from the Saxon period through to the late 17th century. In order that the characteristic technical attributes of each generation should be readily identifiable, each one must have had a relatively short life, so that major repairs and modifications of a later era cannot have been effected, obscuring essential detail. Each structure should be of the same class and the same type, designed to serve the same function, so that like may be compared with like, century for century. Finally, each structure must be demonstrably functional and 'vernacular', *ie* representative of common practice (cf. Brunskill 1971, 20-9).

Although archaeologists in London have not as yet recovered such a sequence of domestic structures, just such a series of riverfront installations has been recorded during the excavation of sites along the London waterfront from 1972 (Fig 2). These revetments feature most of the attributes listed above, and many can be closely dated by consideration of their stratigraphic position combined with artefact studies and dendrochronology. But before the detailed study begins, it must be established that these structures are truly representative examples of medieval timber-building practice in general, and were not the product of specialist carpenters, like coopers, wheelwrights or boat builders.

2. A sequence of vernacular structures exposed on the Trig Lane site in 1975, looking south-east. The front braces of late 13th-century TL3 *revetment can be seen on the north edge of site, partially obscured by the chalk wall. In front of that is reverse face of 14th-century back-braced* TL7 *revetment which was later extended westwards by stave-built* TL10 *structure; the 10 x 100mm scale rests on infill material thrown in behind it. The partially dismantled* TL11 *revetment (supported by scaffolding) extended the waterfront in c.1380, and was replaced in c.1440 by stone river wall to south.*

Who built the waterfront installations in medieval London?

There is little evidence to suggest that London's riverfront revetment construction was the work of specialists. It was once thought that the Custom House II revetment was the work of John de Tottenham, the carpenter sworn to check complaints relating to carpentry in the City from 1325-47 (Tatton-Brown 1974, 138) but although he is known to have erected a timber fortification on the site in 1339 at the start of the Hundred Years War, there is no reason to connect the defensive work with the waterfront feature (Milne & Milne 1982, 54). The only named carpenter known to have built revetments in the City is Richard Cotterel, who was employed not only to rebuild the timber face of Broken Wharf in 1347, but also to construct the jetty, fence and sheds (Salzman 1952, 435). The three carpenters engaged to work on a Southwark wharf in 1389 were required to rebuild two watermills and the millhouse as well (Salzman 1952, 467-9); Ailnoth the engineer was contracted to repair the wharf, wall and King's landing stair at Westminster in 1188 (Harvey 1954, 16), while two carpenters employed to work on the roof of Westminster Abbey were also mentioned in a contract for a wharf at Vauxhall in 1476-7 (Woodward-Smith & Schofield 1977, 284). Even Hugh Herland, 'the disposer of the Kings's works touching the art and mistery of carpentry' and architect of the magnificent hammer-beam roof at Westminster Hall, assisted with the harbour works at Great Yarmouth (Harvey 1954, 130).

The evidence from urban excavations where harbour installations and contemporary buildings have been found supports the general proposition that the construction of both types of structure, although clearly different in function, utilised the same range of techniques. That this approach differs from the methods employed by other specialist woodworkers, such as boat builders, is also apparent. The most cursory examination of the Scandinavian material makes this point emphatically: the solid, block-house tradition of house-building using horizontally-laid logs with lap-jointed corners (Long 1975; Reimers 1982; Hertieg 1975) is obviously reflected in the form of the waterfront *kar* structures (Harris 1973; Herteig 1981) and contrasts starkly with the graceful planked form of contemporary shipping (Crumlin-Pedersen 1970). In Dublin, the relationship between the construction of domestic buildings and waterfront installations is so close that major changes in the form of one is exactly paralleled in the other. An analysis of 48 buildings from Dublin shows that a wattle-wall tradition was predominant from at least the 10th into the 12th century (Murray 1981, Groups 1-3) with some stave-building towards the end of this period (Group 4), and that it was gradually superseded by the introduction of timber-framed structures in the 13th century. The parallel between this and the replacement on the Wood Quay site in *c*.1210 of 10th- to 12th-century wattle or stave-retained embankments or extensions by timber-framed revetments (Wallace 1981) is significantly close. The elevation of the timber-framed cellar wall on this site (Murray 1981, 65, fig 17) bears a striking resemblance to the Liffey revetments (Wallace 1981, 114, fig 110) in its proportions, size of timber used, and even the spacing of the posts. That the same class of carpenters built both types of structure seems certain: indeed, the excavator of the Wood Quay and Fishamble Street sites has already assessed some of the characteristics of Viking, Hiberno-Scandinavian and Anglo-Norman carpentry based on this assumption (Wallace 1982, 263-99).

The London study

Thus the evidence cited, both direct and indirect, supports the proposition that the medieval London waterfront installations were erected by the same persons responsible for timber building elsewhere in the City, and that the same general techniques used on dry land might be anticipated on the riverside.

It is accepted that some particular features used in waterfront installations, such as the manner of the bracing or of the plank cladding, will be peculiar to that class of structure. However, it is argued that the broad range of techniques used and changes in timber-working practice noted in the construction of riverfront revetments would all have been represented elsewhere in the City as much as on the waterfront. To this end, a catalogue of some of the best-preserved medieval waterfront structures is presented in Chapter 3 and assessed in Chapter 4.

About a hundred timber riverfront installations have been recorded in London since 1972, but by no means all of these are illustrated in this report. Many were only observed in the difficult conditions of a contractor's bulk earth-moving operation, some were poorly preserved, much of the timberwork having been removed in antiquity, while other

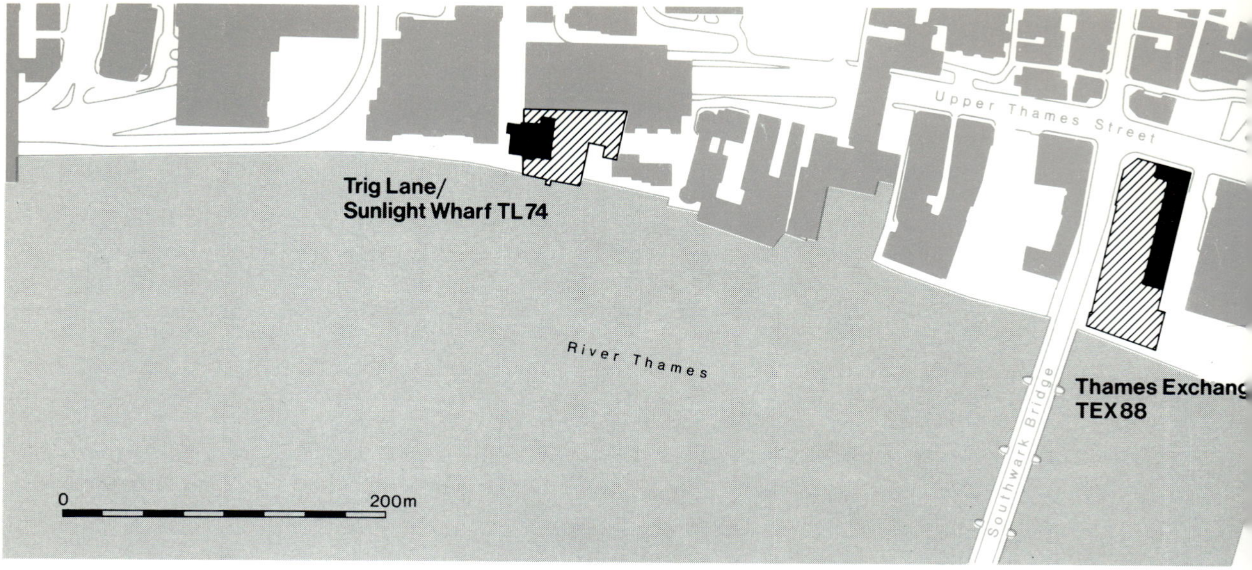

features have proved difficult to date independently. A list of waterfront sites in the London area on which medieval revetments were recorded appears in the appendix to this study, and the relevant archive reports are housed in the Museum of London, where they may be consulted by written request. Rather than describe all known examples in detail in this report, a selection has been made of some of the most complete, better-dated features for which a reasonably comprehensive field record has been compiled, and for which unambiguous stratigraphic relationships have been established. For the present purpose, it was thought that *sequences* of structures would be the most informative, particularly sequences which spanned the transition from earthfast to frame-building. To this end, parts of five sequences are illustrated, one each from the Billingsgate Lorry Park, Seal House and Trig Lane sites, and two from the Thames Exchange excavation (Fig 3). However, the discussions in the later chapters also take into consideration relevant features from several other sites.

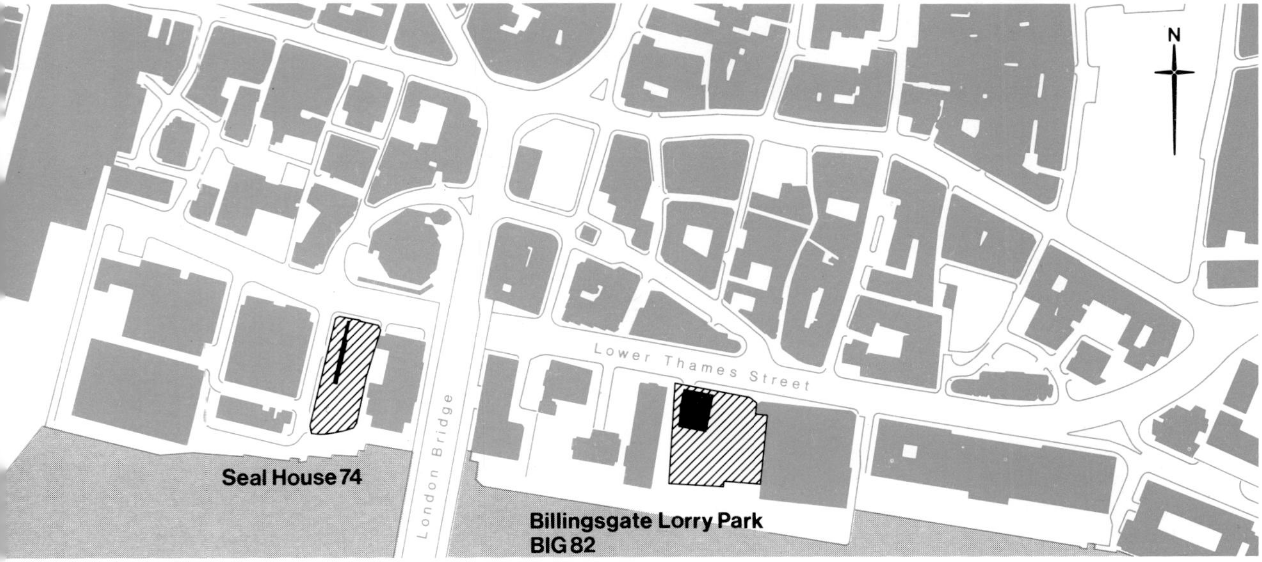

3. Plan of the City waterfront showing sites (hatched) on which structures described in the catalogue (Chapter 3) were recorded: cf. Fig 1. The extent of controlled excavations is shown in black; contractors' ground works were monitored over the rest of the sites.

2: TERMINOLOGY AND DATING

Trevor Brigham, Damian Goodburn, Gustav Milne and Ian Tyers

DEFINING TERMS

Before commencing the study, the terms used must be defined and the dating methodology described. Intensive research over the last forty years has produced a confusing and sometimes conflicting plethora of terms relating to timber buildings, with considerable regional variation. The Council for British Archaeology (CBA) has recently published an illustrated glossary which attempts to provide a logical nomenclature for the subject, which, if generally accepted, will 'continue the trend towards clear and expressive usage' (Alcock *et al* 1989), while previous studies of waterfront material have also included glossaries (Milne & Hobley 1981; Milne & Milne 1982, 109-11; see also MOL 1980 and 1990), based where relevant on data published by Cecil Hewett (Hewett 1980) and Oliver Rackham (Rackham 1976; 1980). All that will be attempted in this chapter is a broad definition of terminology related to buildings and woodland management, illustration of the principal joints recorded in the waterfront structures and a summary of the means whereby the excavations were dated: readers requiring further detail are referred to the works cited.

Building terms

Anchor beam: a horizontal timber, the head of which protrudes beyond the wall post or staves with which it articulates (*eg* Figs 15, 72).
Baseplate: the lower horizontal member of a framed structure, with which wall posts or studs articulate. An *interrupted baseplate* is a series of such plates inserted between principal wall posts.
Brace: a timber which supports another. *Front braces* or *raking braces* are angled braces used to support revetments, equivalent to buttresses in buildings.
Cleft timber: timber which has been split from the log using wedges, rather than sawn.
Earthfast: system of building in which feet of the load-bearing members (principal posts, wall posts or staves) are set firmly in the ground in post pits or wall trenches (cf. timber-framing). Earthfast posts are prone to rot at ground level.
Fillet: a thin strip of timber, sometimes used to link grooved staves.
Normal assembly: method of construction where top-plates are attached to the heads of wall posts and studs, with tiebeams lapped over (cf. *reversed assembly*).
Post: any upright timber. An *aisle-post* or *arcade-post* is a load-bearing post in an aisled hall; a *principal post* is a general term for a load-bearing post, while a *wall post* is a principal post set in the line of the wall (not to be confused with *stud*).
Reversed assembly: method of construction where tie-beams are attached to the heads of paired wall posts. The top-plates are then lapped to the upper surfaces of the tie-beams (cf. *normal assembly*).
Reused timber: a timber usually bearing features such as empty mortises or pegholes which have no apparent function in the context in which the timber was found.
Scantling: dimensions of a timber in cross-section.
Soffit: underside of a timber or joint.
Squint: oblique; a term describing an angle other than 90 degrees.
Staves are elements from a wall formed of contiguous vertical members of roughly equal dimensions in cross-section, which may be load bearing. Staves may be square-butted, tongued and grooved, or filleted (Fig 4).

Staggered staves: alternate staves offset to create two lines of uprights supporting a central woven panel; *paired staves* are set side by side to support a central woven panel, but with gaps between pairs giving the external appearance of stud and panel work.

Stave building: this term is used here to refer to walls in which vertical timbers provide both the rigidity for the structural frame and the cladding, in contrast to structures where thin planks which are not structurally integrated with the building are

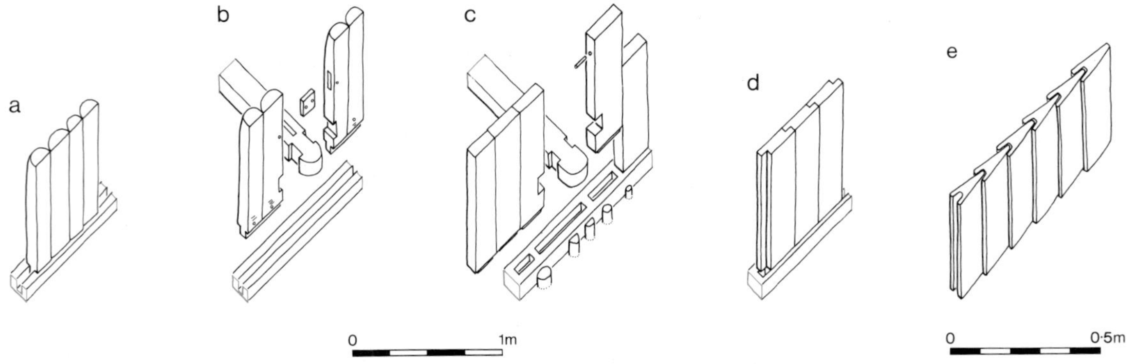

*4. Post-Conquest stave wall construction techniques represented on the London waterfront: a) butted flush (*TL74, TL10*); b) joined with free tenons (*TL74, TL10*); c) joined with dowels (*TL74, TL11*); d) rebated (*TL74, TL11*); e) vee-edged boards (*BC72*).*

simply applied to the outer face of extant posts, an important distinction made by Meeson (Meeson 1983, 35).

It is worth quoting a note which averts potential confusion over the meaning of *stave* as used in Scandinavian and German literature: 'In Norway, the *stav* is the solid corner post (Danish *stople*), while the Danish and Swedish *stav* is one of the upright planks of the walls (Norwegian *planke*). The German *stab* follows the Danish and Swedish meaning ... some Scandinavian wooden churches have no special corner posts and in Norwegian terminology those buildings are palisade churches' (Christie *et al* 1979, III, note 15). The German term *Palisadenbau* also describes the earliest forms of stave building, in which all vertical wall elements are earthfast (Herrnbrodt 1958, fig 78a & b). By the 12th century, such palisade-type walls were superseded by sill-beam based walls in Scandinavia (Hauglid 1976, 411) and Germany (Herrnbrodt 1958, fig 78e & f).
Stud: an intermediate post which does not generally carry load, although it may do so in the absence of wall posts. A stud may be grooved or pegged to accept the wall infill material. A *stud and panel* wall comprises studs with intervening wattle panels, whereas a *stud and plank* wall has vertical or horizontal planks set between the studs.
Tie-back: a horizontal brace retaining a riverfront revetment from the landward side to counteract the weight of the landfill material.
Tie-beam: horizontal brace retaining opposite walls of a building to resist the spread from the roof.
Timber framing: a system of building in which all the framing members *(posts, studs, beams, rafters etc)* are jointed together forming an integrated framework which is normally set upon a stone or brick sill, and is therefore independent of its site (cf. *earthfast building*).
Top-plate: the upper horizontal member of a framed building or waterfront revetment, to which the heads of wall posts or studs are attached.

Joints in medieval waterfront structures

Useful insights into medieval timber building practice in London can be gained from a study of the joints used, a system pioneered in this country by Cecil Hewett. To this end, a range of mortises and tenons, lap and scarf joints recorded on the medieval London waterfront is illustrated.

Mortise and tenon

This category of joints, basic to post-Norman Conquest carpentry and joinery, is one in which a slot *(mortise)* is cut in the edge or face of one timber to accommodate a tongue *(tenon)* cut at the end of another (Figs 5, 6). The development of this joint is crucial to the evolution of timber framing, and this point is discussed in Chapters 4 and 5.

No rectangular 'long' mortises are known from pre-Conquest contexts in London, but baseplates with 'square' mortises have been found on the Billingsgate site (Fig 5) associated with structures of 11th-century date or earlier (Chapter 5): the precise form of the associated tenons, if any, is less well known, and it seems that these early 'square' mortises simply accommodated the feet of the posts, dressed but not jointed.

By the 13th century, revetment posts with standard central (two-shouldered) or bare-faced (single-shouldered) tenons cut on their feet and set

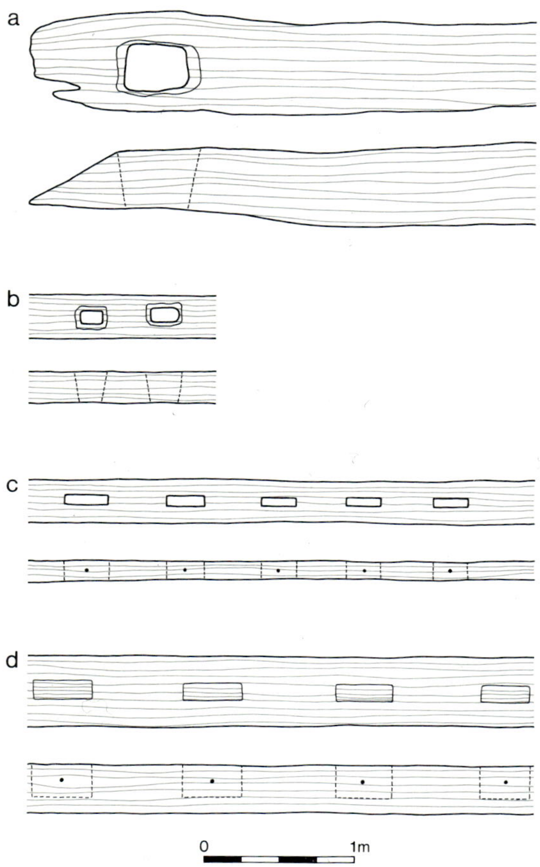

5. Types of mortise represented on the London waterfront:
*a) & b) 10th to 11th-century roughly-cut through-mortises (*BIG82*);*
*c) rectangular through-mortise in 13th-century baseplate (*BIG82*);*
*d) standard rectangular mortises in 14th-century baseplate (*TL74*).*

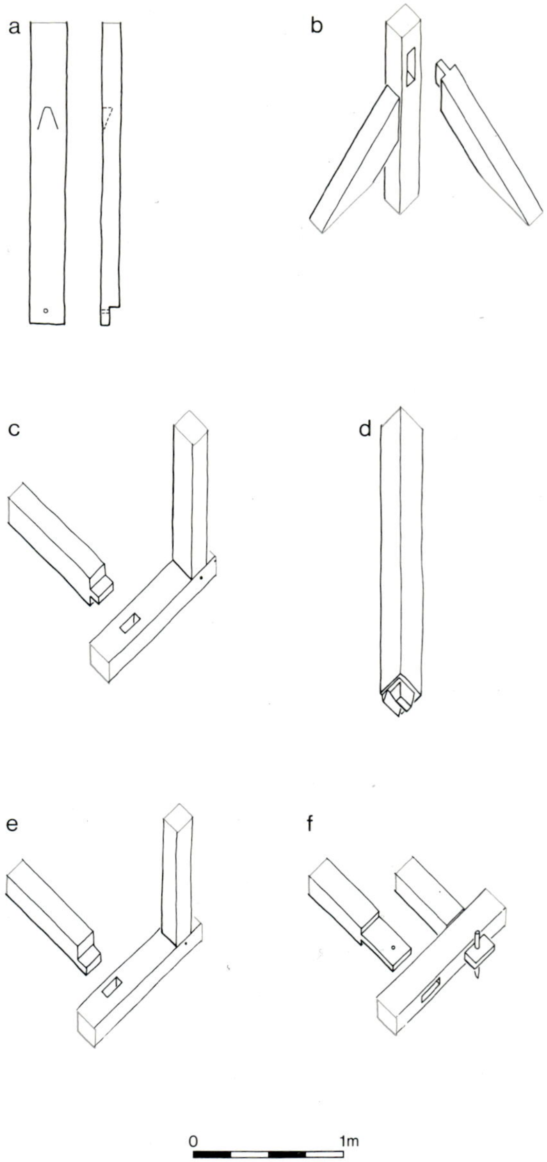

*6. Mortise and tenon type joints represented on London waterfront: a) 13th-century splayed recess in face of timber; bare-faced tenon on foot (*BIG82*); b) late 13th-century chase mortise and tenon joining head of brace to post (*TL74*); c) late 13th-century central tenon in rectangular mortise (*TL74*); d) 13th-century spurred tenon on reused timber (*TL74*); e) bare-faced tenon (*TL74*); f) 15th-century tusk tenon protruding through open mortise (*TL74*).*

in long mortises are recorded (Fig 6), but although chase mortises (see below) are found on the feet of the braces, the tapered head was sometimes set in a tapered *splayed recess* in the face of the post (Fig 6a). These joints resemble *scotches* which have been found in the wall frame members of houses and barns with simple rectangular panels and full height studs (Charles 1974, 21). The function of a scotch was to accommodate the head of a temporary shore to facilitate the raising and supporting of a main post during the erection of a timber building. It has also been argued, however, that 'the presence of scotches denotes the very opposite of rearing (the raising of a prefabricated building frame by frame) the assembly of a frame timber by timber in the vertical' (Charles 1974, 21). In London, the presence of such features in 13th-century contexts (BG14) is clearly a reflection of the methods used to erect earlier post-built structures (*eg* TX7).

The joint used on the foot of 13th- and 14th-century braces was invariably a *chase tenon*, that is, a tenon in which the shoulders were cut at an acute angle and the end of the mortise was similarly raked. In subsidiary baseplates of medieval revetments, a crudely cut bare-faced form was used, but often in an over-long mortise which was subsequently packed with wedges once the final adjustment to the supported post had been made.

A rare form of mortise and tenon recorded on the waterfront is the central tenon with a *spurred shoulder* found on a reused timber in a mid 13th-century structure; this type of joint was in use from at least the 12th century (Fig 6d).

A *free tenon* is a small plate of timber buried at both ends in mortises cut into adjacent edges of abutting timbers (Fig 4a). The only other type of tenon which deserves special mention is the *tusk tenon,* used in an early 15th-century revetment (Fig 6f), in which the tenon protrudes beyond the plates into which it is set, and is secured with a peg or key. Although the Saxon mill at Tamworth affords a parallel (Rahtz & Sheridan 1972, fig 2), few examples of the joint are known from later medieval contexts.

Lap joints

The range of lap joints found in London includes *notched lap joints* dated to the late 12th (Fig 7c) to 13th centuries at the Mermaid Theatre (Fig 7d), but *squint laps* were found in structures ranging from pre-1250 to the early 15th century. Elsewhere in England, notched lap joints have been found in over 30 buildings more or less securely dated from the mid 12th to the early 14th century, but none of these are considered to be vernacular (Hewett 1973). The 13th-century London revetment (Fig 84) is therefore of especial interest, since at least some of the examples were *secret notched laps, ie* the notch was obscured by a small rebate on the foot of the brace when in position. A variety of forms of the same joint in the same structure is not unusual: six variations of the notched lap were recorded in the Blackfriars roof at Gloucester, for example, where the choice was 'influenced by the stresses expected and by the vagaries and imperfections of individual timbers' (Rackham *et al* 1978, 117).

A brace with lap joints cut on the ends must be applied to a frame as a secondary member (Hewett 1980, 289-92), whereas a tenoned timber is assembled as an integral part of the frame. The increasing 'preference' for chase-tenons rather than lap joints from the 14th century onwards therefore implies changes in the design and erection of buildings.

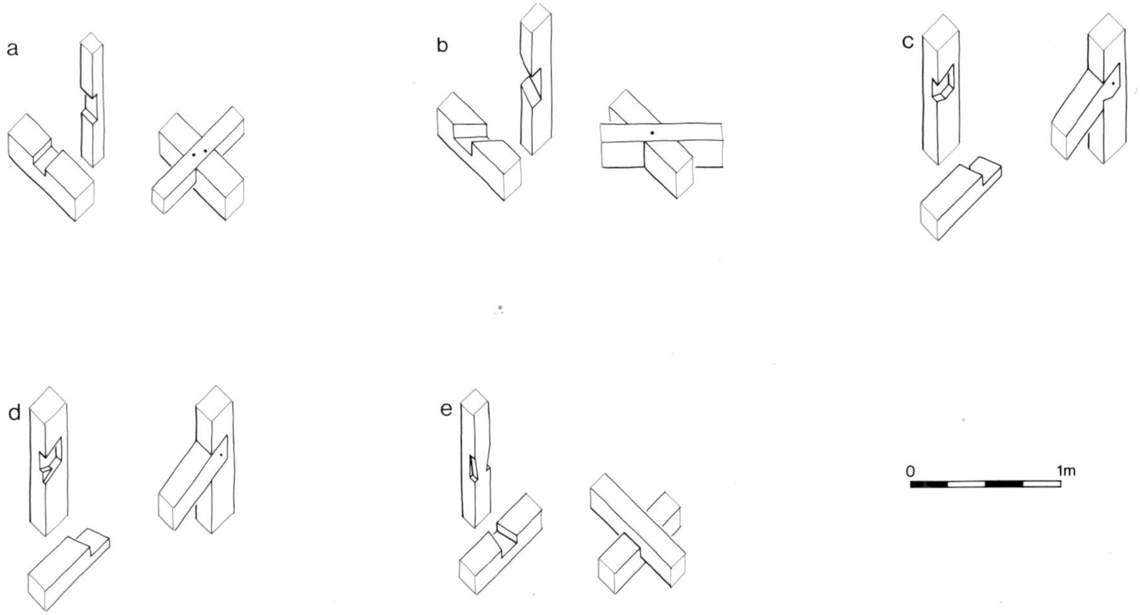

7. Lap joints represented on the London waterfront: a) halving (13th century TL74*); b) diagonal halving (13th century* TEX88*); c) notched lap (late 12th century* TEX88*); d) secret notched lap (13th century* THE79*); e) lap dovetail (early 14th century* TL74*).*

Scarf joints

Scarf joints are used to join the ends of two timbers to form a greater length, and some examples from the London waterfront are shown on Fig 8. The simple *edge-halved scarf with square vertical butts* (Fig 8a) appears in supported baseplates from the 13th to the mid 14th century, and in an unsupported position on the heads of braces in the late 14th century. This joint has been dated to the late 12th century in Essex (where it is considered to be rare: Hewett 1980, 263), the 13th to 14th century in Kent (Brown 1976, 37) and from the 15th to the 18th century in Yorkshire (Hutton 1981, 30). Examples of *splayed* scarf joints come from the early 13th-century TX7 revetment and from a reused timber at Baynard's Castle (Fig 8b) which must be 14th-century or earlier. Three examples of *through-splayed and tabled* scarf joints are illustrated. One is from a 14th-century baseplate at the Custom House site (Fig 8c), the other two from mid 14th- century braces at the Winchester Palace site (Yule 1989); one had a key, the other a wedge (Fig 8d, e). According to Hewett (Hewett 1980, figs 245-7) and Currie (Currie 1972, class 2) such splayed scarf joints are found in buildings from *c.*1190 to the end of the 13th century, although some examples from Kent may be later (Brown 1976, 37), as are some stop-splayed joints from Yorkshire (Hutton 1981, 30).

The late 14th-century scarf joint with *bridled-butts* (Fig 8f) recorded on the Trig Lane site is well known (Harrison 1975, 59; Hewett 1977, 292; 1980, 267; Milne & Milne 1978, fig 10; 1982, fig 25) and is as yet the earliest dated example of a type that continued into the 17th century (Brown 1976, 37; Hewett 1980, 207; Hutton 1981, 31).

The introduction of the *face-halved scarf* seems to have occured in the mid 14th century in Yorkshire (Hutton 1981, 31) and certainly by the early 15th century elsewhere (Hewett 1980, 269): an early 15th-century face-halved scarf from the G12 revetment at Trig Lane is shown here (Fig 8g).

In the conclusion to his monumental work on English carpentry, Cecil Hewett declares that 'the hypothesis that carpenter's joints underwent processes of development towards mechanical efficiency has now been illustrated... It might have been possible, as an exercise in ineptitude, to select a series that did not establish the developments but it is unlikely that any series, chosen at random, would have disproved it' (Hewett 1980, 325). The range of joints found on the London waterfront could be considered as a series chosen at random and thus presents itself as a control group against which to test his hypothesis. The small selection of vernacular scarf joints illustrated here for example,

8. Scarf joint types represented on the London waterfront: a) edge-halved (13th-14th century: TL74*); b) part of through-splayed scarf (pre-15th century:* BYD81*); c) through-splayed and tabled (14th century:* CUS73*); d) & e) part of through-splayed and tabled scarf with key; through-splayed and tabled with wedge (both mid 14th century from Winchester Palace site, Southwark:* WP84*); f) edge-halved bridled butts (14th century:* TL74*); g) faced-halved (15th century:* TL74*).*

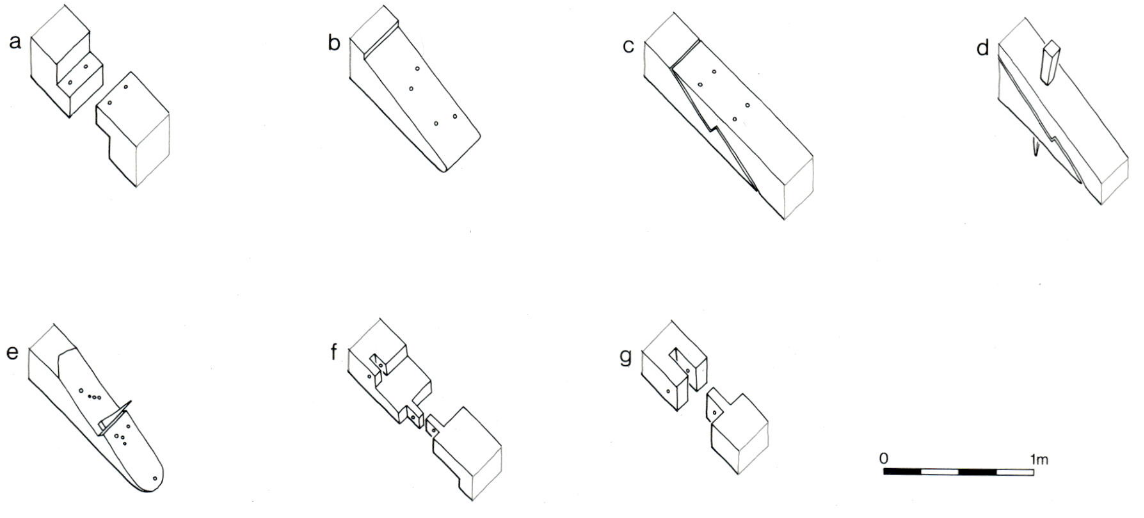

suggests that splayed and edge-halved scarf joints were introduced before bridle-butted examples, which in turn made their appearance before the face-halved variety. This succession is not as such at variance with that proposed by Hewett (Hewett 1980, 270-1). However, it seems clear that several forms continued to be used after others had been developed, and so 'a single simple chronology cannot be held to apply equally throughout England' (Hutton 1981, 36). Thus the edge-halved and the splayed and tabled scarf joints are found in contexts later than might be expected, while the edge-halved bridle-butted scarf joint is slightly earlier. The London material is therefore of especial importance, since its closely dated vernacular examples contribute positively in kind, date and duration to the Hewett model.

Timber and woodland terminology

(after Rackham 1976; 1980)

Coppice: a) young trees cut to near ground level every few years and which grow again from the stool; b) managed woodland which produces crops of poles from such stools; c) (verb) to cut wood from the stools.
Standard: a woodland or hedgerow tree suitable for *timber;* also known as a *timber tree.*
Timber (Meremium): trunks of trees of a size suitable (*ie* greater than *c.*0.2m or 8 inches in diameter) for converting into major structural elements such as beams or planks for timber buildings, as opposed to *Wood (Boscus):* rods, poles or branches used for firewood or for light construction work such as wattle- or hurdlework.
Wane: the surface of the solid wood or timber under the bark (live edge); its presence on an ancient timber is of importance when calculating the dimensions of the parent tree or the felling date, and in indicating the type of conversion used (see Chapter 6).
Wildwood: unmanaged woodland that has not been substantially modified by man.
Woodland management: the system of rotational felling of standards and coppice *etc* to provide a succession of crops. In medieval England this usually took the form of *coppice with standards*, extensive stands of coppice interspersed with standards (the *Silva minuta* mentioned in Domesday Book), or *wood pasture*, stands of managed trees set within pasture for grazing animals (the Domesday *Silva pastilis*).

DATING

Terminology

medieval period: *c.*400 to 1500;
pre-Conquest or *early medieval period:* pre-1066;
post-Conquest or *later medieval period:* post-1066;
mid Saxon: *c.*600 to *c.*900;
late Saxon: *c.*900 to *c.*1100;
Saxo-Norman: *c.*950 to *c.*1150.
Other adjectives used in this report such as *Norman* or *Scandinavian* refer to ethnic origin, and are not used specifically to define a particular date range.

Methodology

The suggested dates given in the description of the structures considered in Part 3 are based principally on dendrochronological study supported by stratigraphic analysis. To take the last first: on the completion of each excavation, the field records are assessed and a *relative sequence* of activity is established during the compilation of the archive report. Such a report presents the stratigraphic evidence that Structure C must have been erected later than A, could have been contemporary with B, but was clearly replaced by Structure D, for example.

For the majority of the structures described here, the broad sequence was the same. The earliest structure was erected on the contemporary foreshore, after which further waterlaid deposits of silt or sand began accumulating against its riverward face. The next phase of development saw another structure erected, usually some metres to the south of the old, upon the new foreshore. Dumped deposits then infilled the area between the new and old frontages. Thus, barring repairs and erosion horizons, a relatively straightforward stratigraphic succession was established in which layers and features developed both horizontally and vertically, rather than solely in horizontal bands as on many other archaeological sites.

Working with this basic relatively-dated framework, an attempt was then made to impose *absolute* or *calendar dates* upon that sequence, taking into consideration the date-range of artefacts (coins, pottery *etc*) recovered from contexts associated with those structures. With most long sequences on medieval sites from controlled excavations in London, it is possible to determine the date of a major structure to within 25 or 50 years. Even greater precision is possible for waterfront sites where dendrochronological studies can be related to a sound relative sequence of structures for which some broad artefact dating is already available.

Dendrochronology

The basic principles and limitations of dendrochronology are well established (Baillie 1982; Schweingrüber 1988) and may be summarised thus: tree-ring dating employs an aspect of the biological processes of tree-growth to provide calendar dates for the period during which the sampled trees were alive. In temperate parts of the world, trees have a growing season marked within the wood as an *annual ring*, with a resting season in the winter months. The amount of wood laid down in any one year by most trees is determined by the climate and other environmental factors. Since trees over relatively wide geographical areas exhibit similar patterns of growth, dendrochronologists are able to assign dates to samples by matching the growth pattern with other ring-sequences that have already been linked together to form *reference chronologies*.

The successful matching of a particular ring-sequence with a specific reference chronology, while providing absolute calendar dates, does not of itself always provide a precise date for the felling of that tree. This is simply because there is often an incomplete ring-sequence, and the full complement of annual rings right to the bark-edge of the tree is required for the felling date to be established with absolute precision. There are several reasons why many of the dendrochronological samples considered in this report had an incomplete sequence and, as a consequence, cannot be used to provide a precise date for the construction of the structure with which they were associated. Firstly, the outermost *sapwood* rings of an oak tree are significantly less resistant to physical damage and to insect and fungal attack than the *heartwood*, and so do not often survive. Secondly, sapwood is often lost during the physical conversion of the whole, round log into squared timbers.

In such cases, the dendrochronologist can only assign a date after which the timber must have been felled if no sapwood at all survives, as is the case with the samples from the TL1 revetment from the Sunlight Wharf site, built from timber felled sometime after 1186 (Figs 9, 66). However, a date range within which felling took place can be estimated if some sapwood rings are present, based on the assumption that the tree would have had a minimum of 10 and a maximum of 55 sapwood rings (Hillam 1987). The TX1 revetment from the Thames Exchange site contained timbers which must have been felled in the period AD 967-89, for example. Where the full sapwood complement survived on the samples analysed, as on the staves from the TX2 structure (Figs 9, 39), then the date of the felling can be determined with absolute historical precision, in this instance to the winter of 1066/7.

However, even such an infamous date as that cannot be taken without qualification as the date at which the associated structure was actually *built*. Timber need not be used immediately after felling, although there is little evidence for long-term storage of timber or of widespread use of seasoned, rather than green, timber in the early medieval period. Confidence in a particular felling date as an indicator of the time of construction can only be attained whenever it seems to be replicated after analysis of a number of samples from the same structure. Such an assessment of many supposedly contemporary samples helps to highlight any potentially reused timbers incorporated within the structure, timbers which on their own would furnish a felling date misleadingly earlier than the actual construction date of the new building. Careful timber recording which notes the presence of pegholes or joints which are not functional in the structure as found is the principal solution to the problem of identifying reused timbers in the field.

The Trig Lane (TL74) samples were initially examined by Dr Donald Brett and Charlotte Harding at Bedford College, London, while work on the Seal House (SH74) material was conducted by Dr Ruth Morgan at the Laboratory in Sheffield University (Morgan & Schofield 1978), where Jennifer Hillam and Cath Groves subsequently studied samples from the Billingsgate Lorry Park site (BIG82). The Museum of London's dendrochronological research team of Ian Tyers and Nigel Nayling prepared the more recent reports on the Sunlight Wharf (SUN86) and Thames Exchange (TEX88) sites. References to the relevant reports are given in the Catalogue (Chapter 3).

9. Summary phasing of waterfront features discussed in the Catalogue, based on results of tree-ring analysis.

KEY
├──┤ felling range
│ felling year
├► felling after

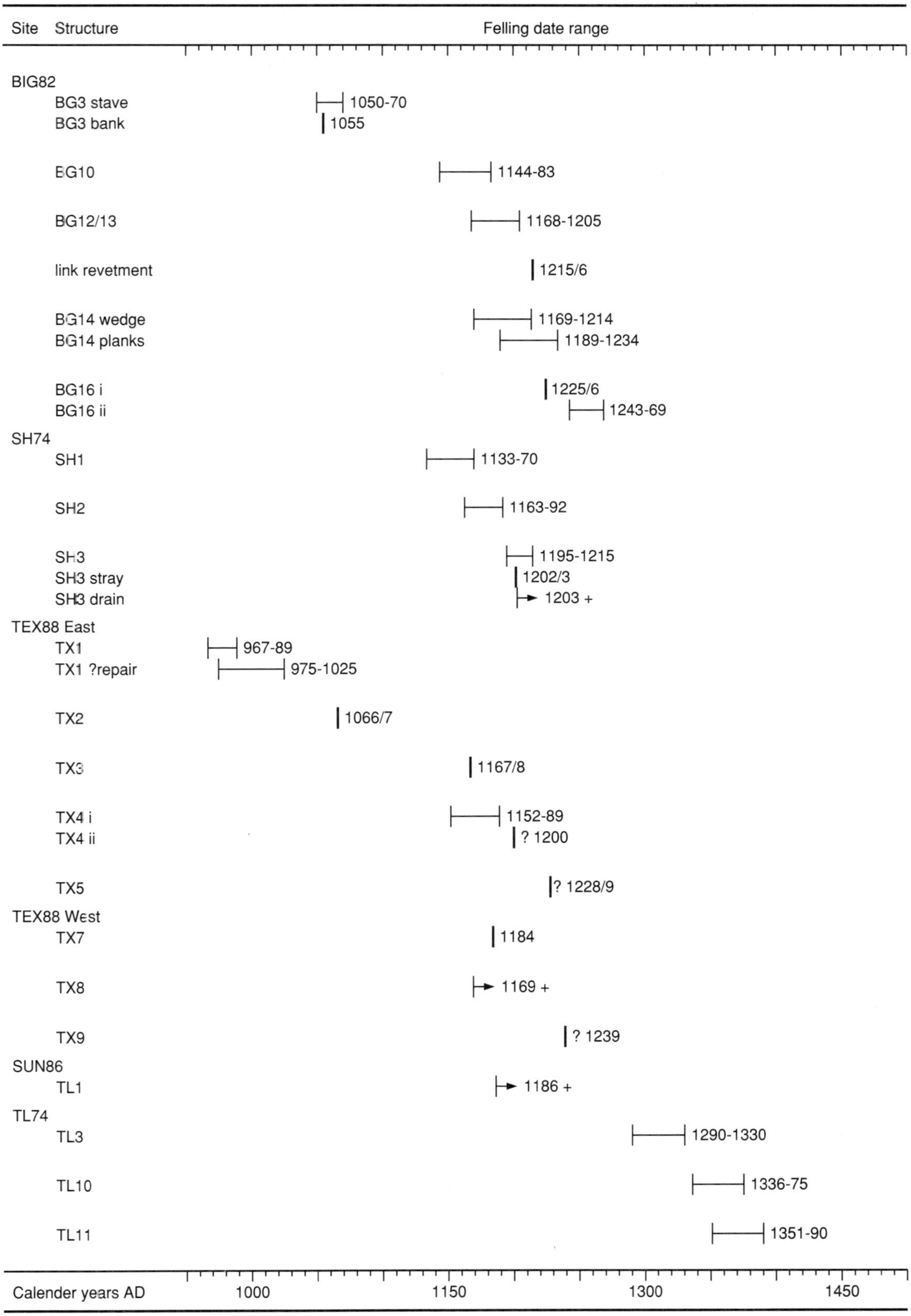
Site Structure
Felling date range
BIG82
BG3 stave 1050-70
BG3 bank 1055
BG10 1144-83
BG12/13 1168-1205
link revetment 1215/6
BG14 wedge 1169-1214
BG14 planks 1189-1234
BG16 i 1225/6
BG16 ii 1243-69
SH74
SH1 1133-70
SH2 1163-92
SH3 1195-1215
SH3 stray 1202/3
SH3 drain 1203 +
TEX88 East
TX1 967-89
TX1 ?repair 975-1025
TX2 1066/7
TX3 1167/8
TX4 i 1152-89
TX4 ii ? 1200
TX5 ? 1228/9
TEX88 West
TX7 1184
TX8 1169 +
TX9 ? 1239
SUN86
TL1 1186 +
TL74
TL3 1290-1330
TL10 1336-75
TL11 1351-90
Calender years AD
1000
1150
1300
1450

Although the dendrochronological results presented here therefore incorporate work by several dendrochronologists working over a period of nearly twenty years, the tree-ring dates were all established using the same basic method. For each oak sample (*Quercus spp*), the presence of sapwood or bark edges were noted as appropriate, and the series of ring widths across a radial section was measured sequentially. This series of widths was then plotted on graph paper to aid visual comparison, and then a variety of computer programmes compared the ring pattern with other samples and material from other sites. Where significantly good cross-matching occurred, the sample was assigned the dates relative to the chronology or other samples with which it had been matched. A felling date or date-range was then established, dependent upon the presence or absence of sapwood and bark, as discussed above. This information could then be passed back to the excavators to assist them in their interpretation of the structures and the development of the site.

Only one radius was measured on each sample, unless particular problems dictated otherwise. The resolution of the measurements has steadily increased over the last twenty years, with some of the earlier samples being measured at 0.10mm, 0.05mm or 0.02mm, while the most recent samples were measured at 0.01mm resolution. Other changes in approach worth mentioning are that it is now common practice to measure only those samples with more than 50 rings, whereas previously some shorter sequences were measured.

Sapwood estimates have also been revised, since the original range quoted of up to 30 years was not broad enough to cover the natural variation. Estimates are now based on the assumption that trees have between 10 and 55 sapwood rings. These changes have resulted in minor modifications to some of the results published previously.

Dating the Catalogue

To the description of each structure illustrated in Chapter 3, a summary of the relevant dendrochronological report is appended. These abstracts are presented to provide a common framework upon which to determine the relative and absolute dates of the structures, while allowing a critical assessment of the reliability of that dating. In general, the results seem to be exceptionally reliable, since most are based on multiple samples supported by several timbers of a similar age. Less reliance should obviously be placed on those results which depend upon a single dated sample.

It will be noted that the length of the abstract varies from site to site and from structure to structure. This is because some results have been published elsewhere (*eg* Hillam forthcoming), while others are presented here for the first time. All the Thames Exchange material comes into this latter category, as does the BG14 and TL1 structures. In addition, the opportunity has been taken to publish a revision of the Trig Lane dating (Fig 63).

3: CATALOGUE OF WATERFRONT INSTALLATIONS

Compiled by Gustav and Chrissie Milne

In this chapter, representative sections of 25 waterfront structures are described and illustrated at common scales to aid comparison. The selection of examples concentrates particularly on 11th- to 13th-century features, to focus on the period which saw the introduction and development of fully-framed timber buildings, although one post-medieval structure is included (BY1) to represent techniques and developments at the end of the period. Each group of revetments has been numbered as part of a site sequence (*eg* the Thames Exchange revetments are TX1 to TX9), but where features have been published elsewhere, the nomenclature in this catalogue has been adapted to complement the scheme used in that publication. Thus the Billingsgate structures referred to as W3 and W10 elsewhere (Steedman *et al* forthcoming) are described in our catalogue as BG3 and BG10, while those from Seal House, known as W2 and W3 in Schofield 1975, are published as SH2 and SH3 here. A chronological table comparing the structural attributes of the revetments is included in the index (Fig 120).

A list of unpublished archive reports concerning the excavations and the dendrochronological analysis of the structures considered in this catalogue is appended to the Bibliography.

All measurements cited in the catalogue are approximate figures, given to provide a general impression of size and to aid comparison of timbers and structures: they should not be used to calculate the units of measurement initially employed to construct the revetments.

BILLINGSGATE LORRY PARK
TQ33008065 Site code: BIG82

The controlled excavation of a 24m by 18m part of the Billingsgate Lorry Park site began in February 1982 and concluded in February 1983, under the supervision of Steve Roskams (Figs 10-11). The site lay immediately south of Lower Thames Street, abutting the St Magnus House and New Fresh Wharf excavation site of 1973-6 to the west, with the Billingsgate Market building to the east. One of the earliest features located was the remains of a Roman quay (W1) sealed beneath a thick foreshore deposit (Brigham 1990, 100-7). On top of that, an artificial embankment had been raised in the 11th century, divided by an inlet. The face of this embankment had been refaced several times (W2 to W9; W11) and the inlet finally blocked (W10: see BG10), all this activity taking place before 1190 (Steedman *et al* forthcoming).

Unfortunately, much of the timberwork used in these revetments had been robbed in antiquity, but the W3 and W10 structures were particularly well preserved, and are described below as BG3 and BG10. The waterfront was then advanced with the erection of a series of timber revetments (W12 to W16) of 12th- and 13th-century date (BG12-14; BG16). Waterfront buildings, warehouses and part of the church of St Botolph were also recorded. Medieval reclamation to the south of the controlled excavation was investigated in difficult conditions during a subsequent watching brief (Site code BWB83).

10. Billingsgate Lorry Park site (see Fig 3). Plan series showing stages in waterfront development from the 11th to late 13th century, and position of structures described in Catalogue. Scale 1:1250.

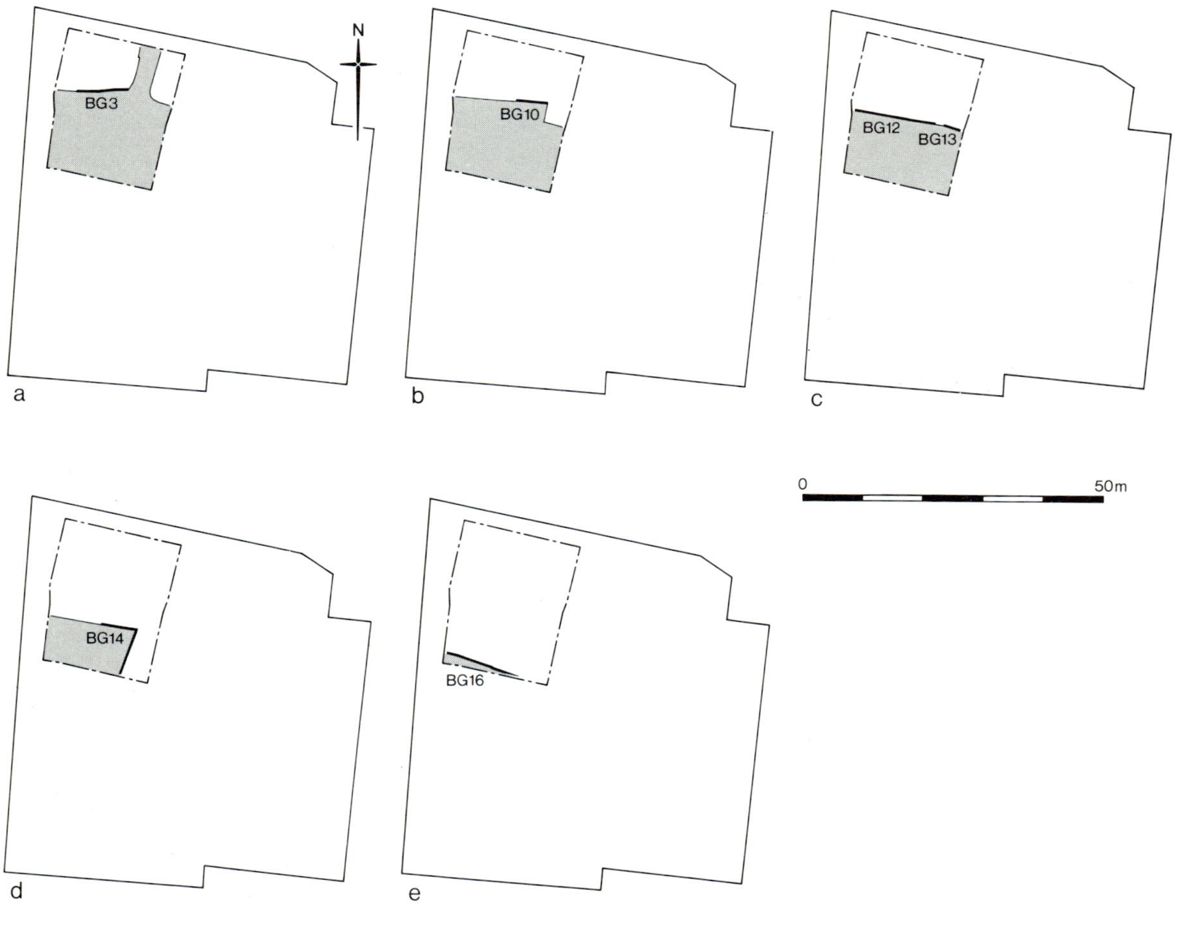

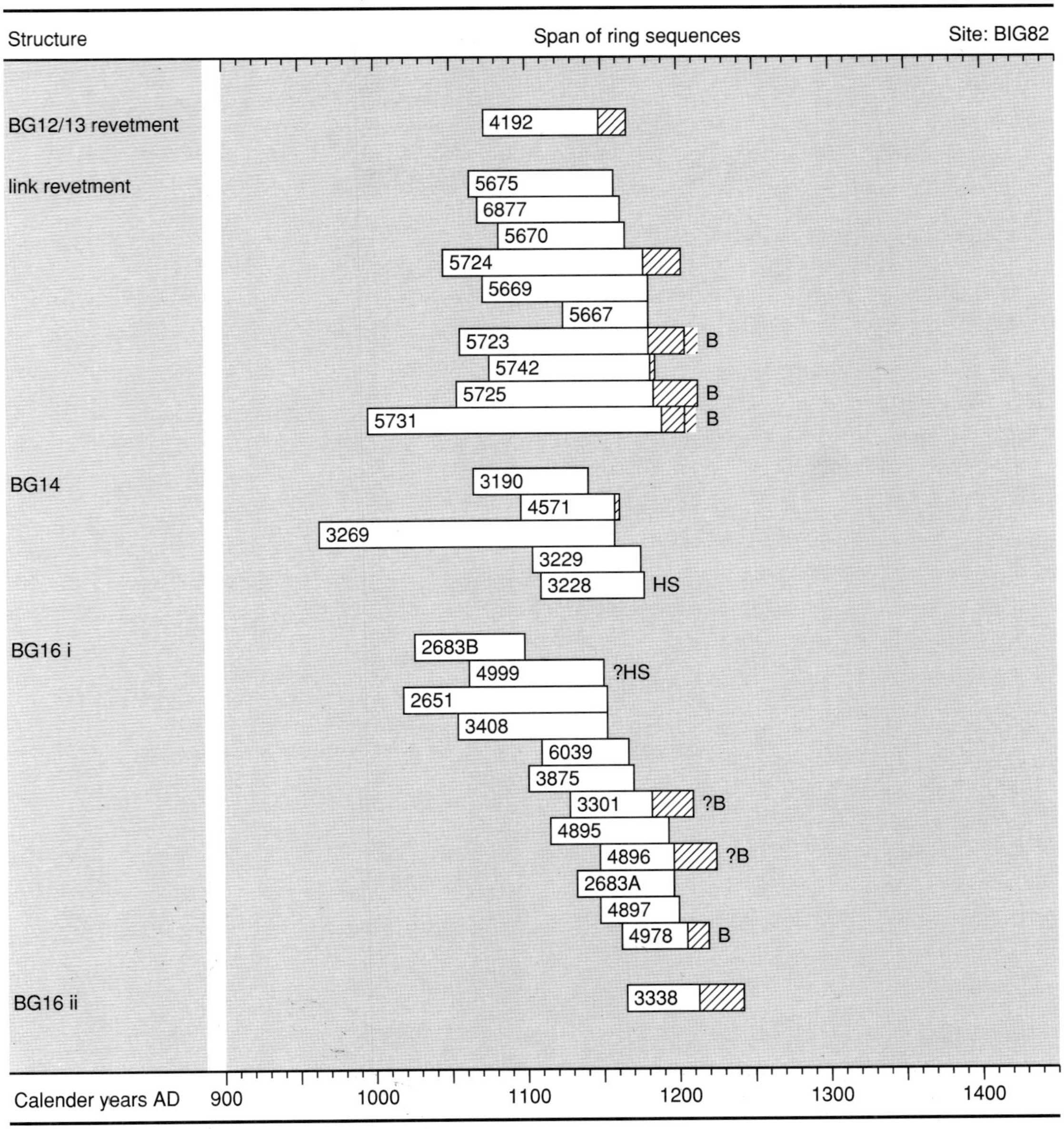

11. Bar diagram showing tree-ring results from later medieval waterfront structures from Billingsgate Lorry Park site (BIG82).

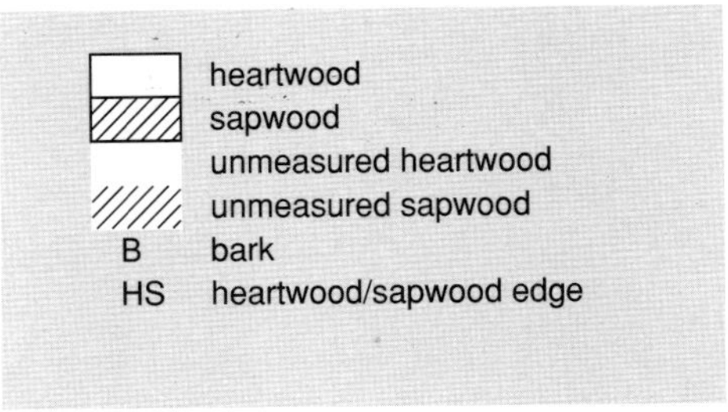

STRUCTURE BG3

(Figs 12, 13)

The BG3 structure was recorded in the western half of the site, immediately south of a major waterfront embankment (Steedman *et al* forthcoming). It comprised at least 21 displaced split oak staves which were up to 3.4m long, 0.4m wide and 150mm thick. Their feet had been set earthfast into the foreshore, although the staves had subsequently collapsed southwards. It is not certain precisely how, or even if, this stave wall was initially braced, but it has been suggested that it was raked back at an angle over the face of the embankment, rather than stood vertically. Beneath the collapsed timbers was a substantial grooved baseplate at least 7.6m long and 0.5m in cross-section. Since the displaced staves had not been set in that groove, the baseplate presumably represents an earlier phase of waterfront activity accommodating stavework.

Archive reference: BIG82 IV.4

Dating: A gravel layer associated with the earliest phase of the main waterfront embankment contained a coin minted after 959, but officially out of circulation by 973.

The BG3 staves were not the primary facing of that bank. They must have collapsed after *c*.1080, since they overlay a foreshore deposit from which a lead 'trial piece' coin of William I was recovered.

Dendrochronological summary: Timbers from the bank to the north of the staves were extensively sampled and 84 were dated, of which eight came from trees felled in 1055 (Fig 11). Out of 21 samples from the BG3 structure itself, 10 were dated, four of which included sapwood (Hillam forthcoming). A felling date range of 1050-70 is estimated.

12. Billingsgate Lorry Park, 11th-century Structure BG3*: plan of collapsed earthfast stave wall lying over a substantial baseplate which may have accommodated an earlier phase of stave work.*

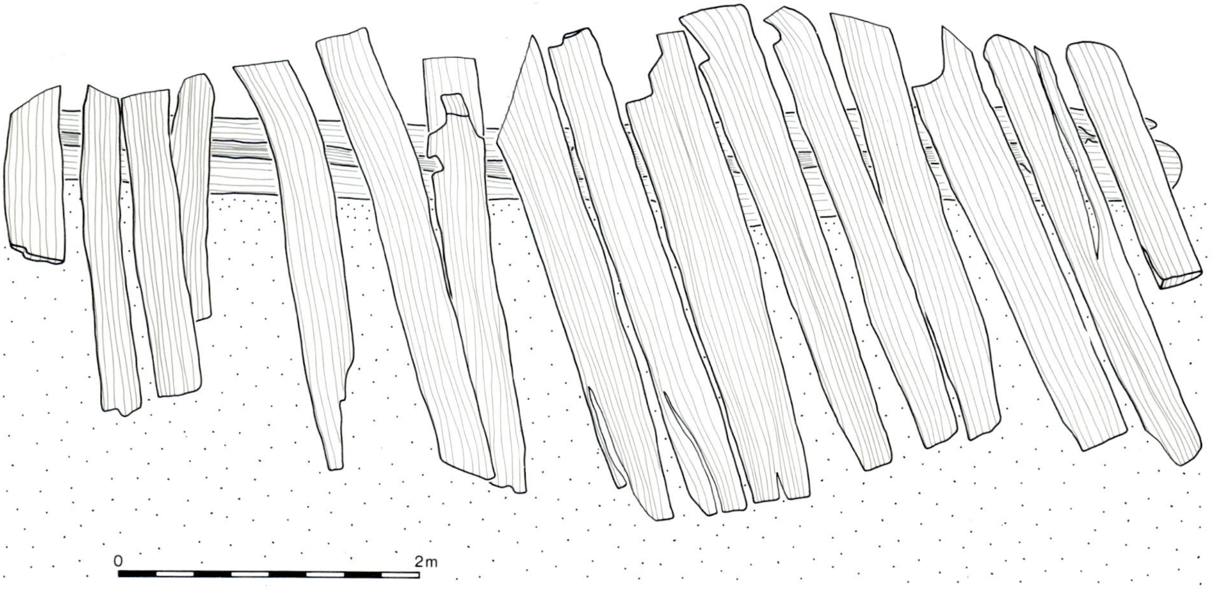

13. Billingsgate Lorry Park: the landward face of the collapsed staves from the BG3 *structure, looking south-east. Scale 10 x 100mm.*

STRUCTURE BG10

(Figs 14-16)

The back-braced BG10 stave revetment was recorded for over 4.3m east-west, and had been built across the mouth of an inlet in the eastern half of the site. It represents one of the last phases of repair and modification to the Saxo-Norman embankment and its associated inlet before the waterfront was extended further to the south with the construction of the BG12 and 13 structures. The BG10 revetment incorporated 22 vertical members up to 1.2m tall, 0.2m wide and 40mm thick. They were set in a groove cut into the upper face of a roughly-dressed baseplate some 0.25m wide. The one complete north-south back brace which survived was 3.6m long and was secured at its north end by a crosspiece passed through a square mortise and retained to the south by piles. Its south end protruded *c.*0.4m beyond the riverward face of the revetment and was also cut by a square mortise, this time for a horizontally-laid lockbar which retained the heads of the staves (Fig 15).

Archive reference: BIG82 VII.I

Dating: The BG10 structure is stratigraphically later than BG3 (1050-70) and earlier than BG12 and 13 (1168-1205). Pottery from the infilled inlet to the north could be of early to mid 12th-century date.

Dendrochronological summary: Out of 17 samples, 14 were dated, three of which included sapwood (Hillam forthcoming). A felling date range of 1144-83 is estimated (Fig 11).

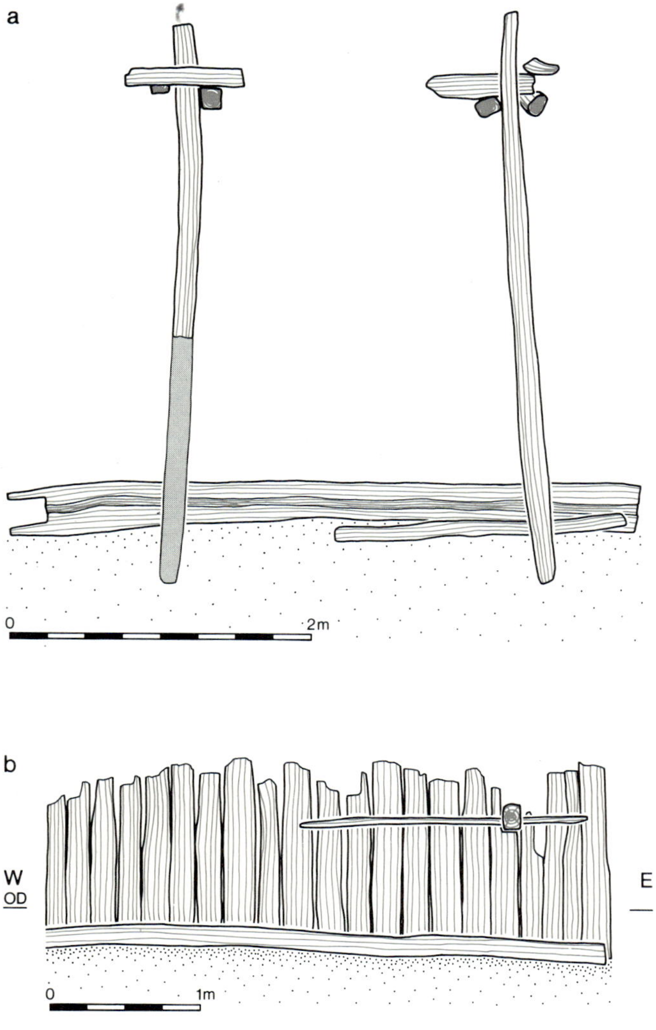

14. Left: Billingsgate Lorry Park, 12th-century BG10 *stave revetment: a) plan of baseplate, back braces and lockbar with staves removed; b) south-facing elevation of stave wall with back brace and lockbar (cf. Fig 10).*

15. Top right: Billingsgate Lorry Park. Detail of BG10 *revetment, looking north-east. The 2 x 100mm scale rests on arbitrary excavation level on southern (riverward) side of the partially excavated structure. The decayed heads of some staves are retained by a lockbar passing through the protruding head of the back brace (cf. Figs 14, 16).*

16. Bottom right: Billingsgate Lorry Park. The southern (riverward) face of BG10 *revetment fully exposed, looking north. The 5 x 100mm scale rests on the foreshore next to the substantial, grooved baseplate. The back brace and lockbar shown on Fig 15 have been removed.*

STRUCTURES BG12 & BG13

(Figs 17-19)

The BG12 and BG13 revetments mark phases of activity stratigraphically later than those represented by the stave-built BG3 and BG10 structures. Unfortunately most of the superstructure for the western revetment (BG12) had been removed in antiquity. All that survived was a 0.7m-deep robber trench in which post pits were recorded, with an unmortised timber baseplate parallel to it, but *c.*0.5m to the south and retained by piles. The plate comprised at least three timbers roughly scarfed together (Fig 19). It is suggested that the revetment comprised an earthfast post and plank revetment braced to the south by shores lodged against the subsidiary plate, or a structure similar to that described for TL1 at Trig Lane.

The BG13 revetment continued the alignment of the BG12 structure across the western half of the site, and was broadly contemporary with it, although a different construction technique seems to have been used in the disturbed fragment which survived. At least three levels of horizontal softwood planking were evidence for the importation of building timber into medieval London. They had been sawn, were over 3m long, up to 0.36m wide and 50mm thick, while the presence of numerous pegholes suggests they may have been reused.

Unfortunately, the manner in which the structure was supported is uncertain, since no principal posts were observed *in situ,* although a timber which may have been associated with the revetment was recovered from a later phase of dumping. (This timber provided the sole dendrochronological sample for this phase.) However, the northern ends of two tie-backs secured with pile-retained crossbars were recorded on the landward side of the plank cladding, showing that this revetment was back-braced, although how the braces articulated with the frontage is unknown.

Archive reference: BIG82 VIII.1/2

Dating: The BG12 and BG13 structures are stratigraphically later than BG10 (1144-83) and earlier than BG14 (1216+). The revetments retained reclamation deposits containing 12th-century pottery, pilgrim souvenirs of 1170+, and coins of 1180+.

Dendrochronological summary: The sole sample had 95 rings (Figs 9, 11), including 17 sapwood, and has an estimated felling date of 1168-1205 (Hillam 1990).

17. Billingsgate Lorry Park, Structure BG12*: plan showing position of robbed-out posts in relation to the pile-retained plate against which the front braces would have butted; cf. Fig 10.*

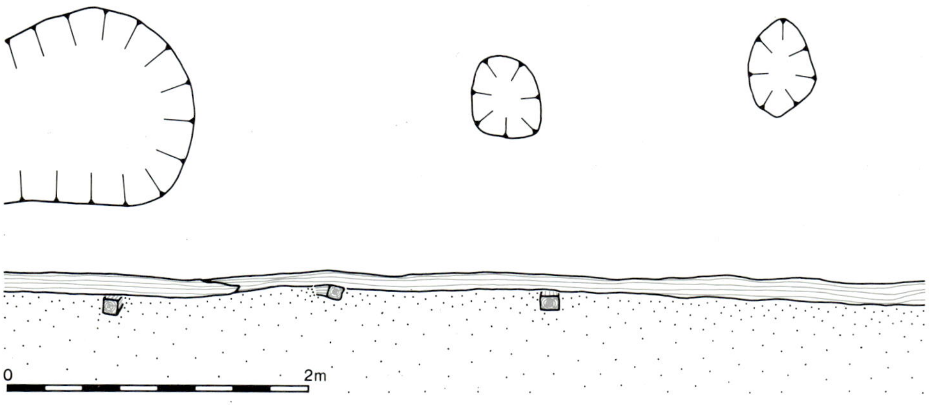

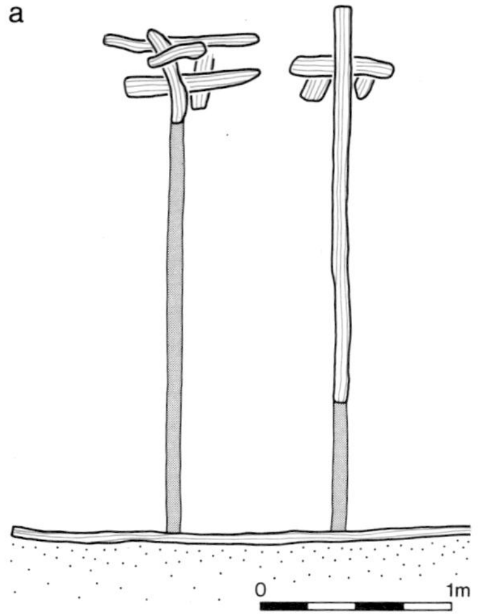

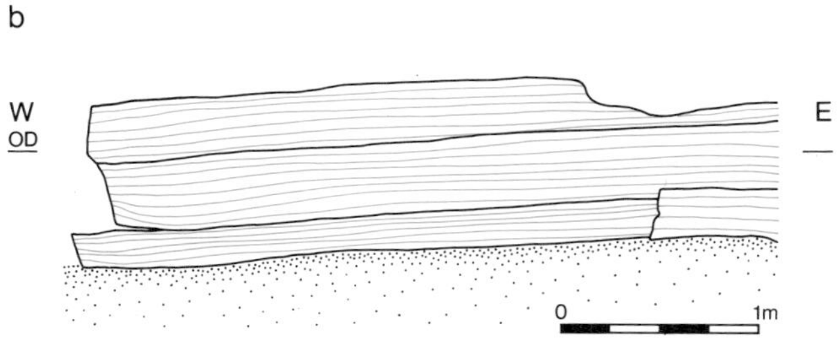

18. Above: Billingsgate Lorry Park, Structure BG13.
a) plan of back braces in relation to plank cladding of revetment;
b) south facing elevation of plank cladding.

19. Below: Billingsgate Lorry Park. Detail of the BG12 *structure, looking south-east. The 10 x 10mm scale lies next to the junction of two members which formed the plate retaining the feet of the front braces; cf. Fig 17.*

STRUCTURE BG14

(Figs 20-3)

The front-braced BG14 post and plank revetment lay 3m to the south of the BG13 structure. A north-south revetment (not illustrated: Archive reference BIG82 VIII.2) ran between the two and presumably operated for a short time during the construction of BG14. The temporary structure comprised a north-south mortised baseplate into which squared posts were tenoned and pegged, and these were supported to the west by diagonal braces set into subsidiary baseplates laid on the foreshore. This structure was extensively sampled for dendrochronological analysis.

The broadly contemporary BG14 revetment survived to a height of 2.25m in the centre of the site. It comprised a squared east-west baseplate into which rectangular mortises had been cut, some passing through the plate where it was only 0.6m thick. The mortises accommodated shouldered, pegged tenons cut on the feet of the principal posts, many of which were reused timbers (see *eg* Fig 92). The posts varied in size, but were at least 2m tall, up to 0.3m wide and 150mm thick. They were in turn supported by barely-dressed branches, sometimes curved and still in the round, acting as front braces. The head of each brace tapered to a point which was housed in a splayed recess in the face of a principal post, while the foot was cut to a rough chase tenon wedged into a through mortise in a subsidiary baseplate running north-south on the foreshore.

An additional post and brace to the west end of the surviving section (see Fig 20) is interpreted as a later repair.

20. Billingsgate Lorry Park. A general view of BG14 *revetment surviving virtually to full height, looking north. The structure incorporates squared posts tenoned into a squared baseplate, but the braces are all roundwood branches.*

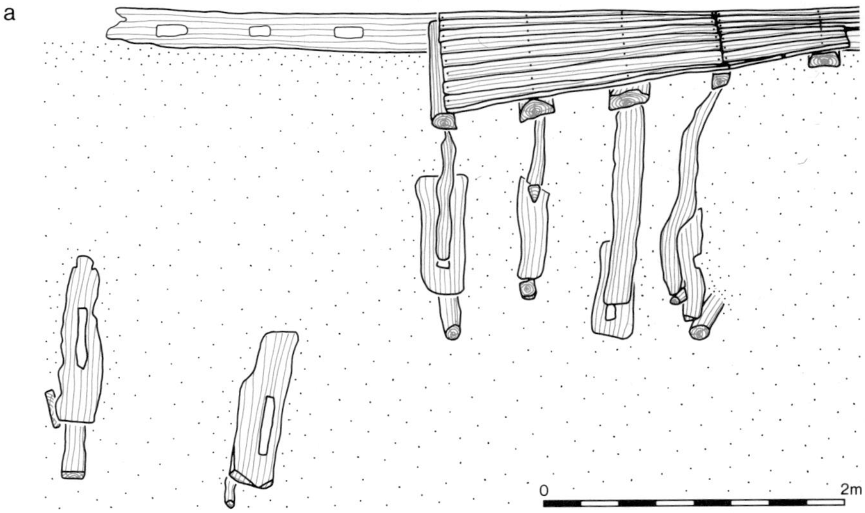

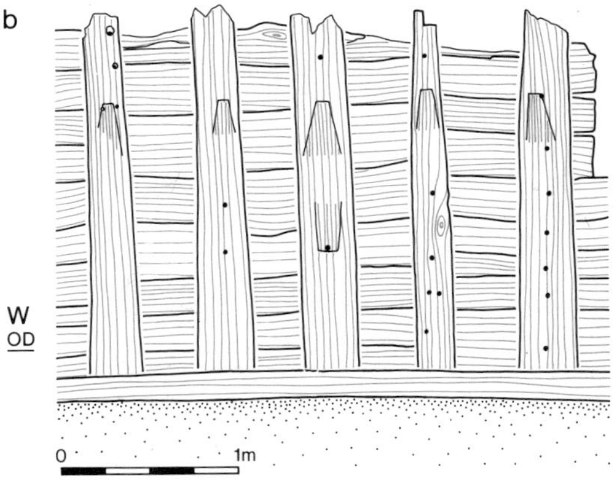

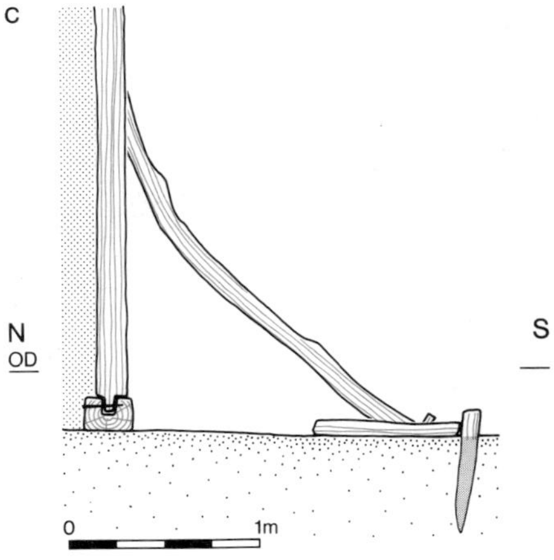

21. Billingsgate Lorry Park, 13th-century Structure BG14*: a) plan showing baseplate with posts and cladding removed in west, and subsiding as found in east; b) south facing elevation of revetment (but with the front braces removed); c) side elevation, semi-reconstructed, showing the branch used for the front brace.*

22. Above: Billingsgate Lorry Park. Reverse (landward) face of BG14 *revetment cladding, looking south. The unenhanced assembly marks (cf. Fig 23) show that it was prefabricated; scale 5 x 100mm.*

23. Below: Billingsgate Lorry Park. BG14 *revetment cladding as on Fig 22, but with the assembly marks enhanced with chalk.*

The cladding comprised up to ten runs of sawn planking up to 2m long, 0.36m wide and 30mm thick, laid horizontally edge to edge and pegged onto the north face of the posts. Three discrete sections of cladding were identified by different sets of assembly marks incised on the north face, demonstrating that the structure had been prefabricated. Roman numerals were not used, every run of planking simply being marked with the number of strokes that corresponded to its level. The marks on each 1.8m-wide section were differentiated: units in the east were incised diagonally, unlike the vertically-set ones to the west, while the central ones had an additional stroke scored horizontally across them.

Archive reference: BIG82 IX.1

Dating: The BG14 revetment is stratigraphically later than BG12 and BG13 (1168-1205); earlier than BG16. Taking into consideration the dendrochronological evidence discussed below, a date of *c.*1220 is suggested for the construction of BG14.

Dendrochronological summary: The BG14 revetment was conserved in its entirety for display, but was extensively sampled in as non-damaging a way as possible (archive report: Hillam & Groves 1985). Initially 20 samples were taken but of these only six were viable and three were dated (Figs 9, 11), and an additional wedge was taken (archive report: Hillam 1990). This may have been from a reused timber, but had nine sapwood rings and an estimated felling date of 1169-1214. Some of the timbers were also X-rayed (Tyers 1985), and the two dated samples were combined to produce an estimated felling date of 1189-1234.

However, 31 samples were taken from the broadly contemporary north-south structure (archive reference BIG82 VIII.2; link revetment on Fig 11), from posts, planks, braces, baseplates and piles. Of these ten were dated, suggesting that at least two of the posts and four planks were contemporary. The bark and sapwood survived on one sample, and a felling date of 1215/16 is suggested.

STRUCTURE BG16

(Figs 24-6)

The front-braced BG16 post and plank revetment was erected between 6m and 8m to the south of the BG14 structure. Although a substantial section of the north (landward) face was recorded, the front (riverward) face of the structure was only recorded in the western corner of the controlled excavation. It survived for a length of 13m and to a height of 1.8m. In form, it closely resembled the BG14 structure which it replaced, and some of the timber elements may have been removed from the western section of the earlier revetment for reuse in it. It comprised sections of squared baseplate joined with through-splayed and pegged scarfs, into which posts had been set at 0.6m to 0.8m centres with standard pegged mortises and tenons. The planking had originally been pegged to the posts, but nails were used in a small area which had been repaired.

A point of particular interest is the survival of decayed fragments thought to represent part of a wallplate, with pegged mortises in the underside to accommodate the heads of the principal posts. The posts were supported by diagonally-set front braces, the feet of which were tenoned into subsidiary baseplates on the foreshore to the south, as in the BG14 structure.

Archive reference: BIG82 XI.1

Dating: The BG16 revetment is stratigraphically later than the early 13th-century BG14, and retained reclamation dumps containing 13th-century pottery and a group of coins deposited shortly after *c.*1250.

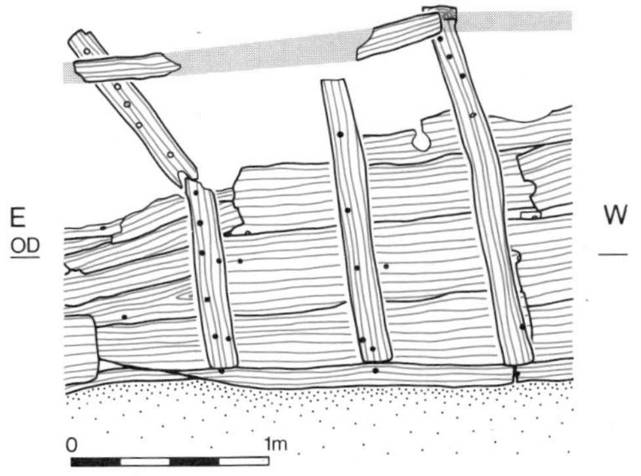

24. Billingsgate Lorry Park, 13th-century Structure BG16*: elevation of the south face of revetment (drawn in reverse from field elevations of the north face). Note displaced top-plate.*

25. Billingsgate Lorry Park: landward (north) face of BG16 *revetment excavated on the edge of the sheet-piled southern limit of excavation. The 5 x 100mm scale stands on baseplate into which posts were set. Note rebates on two posts in west (right), showing that they were reused timbers (cf. Fig 24).*

26. Right: Billingsgate Lorry Park. Detail of displaced top-plate from BG16 *revetment, disturbed by sheet piling (cf. Fig 24). The 10 x 10mm scale rests on the top-plate, which has a mortise cut in it to accommodate rough tenon on the head of the (once) vertical post.*

SEAL HOUSE 1974
TQ32778067 Site code: SH74

From May to December 1974, a 40m-long north-south trench 3m wide was excavated on a site south of Upper Thames Street, east of Swan Lane and west of Fishmongers Hall, which itself lies adjacent to the modern London Bridge (Fig 27). The work was supervised by John Schofield (Schofield 1975; Hobley & Schofield 1977, 37-8). Among the earliest features recorded were parts of Roman waterfront installations, over which a thick foreshore deposit had accumulated (Brigham 1990, 107-111). Several phases of riverfront structure marked subsequent extensions of the waterfront in the 11th to 13th centuries, and these were labelled W1 to W3 (Steedman *et al* forthcoming).

In 1976 a watching brief was conducted on the area to the south and west of the trench during contractors' earth-moving operations. Fragments of five other timber riverfront structures (W4 to W8) were investigated in this period, marking further stages in the reclamation of this part of the medieval waterfront, culminating in the construction of a masonry river wall (W9), thought to be 15th-century in date. A similar sequence was observed during contractors' site work on the west side of Swan Lane (Site code: SWA81). Since few of the structures were planned *in situ,* they are not included in this catalogue (but cf. Egan & Pritchard 1991).

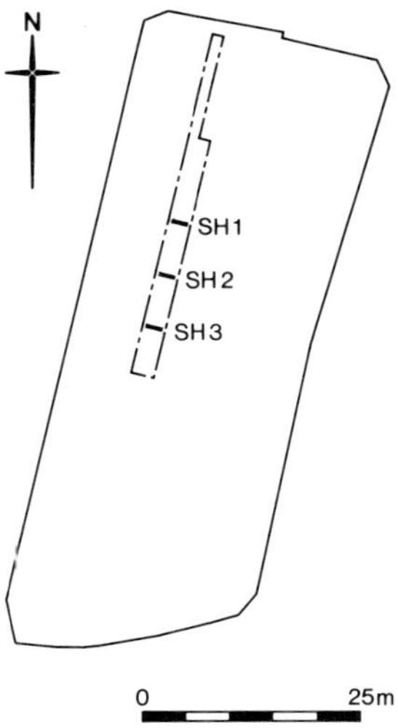

27. Seal House site (see Fig 3). Plan of controlled excavation and position of the structures described in Catalogue. Scale 1:1250.

STRUCTURE SH1

(Figs 28-30)

The SH1 structure or structures incorporated a displaced baseplate presumably for a stave revetment, with fragments of a back brace to the north set into an embankment stabilised by planked cribwork. The embankment had been raised over the remains of the 3rd-century Roman quay at the north end of the site. The highest surviving levels comprised a dump of organic material in which the fragmentary remains of an internal revetment were recorded. This phase of the development is not

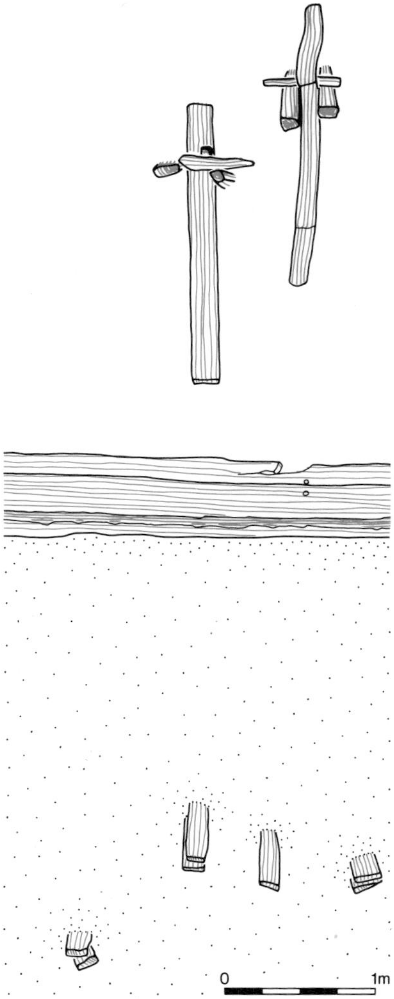

28. Seal House, 12th-century Structure SH1: plan of severed back braces and baseplate.

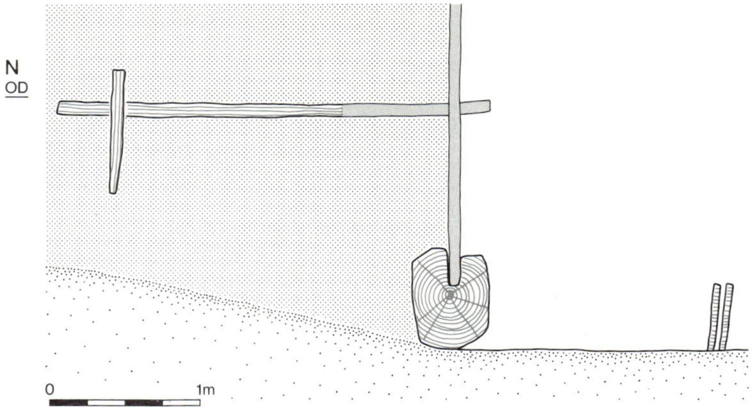

29. Above: Seal House, Structure SH1*: side elevation, semi-reconstructed.*

30. Below: Seal House, baseplate of SH1 *structure, looking north: the superstructure had been removed in antiquity. The 2 x 100mm scale stands on the foreshore against the displaced baseplate: the groove in the upper face presumably accommodated a stave wall.*

illustrated here. The south edge of the compartment had broken away in antiquity, suggesting that the south face of the embankment had collapsed.

This feature was sealed by another phase of dumps, presumably representing material thrown behind a new revetment constructed to the south. Although much of this structure had been dismantled, the baseplate survived. It was aligned east-west, and was 0.5m deep, 0.36m wide and at least 2.7m long. There were two small notches 1.2m apart in the top of the south edge, and the upper face was cut along its length by a slot 110mm wide and 120mm deep. This may have accommodated the feet of the staves forming the revetment face.

Two closely-spaced but severed back braces set at a higher level to the north of the baseplate probably once articulated with the stave wall. Each comprised a horizontal north-south beam pierced at the north end, through which a pile-retained east-west crosspiece passed.

Archive reference: SH74 W1

Dating: The SH1 structure was laid on a foreshore stratigraphically later than the remains of a Roman quay, and presumably retained material within an embankment containing 12th-century pottery (but with some intrusive 13th-century material). It was stratigraphically earlier than SH2 (*c.*1163-92).

Dendrochronological summary: Of the nine samples taken from this structure, five were dated but only one had sapwood (Hillam forthcoming): the estimated felling date range is 1133-70 (Fig 9).

STRUCTURE SH2

(Figs 31-3)

The post and plank SH2 structure was constructed on the foreshore 5m south of the SH1 baseplate. Two earthfast posts were set 1m apart north-south. The southern one was 3.25m tall and 0.34m x 0.34m in cross-section at the base, its head tapering to 0.28m x 0.28m. The northern one, which was at least 0.2m x 0.2m in cross-section, had been cut down to only 0.8m in height. Both timbers were listing southwards when found, but were presumably set vertically when built. Grooves cut in adjacent edges and faces along the length of the timbers accepted up to six tiers of planking running north-south and east-west, forming compartments. The planks were up to 0.38m wide and up to 350mm thick, and were additionally supported by piles driven against their faces. Although much of the timberwork had been removed on the eastern side of the excavation, the presence of a plank in the 50mm-deep groove cut vertically in the east face of the south post demonstrated that the cladding once extended eastwards. There were no slots in the south post to accept planks heading southwards, or in the north or east faces of the north post.

Archive reference: SH74 W2

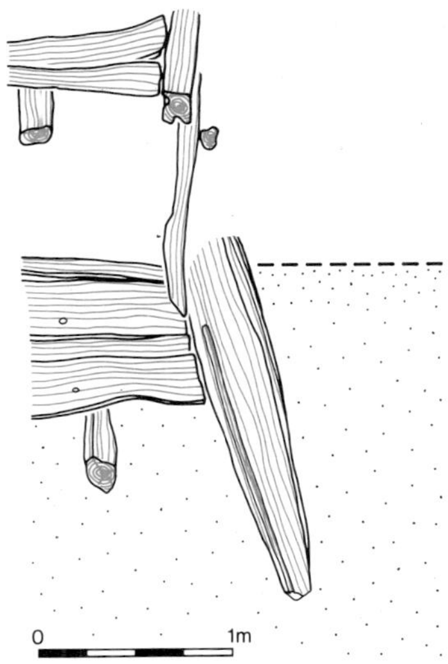

31. Seal House, 12th-century Structure SH2*: plan of collapsed revetment as found.*

Dating: The SH2 structure was stratigraphically later than SH1 (*c.*1133-70), was associated with pottery of late 12th-century date, and was sealed within the dumps thrown behind SH3 (*c.*1195-1215).

Dendrochronological summary: Of the seven samples taken from this structure, four were dated but only one had sapwood (Hillam forthcoming): the estimated felling date range is 1163-92 (Fig 9).

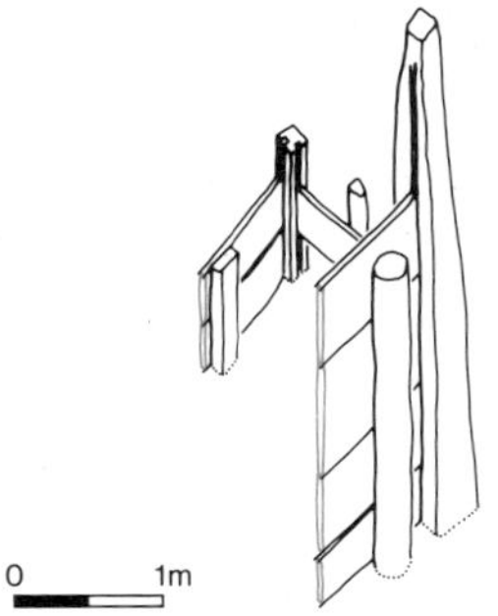

32. Seal House: semi-reconstructed axonometric projection of part of Structure SH2.

33. Seal House: part of SH2 *structure, looking south. The 5 x 100mm scale rests on the foreshore upon which the structure was built: the main post to east (left) of scale is earthfast. The plank cladding is set into grooves cut in the edge of the post.*

STRUCTURE SH3

(Figs 34-6)

A 2.5m-wide section of the front-braced post and plank SH3 revetment was recorded 6m to the south of the SH2 structure. A series of subsidiary baseplates aligned north-south had been laid over the sloping foreshore, of which two were recorded. Both had retaining piles driven against the south end, while chase mortises had been cut in the upper face to accept the tenon on the foot of the front braces. One of these baseplates passed beneath the principal east-west baseplate. The latter was 0.33m x 0.12m in cross-section and comprised at least two sections of timber, apparently joined with a through-splayed scarf. Through-mortises set in the upper face of the plate accommodated pegged tenons on the feet of five squared vertical posts up to 0.2m x 0.2m in cross-section, one of which survived up to 2.4m tall. Splayed recesses cut in the south face of the posts accommodated the heads of the front braces, which were clearly reused timbers. No braces survived with the other vertical posts. Splayed recesses cut in the south face 1m above baseplate level may have accommodated braces, unless all three members were reused timbers.

The cladding comprised at least six runs of planking up to 0.5m wide and 400mm thick, which was pegged to the north face of the posts. No back braces were observed in the short section of the structure recorded during the controlled excavation.

Archive reference: SH74 W3

Dating: The SH3 structure was stratigraphically later than SH2 (*c*.1163-92), was associated with substantial dumps of pottery of early 13th-century date, and was stratigraphically earlier than dumps containing mid 13th-century pottery.

Dendrochronological summary: Of the 14 samples taken from SH3 posts, planking and braces, eight were dated (Figs 9, 37). Of these, two retained sapwood from which a felling date range of 1195-1215 was estimated (Hillam pers comm). In addition, three samples from a drain which ultimately functioned with it were derived from trees felled after 1203, while a single displaced timber which was probably associated with the construction of the revetment came from a tree felled in the winter of 1202/3.

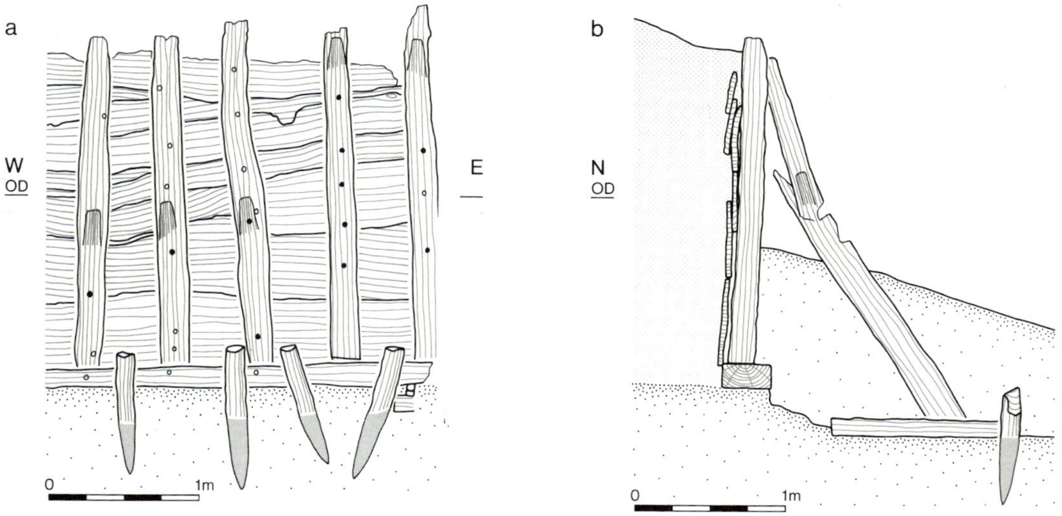

34. Seal House, 13th-century Structure SH3*: a) south facing elevation, with front braces removed; b) side elevation with broken front brace as found.*

35. Seal House: south (riverward) face of SH3 *revetment, looking north. The 5 x 100mm scale rests on the baseplate below splayed recesses cut in the face of the posts.*

36. Seal House: landward face of SH4 *revetment, looking south. The 10 x 100mm scale rests against the plank cladding which has been pegged to the revetment posts.*

37. SH3 *structure: bar diagram showing tree-ring results.*

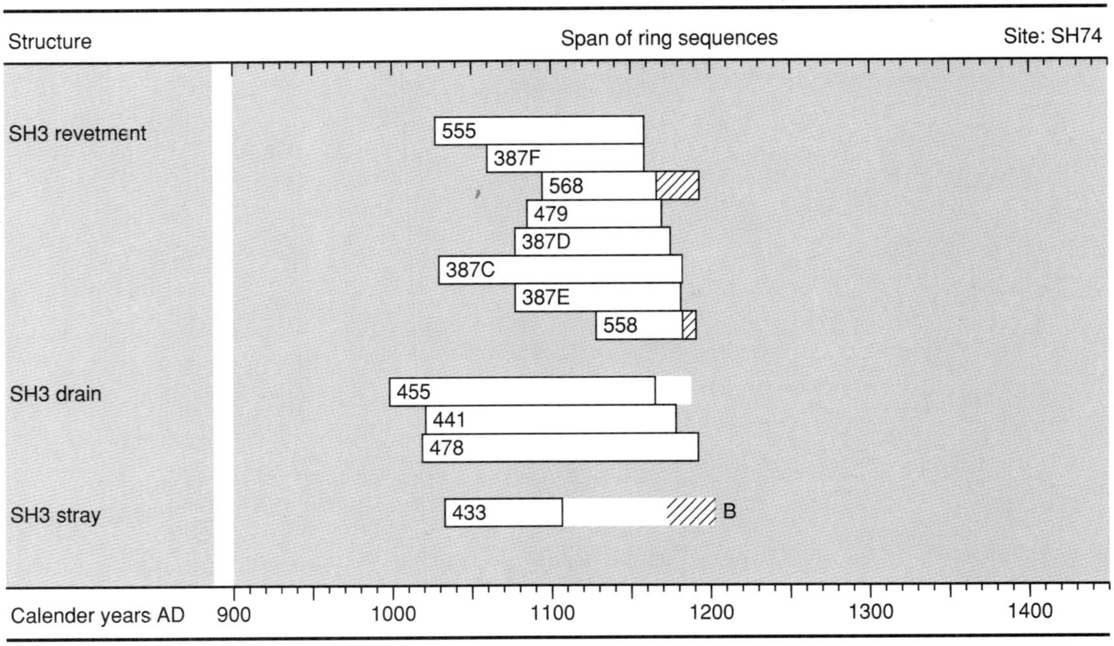

THAMES EXCHANGE

TQ32458075 Site code: TEX88

The 4,000 square metre site lies at the north-east corner of Southwark Bridge, in the area once known as Three Cranes Wharf. Ground works were monitored continuously from January 1988 to September 1989, while a controlled excavation of a 70m x 11m area on the east of the site was mounted in phases between August 1988 and March 1989 (Fig 38). The line of a 3rd-century Roman quay was traced for 35m east-west in the north of the site, and was overlain by a thick accumulation of foreshore material. Over this, a long sequence of development was recorded, incorporating over thirty timber riverfront structures dating from the 10th to the 14th centuries, in addition to associated buildings and other features. It proved possible to examine the development of two waterfront properties, initially set either side of an inlet aligned with the foot of College Hill, a lane on the north side of Upper Thames Street. Six structures from the eastern 'property' (TX1-TX6) and three from the western 'property' (TX7-TX9) are described in this report.

The project was directed by Gustav Milne, with Chrissie Milne supervising the controlled excavations, while Morag Colquhoun and Jo Stevenson were responsible for monitoring the contractors' ground works. They also prepared the detailed archive report upon which the following summaries are based, and prepared the associated illustrative material.

The majority of the field work was funded by the developers, Kumagai-Gumi, with additional support for the watching brief from DUA contingency funds, and for some of the post-excavation work from the City of London Archaeological Trust and from English Heritage. Only that part of the archive report which is summarised here has been completed, since there is no further funding available for the study of the rest of the structural sequence or for the large assemblages of associated finds.

The absolute dating of the structures therefore relies on the dendrochronological study by Nigel Nayling (Fig 39), elements of which are summarised in the dating sections of the following descriptions.

38. Thames Exchange (see Fig 3). a) Plan showing alignments of medieval waterfront structures recorded and observed. The area of controlled excavations is shown within the line broken by dots. b) to h) Plan series showing stages in waterfront development from 10th to 14th centuries: position of structures described in catalogue marked. Scale 1:1250.

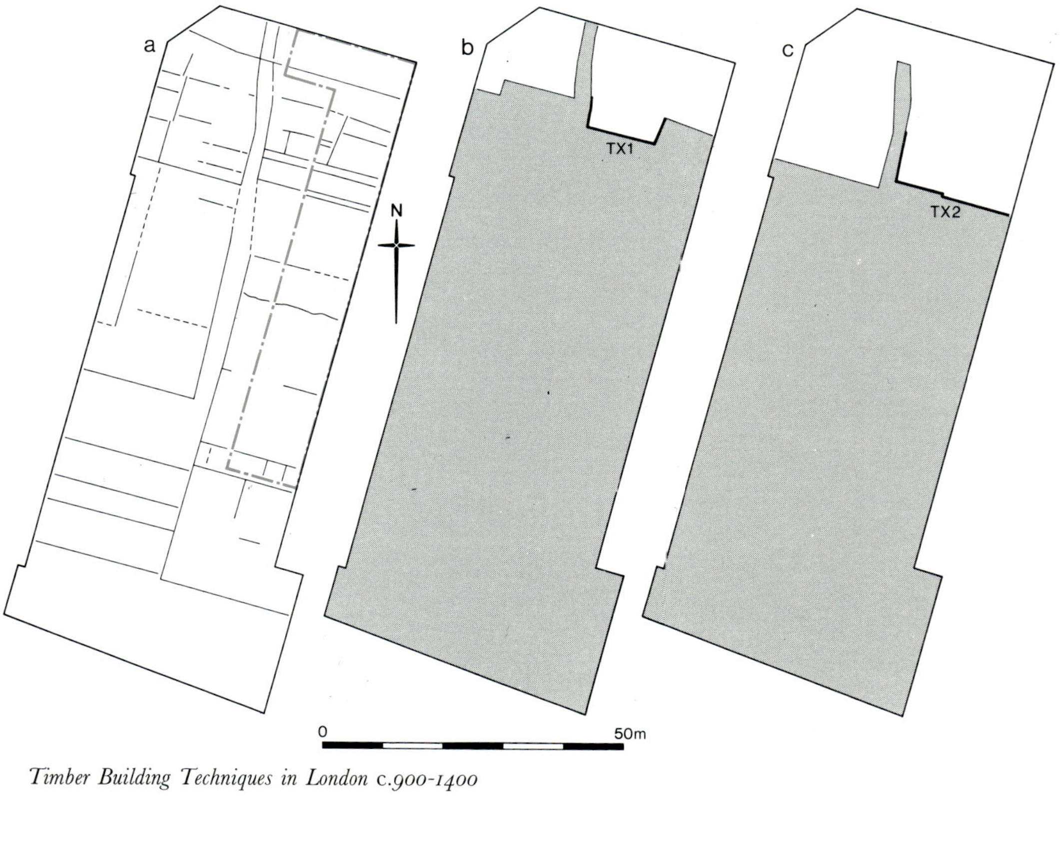

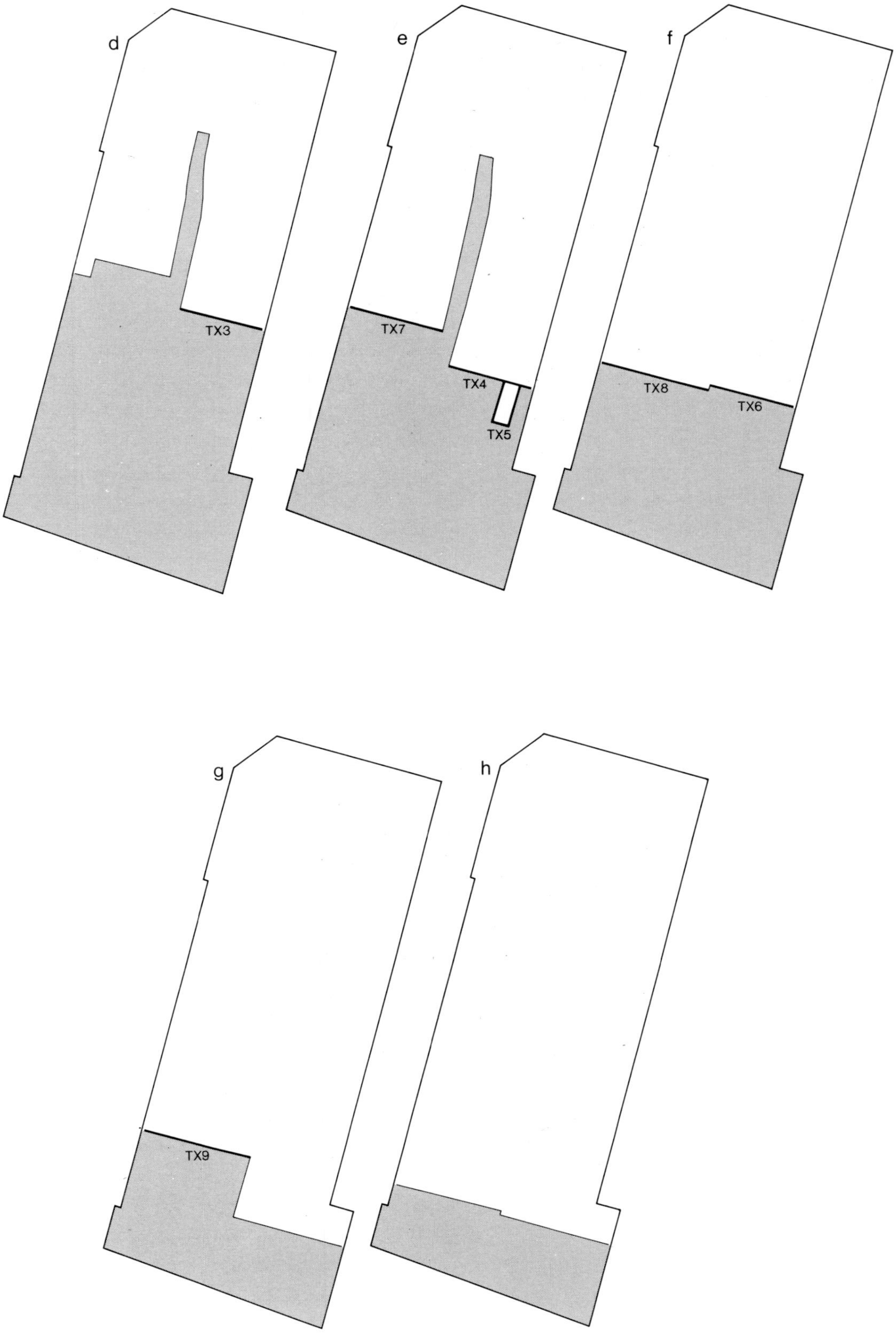
d
TX3
e
TX7
TX4
TX5
f
TX8
TX6
g
TX9
h

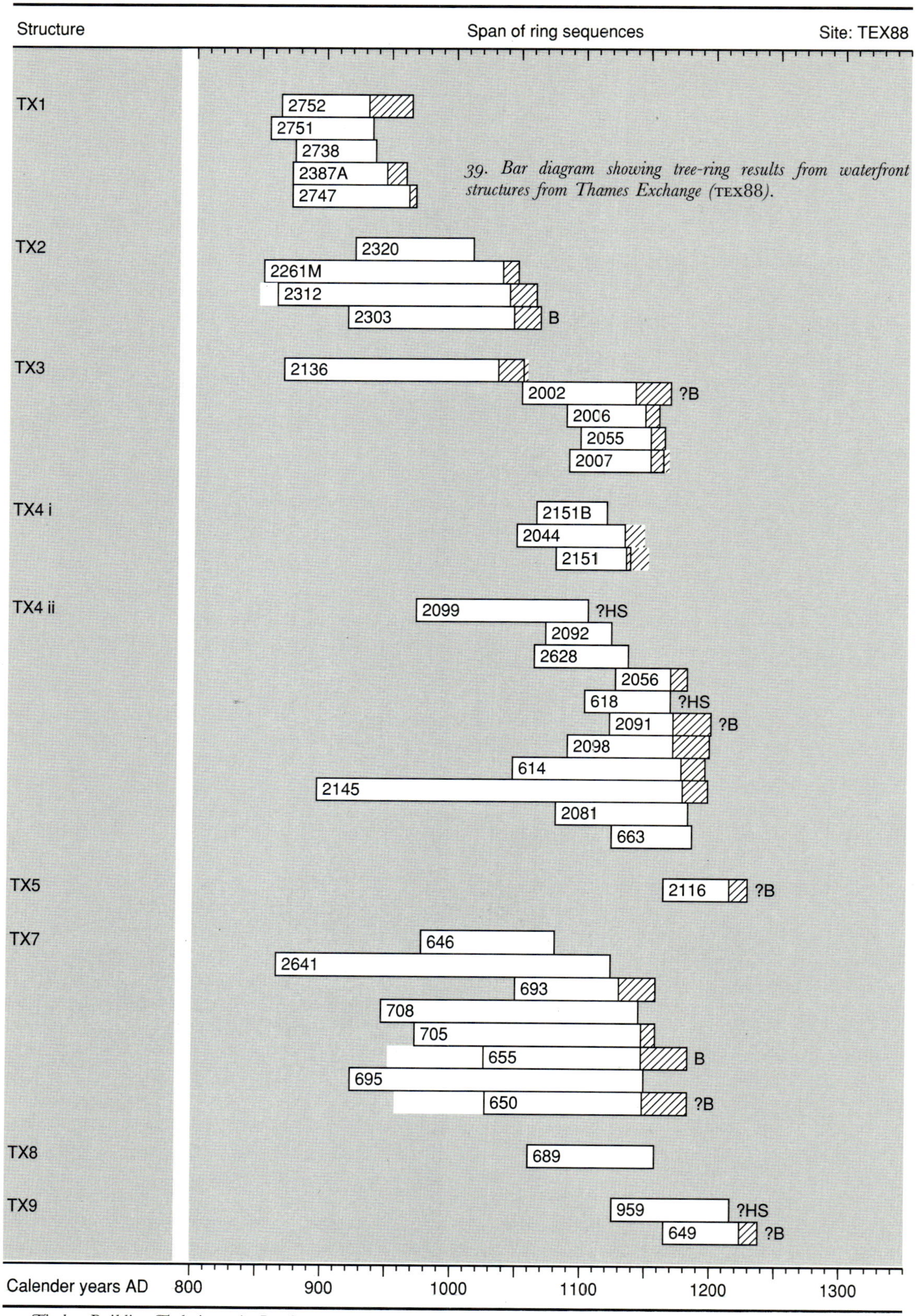

39. Bar diagram showing tree-ring results from waterfront structures from Thames Exchange (TEX88).

STRUCTURE TX1

(Figs 40-2)

The earliest medieval waterfront structures recorded during the controlled excavations of the Thames Exchange site all comprised earthfast post and plank revetments, usually utilising roundwood posts retaining cleft planks. The first structures were laid over the foreshores which sealed the robbed remnant of the Roman quay and at least five phases of repair or advance were identified earlier than (*ie* north of) the TX2 structure (see for example Figs 105, 106: all seem to represent activity before the Norman Conquest.

None of these excavated structures exhibited complex joinery (although one incorporated substantial fragments of reused boat or ship timber), with the exception of revetment TX1. This structure merits special study since the well-built junction of two walls survived; in all other respects, this revetment was no different from its direct predecessors and successors. Consequently, only one Saxon revetment from this site is illustrated in this catalogue.

The TX1 structure extended for 5m southwards from an earlier earthfast post and plank revetment before returning westwards for 6.9m. The extent of the structure seems to have been marked out by driving a line of earthfast piles 0.4m apart, each one at least 2.5m tall and up to 180mm in diameter. The bottom of each pile had been cut to a point some 0.6m long.

At least eight levels of cleft oak boards were laid against the landward face of these piles to retain the infill material, but were not fixed with pegs or nails. However, the ends of the planking of the east-west and north-south walls were interlocked by half-lapping the eastern boards over the southern boards. This shows that each run of planking was laid from west to east and then from south to north. The facing stood to some 1.5m above the level of the contemporary foreshore.

The end of a horizontal brace or anchor beam at least 3.6m long protruded 0.6m through the south plank wall above the seventh level of planking. It was 0.22m x 0.13m in cross-section and had a rough sub-rectangular mortise cut through the south end, which retained the head of one of the earthfast piles. The north end of the brace had been destroyed by later foundations, but it is clear that the brace was laid after the majority of the infill material had been thrown in behind the planking.

These dumps were sealed by a cobbled surface at 0.9m OD. Internal surfaces of buildings which may be contemporary were recorded 9m to the north at *c.*1.65m OD.

Archive reference: TEX88 Structure 1744

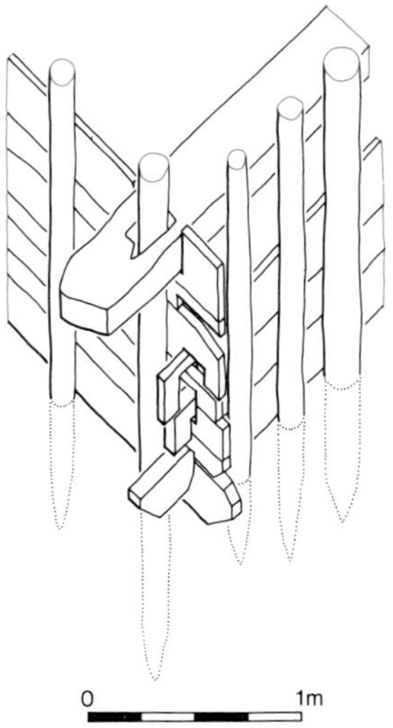

40. Thames Exchange: semi-reconstructed axonometric projection of south-east corner of 10th-century Structure TX1*: see Fig 38.*

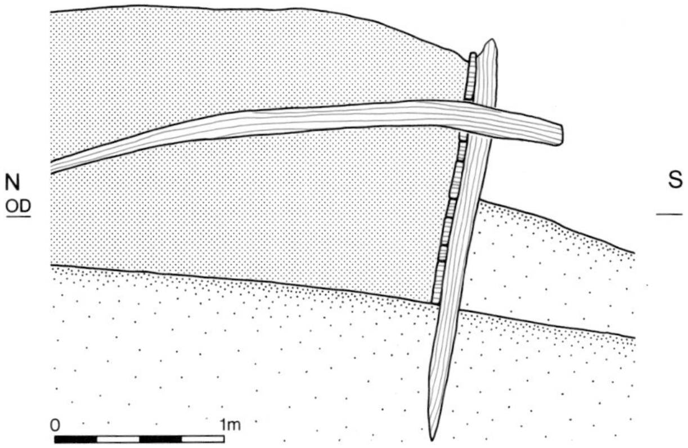

41. Thames Exchange: side elevation of Structure TX1 *(cf. Fig 40).*

42. *Thames Exchange:* TX1 *braced revetment, looking north-west. The 2 x 100mm scale stands on the foreshore: above it a back brace protrudes south. Note interlocking planks forming the south-east corner of structure (cf. Fig 40).*

Dating: The TX1 structure was not the earliest structure on the site (see Structure 1512, Fig 102), but was one of a series of features built onto the foreshore which sealed the remains of a Roman quay. It was stratigraphically (though not directly) earlier than TX2 (1066/7). The finds groups associated with this and the other Thames Exchange structures described in this catalogue still await detailed study.

Dendrochronological summary: Of the 12 samples from the TX1 structure, five were dated, and three had sapwood: the estimated felling date is AD 967-89 (Figs 9, 39). Timber 2747 was recovered during the watching brief and may represent a later repair to the TX1 structure: it was felled between 975 and 1020.

For comparison, five samples were taken from the broadly contemporary Structure 1748 from the same site, two of which were dated. Timber 2402 had six sapwood rings, with an estimated felling date range of AD 952-99, but 2398 had 26 sapwood rings, and may have been felled in 966/7.

STRUCTURE TX2

(Figs 43-5)

Following the construction of the TX1 revetment, modifications were made, which incorporated at least three more earthfast post and plank structures. This activity only advanced the line of the contemporary waterfront some 5m southwards, and so may be interpreted as a succession of repairs rather than as extensions designed to win new land.

The next phase of advance was also modest, some 2.5m, but incorporated a different structural technique, that of earthfast stave building, with the construction of the TX2 structure. Part of this revetment was recorded in the controlled excavation, while two further observations were made during ground works to the west and east. In all, the structure was traced for a distance of 18m east-west. It seemed to comprise two roughly parallel lines of earthfast staves set up to 1m apart, of which the south wall seems to have been free-standing.

The north wall was supported by horizontal back braces and retained a bank of timber and silts. This comprised a dump of horizontally-laid timbers, rough radially-split members and an assortment of waste timber, most of which was laid north-south and ultimately encased in grey silts. This horizon was sealed by a layer of pure grey clay some 0.75m thick which was in turn sealed by another level of rough radially split oak, branches and waste timber, all laid horizontally east-west in a matrix of grey clay. This feature has much in common with the hurdle and faggot silt traps used in the reclamation of the Fens and to help consolidate banks prone to erosion (Rackham 1980, 389). The embankment thus formed extended northwards to the latest of the earthfast post structures, and was sealed by a deposit of peat which covered the sloping surface of the clay and timber bank as well as its south face.

To the south, the embankment was retained by a line of wattle hurdles laid against the north face of the earthfast stave wall, which had been set in a trench in the foreshore some 0.5m deep. The staves which had not been truncated in antiquity, were up to 3m tall, and varied in width from 0.21m to 0.5m and in thickness from 70mm to 150mm. Some of the staves were halved, others radially cleft and some tangentially cleft. All but one had flat bases, and there was evidence of previous use for some of the timbers, principally in the form of peg holes. The staves were irregularly spaced, and five were supported by back braces laid horizontally north-south at intervals of 2m, at a height of 1.15m OD. The braces were up to 4.2m long, 0.35m deep and 0.10m wide, set on edge. At the north end, each brace was secured by a pile-retained crosspiece slotted through the brace. The south end passed through a rectangular notch cut on the eastern edge of the stave, protruding some 0.6m beyond the face of the revetment. A sub-rectangular mortise had been cut in the projecting end, presumably to accommodate a horizontal retaining bar.

The second stave wall lay immediately to the south, and a 7m length was recorded. It comprised at least 11 radially-cleft or halved earthfast staves set 0.6m into the foreshore, 0.2m apart. The staves were up to 0.3m wide, 90mm thick and 3.1m long. Beneath the surface of the contemporary foreshore the staves remained vertical, but immediately above that point those which had not been truncated in antiquity had been bent and twisted southwards.

Wattle hurdles at least 0.6m high had been set 0.1m into the foreshore against the north face of the staves. There was no evidence of any other support

43. Thames Exchange: detail of TX2 *stave structure, looking east. The 5 x 100mm scale stands against a section cut through the foreshore into which the free-standing earthfast stave to the south was set. It was subsequently secured with wattle-work woven around it.*

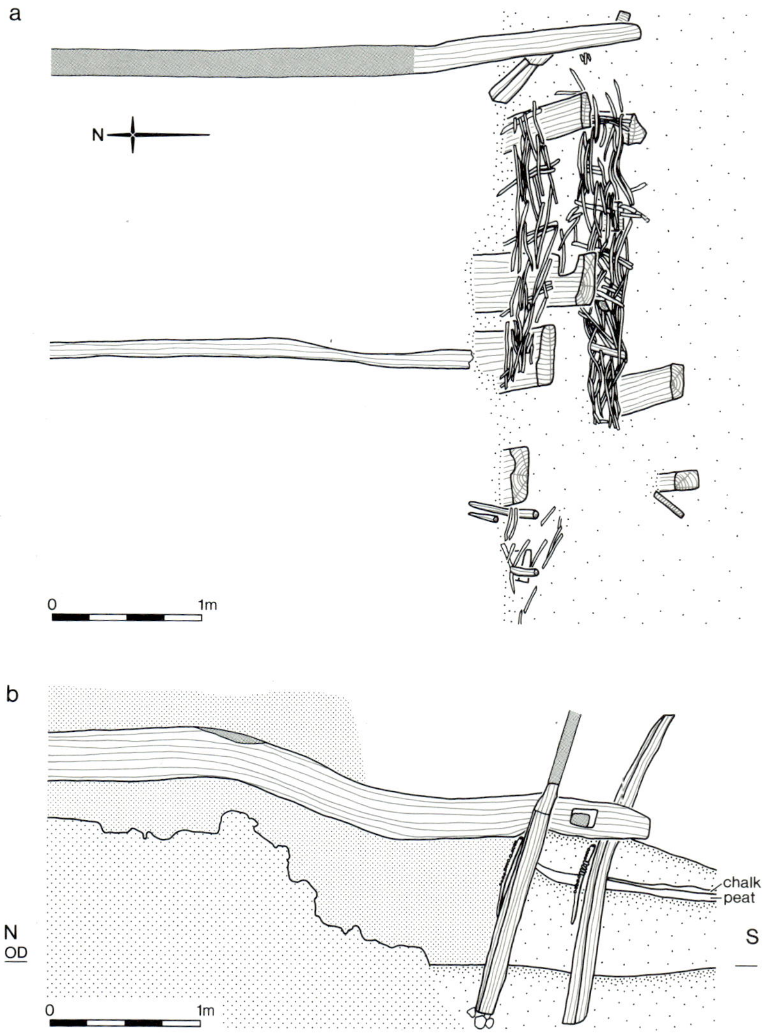

44. Thames Exchange, 11th-century Structure TX2*: a) plan: north to left (see Fig 38); b) side elevation as found. Note the chalk, peat and foreshore horizons demonstrating that the southern line of staves was free-standing.*

for these staves, in the form of front or back braces, and there seems to have been no contemporary dumping behind them. Similar waterlaid deposits accumulated both north and south of this wattle and stave structure, and a tamped chalk surface was also recorded on both sides of it. Taken together, the evidence suggests that the staves formed a free-standing wall, rising up to 2.5m proud of the contemporary foreshore, providing additional protection for the revetment to the north.

Dumping associated with the next waterfront advance engulfed the free-standing stave wall, filled the spaced behind it, and lapped up against the more northerly braced stave wall, demonstrating that both sets of staves were contemporary.

45. Thames Exchange: TX2. *The 5 x 100mm scale stands on the foreshore to the south of the displaced stave, which had been supported by the back brace and lockbar seen in section.*

Archive reference: TEX88 Structure 1437

Dating: The TX2 structure was stratigraphically (though not directly) later than TX1 (*c.*AD 967-89), which was in turn earlier than TX3 (1167/8).

Dendrochronological summary: Of the 12 samples from the TX2 structure, four were dated, three had sapwood, and one also had bark (2303): a felling date in the winter of 1066/7 is indicated (Figs 9, 39).

a

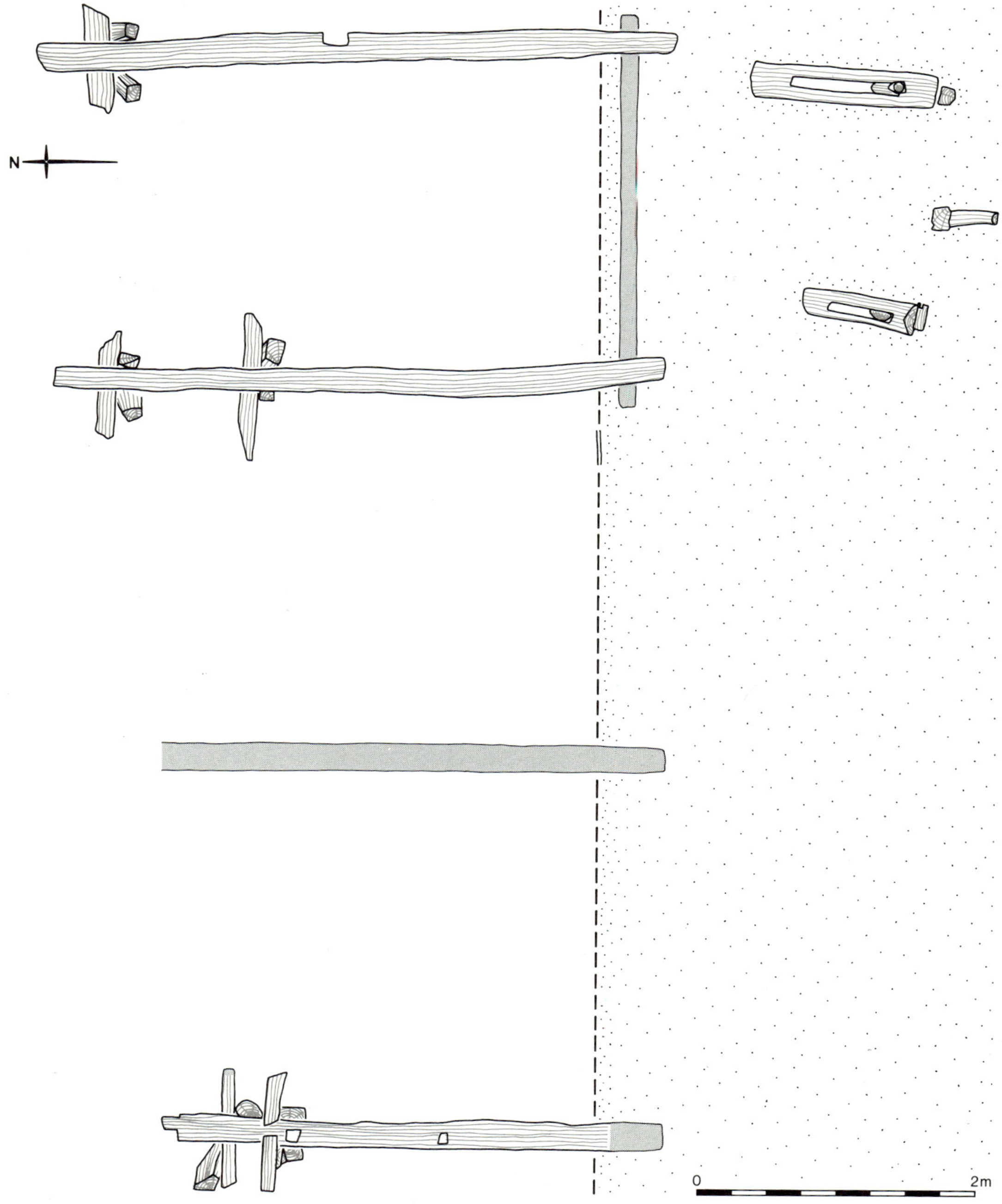

46. Thames Exchange, 12th-century Structure TX3 *(see Fig 38). a) plan, north to left. Dashed line indicates position of the robbed-out front wall which may have been secured with a lockbar passed through the southern ends of the back braces. b) Right: semi-reconstructed side elevation: elements not found are shown toned.*

STRUCTURE TX3

(Figs 46-9)

The waterfront was subsequently extended some 30m southwards, a major reclamation, at which point the remains of the next timber structure, TX3, were recorded. However, it is possible that an intermediate structure may have been used and removed in antiquity. Even the TX3 revetment was extensively robbed, with only four low-level back braces, and evidence for two high-level back braces and up to three front braces surviving. The structure was traced for a distance of at least 10.8m east-west. The lowest back braces were laid horizontally north-south over the dark grey silt and clay dumps, which were some 0.5m thick at this point. The squared braces were up to 4.6m long and 0.20 x 0.25m in cross-section, while two showed evidence of reuse. They were set 2.5m apart, and were secured at the north end by pile-retained cross-pieces passed through a sub-rectangular mortise. The south end of two of the braces survived intact, with a similar sub-rectangular mortise passing through it from east to west. The best surviving higher-level back brace was laid over more dumps, a further 0.5m above the lower brace. It was a roughly-worked elm trunk 4.5m long and 0.22m in diameter, and was secured with two pile-retained crosspieces. At the south end were the remains of an east-west mortise, which had been broken off at the presumed junction of brace and revetment facing.

Although the facing had been robbed out, decayed traces of a vertical plank and imprints of some horizontal planking, perhaps even boat planking, were observed on the clearly-defined south face of the reclamation dumps. The lower 0.7m of this vertical face was well-preserved, suggesting that the facing had been removed quickly and cleanly. This could imply that the frontage was not composed of closely spaced earthfast elements, since the removal of such timbers would have required major disturbance of the underlying and surrounding deposits.

Two baseplates were recorded on the foreshore to the south of the structure, of which one was 1.4m long, with a rectangular through mortise cut in it. It was neither chased nor pegged, but was retained to the south by piles.

Archive reference: TEX88 Structure 1007

Dating: The TX3 structure was stratigraphically later than TX2 (1066/7), which was in turn earlier than the first phase of TX4 (*c.*1152-89).

Dendrochronological summary: Five of the 16 TX3 samples were dated. All had sapwood and one (2002) had 27 sapwood rings and traces of bark: a felling date in the winter of 1167/8 is indicated (Figs 9, 39).

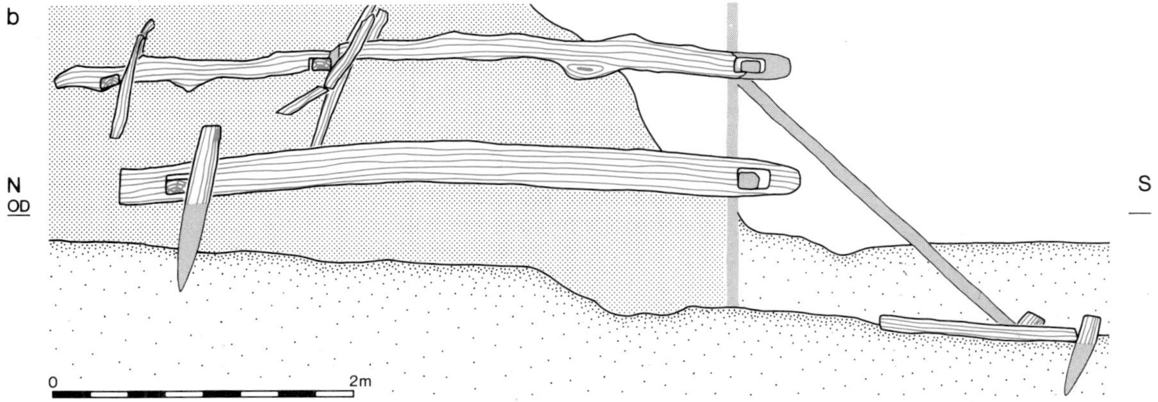

47. Above: Thames Exchange. Back braces from Structure TX3, *looking east. The 5 x 100mm scale rests within the infill deposits behind the revetment. Note the rectangular hole cut in the southern end of the back brace to the south of the scale, marking the position of the robbed cladding.*

49. Below: Thames Exchange, detail of TX3 *revetment, looking north-west. The 2 x 100mm scale rests on the foreshore south of the dumped material behind the revetment. Note traces of timber on the vertical face of the dumps, and the hole in the protruding southern end of the back brace to accommodate a lockbar retaining the cladding.*

48. Thames Exchange: remains of Structure TX3, *looking north. The 5 x 100mm scale rests on the foreshore to the north of which are the lower dumps which had been retained by revetment cladding, secured by the horizontal back braces seen lying within the half-excavated infill material. In the foreground, a trench has been cut through the foreshore deposits, revealing piles and a baseplate which presumably secured the feet of braces supporting the revetment.*

STRUCTURE TX4

(Figs 50-2)

The next advance saw the erection of the front- and back-braced earthfast post and plank TX4 revetment. A length of 8m was examined in the controlled excavation (described below), while observations on four other occasions traced the structure over a distance of 33m east-west. The structure had clearly been repaired, since two severed back braces from the initial phase (Structure 1087) were sealed within the infill deposits behind the replacement planking. This new structure (392) incorporated a series of earthfast posts set in post pits dug 0.5m into the foreshore. The majority of the posts were roughly squared, over 2m long, and of variable cross-section, on average 0.15m x 0.15m.

Every sixth post was a substantially heavier member, being up to 0.4 x 0.3m in cross-section at the base, but tapering towards the head. Rebates 0.1m x 0.6m deep were cut down the north-east and north-west corners to accept the pegged planking. Additional rectangular slots, 70mm x 50mm by 60mm deep, were cut into the east and west faces of several of these posts, and may have been utilised during the initial erection process.

Some of the heavier posts were supported by back braces, of which one still articulated with a revetment post (Structure 1071). This diagonally-set brace comprised a squared timber 0.2m x 0.2m in cross-section, and could have been up to 4m long. The south end articulated with the head of the post some 2m above the contemporary foreshore level. Although the actual junction of post and brace did not survive, a pegged notched lap joint cut on the east face of the post may have been used. A similar joint was used at both ends of the diagonal strut which ran from the brace to the foot of the post, and on the east face of one of the posts (2028) the housing for a notched lap joint, which seems to have been

50. Thames Exchange: the riverward face of TX4 *revetment, looking north. The 5 x 100mm scale stands on the primary foreshore, resting against the plank cladding retained by earthfast posts. In the centre of the photo, foreshore deposits which accumulated against the revetment have been excavated, exposing the feet of the front braces. In the foreground are the remains of the* TX5 *river stair trestles.*

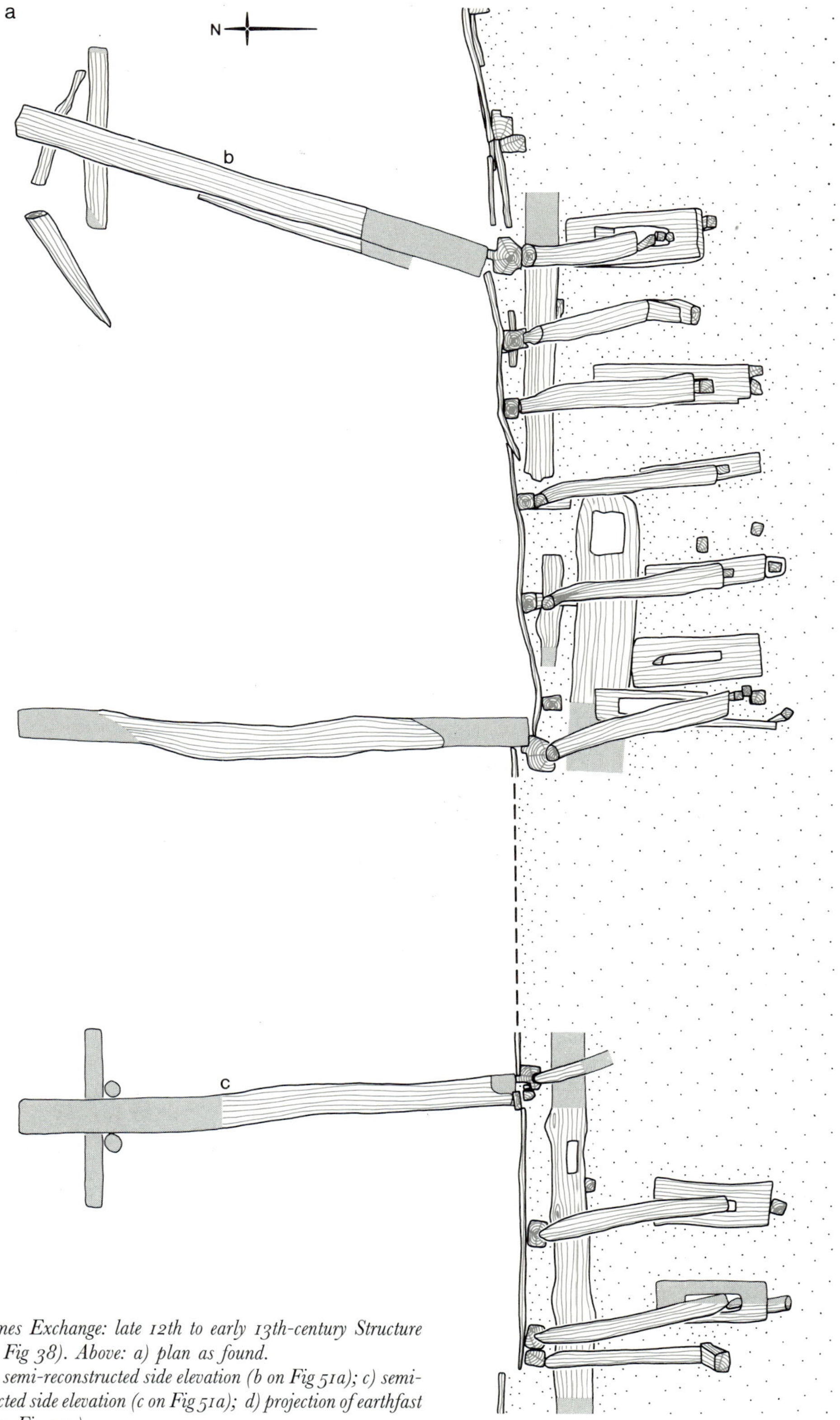

51. Thames Exchange: late 12th to early 13th-century Structure TX4 *(cf. Fig 38). Above: a) plan as found.*
Right: b) semi-reconstructed side elevation (b on Fig 51a); c) semi-reconstructed side elevation (c on Fig 51a); d) projection of earthfast post (d on Fig 51a).

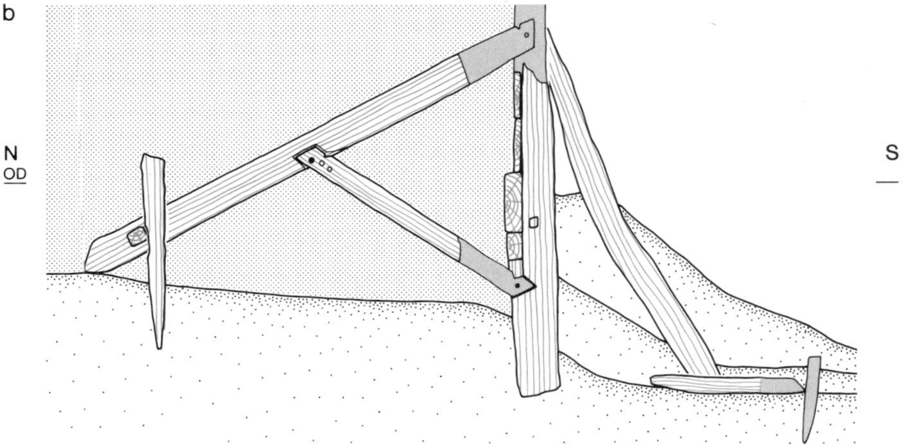

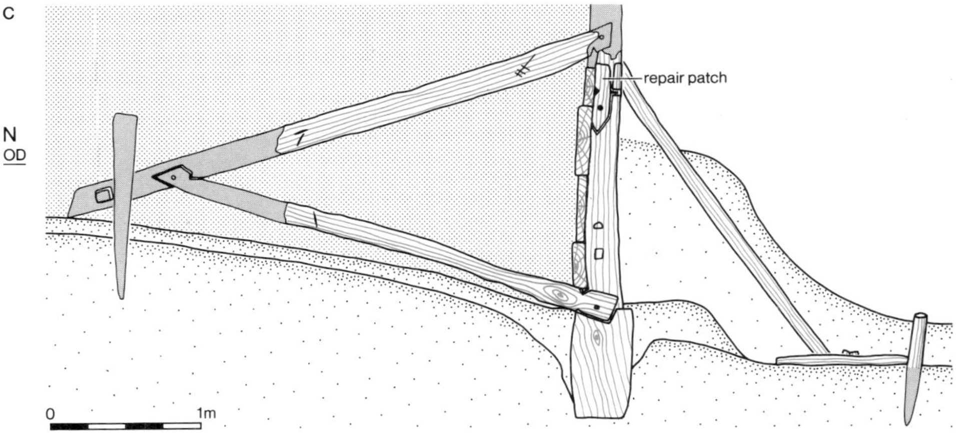

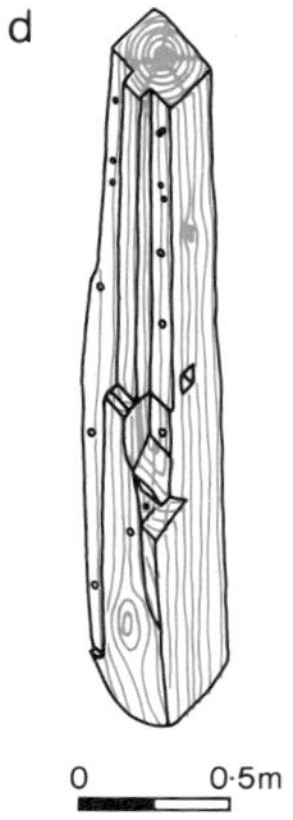

52. Thames Exchange: detail of TX4 *revetment back brace, looking east. The 10 x 10mm scale rests on a squared timber above an incised assembly mark (cf. Fig 51c).*

cut too low to articulate with the back brace, had been infilled with a pegged timber patch. Assembly marks incised upon both brace and strut show that the structure had been prefabricated.

Each of the earlier back braces (1087) was secured at the north end by a pile-retained crosspiece passed through a square mortise in the brace, which rested on the foreshore at this point.

All the posts were supported to the south by front braces comprising a mixture of squared timber and roundwood elements up to 2.4m long and 0.15m across. The tapered head of each brace was set in a splayed and tapered recess cut in the south face of the vertical post, but the foot was cut to a chase tenon and wedged in a mortise in a subsidiary baseplate laid north-south on the foreshore and secured by a pile. Much of the timber for these plates seems to have been reused, as was the irregular series of logs and timbers wedged around the feet of the posts to provide additional support.

The cladding comprised at least five levels of horizontal planking laid edge-to-edge. They were 60 to 100mm thick and were cut to lengths of up to 4m so that the east and west ends were butted and pegged into the rebates cut only on the back-braced posts. In the original scheme, it seems that the planks were not pegged to all the intermediate posts: study of the reset panel of planking from the controlled excavation area revealed vertical lines of unused peg holes 1.2m apart, suggesting that initially it was pegged only to alternate posts.

Archive reference: TEX88 Structures 392, 1071, 1087

Dating: The TX4 structure was stratigraphically later than TX3 (1167/8), but was built earlier than TX5 (1228/9), with which it ultimately functioned. The revetement was built in two discrete phases, of which the severed back braces (archive reference TEX88 1087) were the earliest.

Dendrochronological summary: Of the six samples from the first phase of TX4 (Structure 1087), three were dated and two had sapwood: the estimated felling date range is 1152-89 (Figs 9, 39). Of the 32 samples from the second phase of construction within the main area of excavation, 11 were dated and five had sapwood. An estimated felling date range for these samples is 1198-1224, but one (2091) had 29 sapwood rings with bark: a felling date of 1200 is indicated.

STRUCTURE TX5

(Figs 53-6)

On the foreshore immediately south of the TX4 revetment lay the remains of the TX5 jetty. The surviving structure comprised two trestle fragments 2.25m apart, aligned north-south. Both trestles incorporated a baseplate in which one vertical post and two diagonal braces had been set. All the timbers were squared. The baseplates were 5m long and 0.20m x 0.17m in cross-section. Each had been laid horizontally, after preparation of the sloping foreshore which had begun to accumulate against the face of the TX4 revetment. The south end was butted against a pile-retained east-west timber.

The vertical post was 1.9m tall (excluding tenons) and was 0.18m x 0.18m in cross-section. Its foot was cut to a standard shouldered tenon, which was pegged in a rectangular mortise in the upper face of the baseplate. Remnants of another north-south shouldered tenon survived on its head, suggesting that a north-south timber had passed over it at that height. Diagonally-lapped onto its western face was a brace, 0.12m x 0.12m in cross-section, which was lapped onto the north end of the baseplate and rose southwards at an angle of 45 degrees for a length of 1.6m, at which point it had been broken off at its junction with a second diagonal brace, 0.14m x 0.14m in cross-section. This was 2.65m long and was lapped and pegged to the western edge of the baseplate. It rose diagonally northwards, lapping over both the other brace and the vertical post. Assembly marks incised on the west face of this brace and the vertical post show that the trestle was a prefabricated structure.

It seems that this structure once incorporated a second braced vertical post, but this had been removed in antiquity. The evidence lies in joints cut in the upper face of the baseplate: a shallow trench 2.1m south of the surviving post may have accommodated an east-west plate into which another post may have been set, braced by a strut tenoned into the chase mortise 1.3m to the south.

The partial reconstruction of the jetty shown here incorporates the little evidence that survived for the decking. This was in the form of a collapsed and broken east-west timber, up to 0.2m x 0.2m in cross-section, which may once have spanned the jetty above the heads of the two surviving vertical posts. It was found lying between the two posts, within the dumps which had been thrown over the dismantled jetty when the next phase of reclamation took place. If it formed part of the jetty, it would

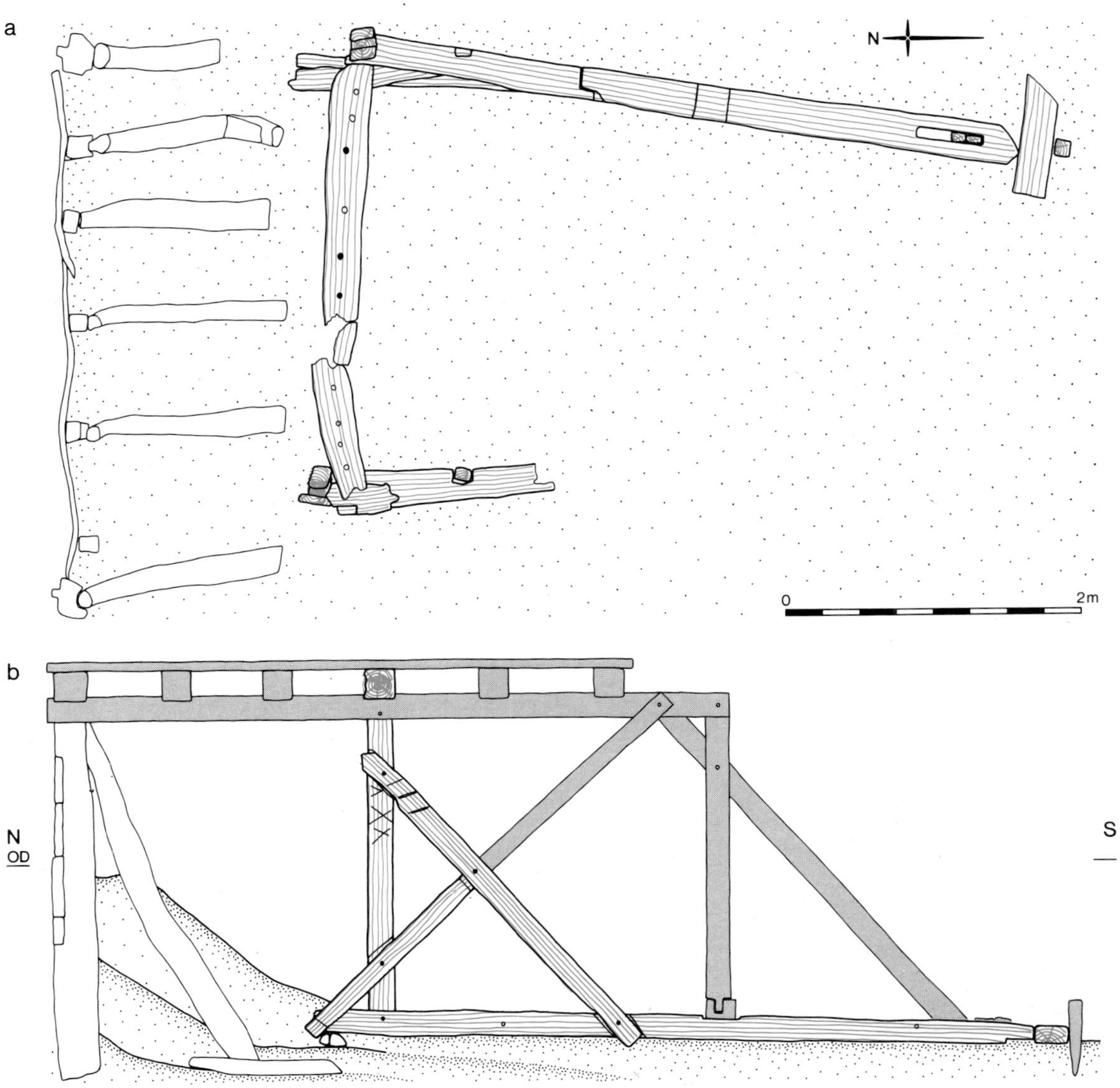

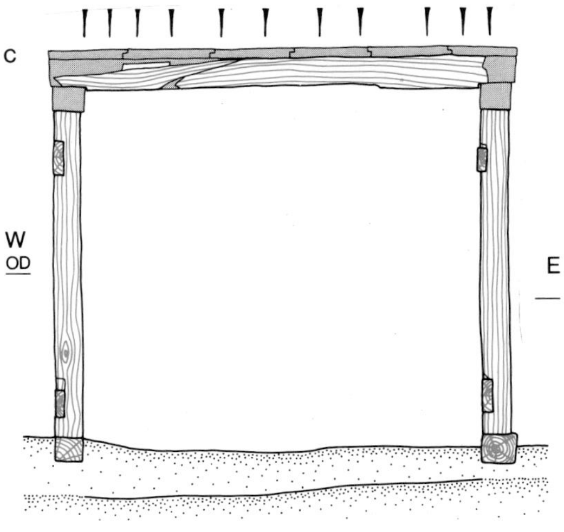

53. Thames Exchange: early 13th-century Structure TX5*: a) plan as found (cf. Fig 38), shown in relation to* TX4 *to north (to left); b) semi-reconstructed west facing side elevation showing possible arrangement of decking for the jetty in relation to broadly contemporary* TX4 *revetment to the north. Left: c) semi-reconstructed south facing cross-section of jetty trestle. Pegs shown over the decking indicate the position of pegholes in the underlying joist.*

have served as a joist laid over north-south bearers: 11 pegholes in what was the upper face as found may therefore mark the position of the boards which formed the actual decking.

Archive reference: TEX88 Structure 1061

54. Thames Exchange: part of the 13th-century waterfront, looking east. The 5 x 100mm scale stands on the foreshore which accumulated against the face of the TX4 *revetment, to right, surviving almost to full height. In centre of area, a trench has been cut down to the base of the* TX5 *jetty trestle, erected in the open river to the south of the revetment.*

55. Thames Exchange: detail of assembly mark on TX5 *jetty trestle next to the 10 x 10mm scale.*

56. Thames Exchange: remains of TX5 *jetty trestle, river to left. The 5 x 100mm scale rests on the foreshore upon which the baseplate was laid: note applied scissor braces. Behind trestle is the north end of the* TX6 *revetment back brace.*

Dating: The TX5 structure was built shortly after TX4 (1200) but earlier than the 13th-century TX6.

Dendrochronological summary: Of the six samples from the TX5 structure, only one was dated, but this had 14 sapwood rings and traces of bark. A felling date in the winter of 1228/9 is indicated (Figs 9, 39).

STRUCTURE TX6

The next phase of reclamation saw the construction of the TX6 revetment 4m south of the TX4 structure. Although only small sections survived to east and west of a later brick foundation, this was sufficient to establish the alignment of the structure, that all posts were front-braced, with back braces at 5m intervals, and that the timbers were squared.

The TX6 extension incorporated dumped deposits which sealed the TX4 and TX5 structures. However, the only complete back brace found was set in a trench cut through these deposits, and may represent a modification to the original scheme. This back brace is unusual, for the north end relied partially on support from the earth on the edge of the trench.

The order of assembly would seem to be as follows. Some 6m to the south of the TX4 structure, a subsidiary baseplate of beech 0.24m x 0.12m in cross-section was laid east-west. Lapping over it was the south end of the 4.8m-long back-brace baseplate, which was 0.27m x 0.2m in cross-section. The upper face of this member had been cut by a chase mortise at the south end, into which a diagonally-set squared front brace had been tenoned. To the north was a trench 0.2m wide and 60mm deep into which was laid the principal baseplate, 0.18m by 0.1m in cross-section. The principal posts were up to 1.9m tall, were 0.23 x 0.2m in cross-section, and were tenoned and pegged into the beech baseplate. The head of the front brace was chase-tenoned and pegged to the post, rather than using splayed recesses as were noted on earlier structures. The brace was 1.95m long and 0.18m x 0.15m in cross-section. Both post and brace had identical assembly marks incised on the west face.

The back brace elements were then assembled. A mortise to the north of the principal baseplate accommodated a vertical member 0.22m x 0.21m in cross-section, standing to a height of 1.35m with shouldered tenons at both ends. The pegged tenon on its head articulated with a horizontal brace 2.9m long and 0.16m x 0.16m in cross-section, supported at its north end by the edge of the trench into which it was set. Its west edge was pegged to the diagonal back brace which lapped over it. This brace was at least 2.7m long and 0.15m x 0.15m in cross-section. Its foot was chase-tenoned into the baseplate, and its head seems to have been lapped over the west face of the principal post. An additional diagonal strut 2.4m long and 0.15m x 0.15m in cross-section articulated with the north end of the brace baseplate, the back brace and the horizontal member, using diagonal lap joints.

The plank cladding for the revetment comprised at least four levels of boards up to 0.6m wide and 0.1m thick. Initially they were pegged to the north face of the posts, although some planks used in later repairs had been nailed into position.

Archive reference: TEX88 Structure 393

Dating: The TX6 structure was stratigraphically later than TX5 (1228/9), and must be mid to late 13th-century in date. No dendrochronological samples from this structure have been dated.

57. Thames Exchange, 13th-century Structure TX6 *(see Fig 38f): semi-reconstructed side elevation showing back brace supported at the north end on the edge of a cut in earlier infill material, shown in darker tone.*

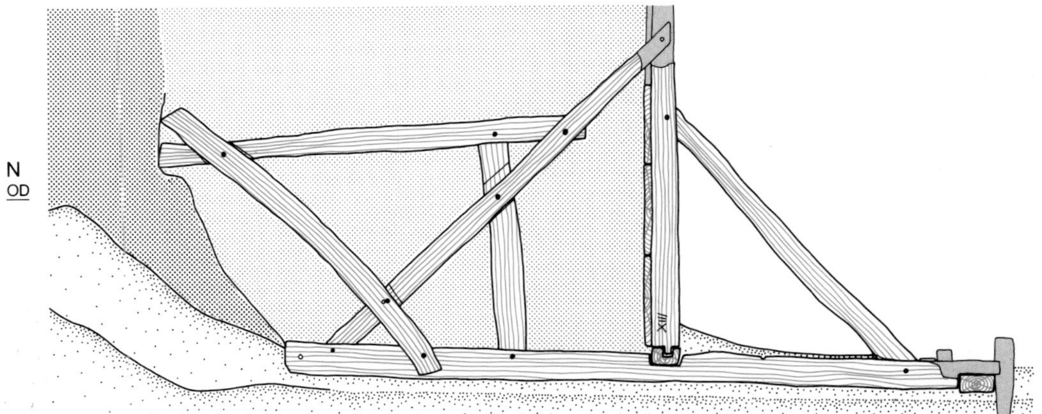

STRUCTURE TX7

(Figs 58-9)

This earthfast post and plank revetment was recorded on six separate occasions during the contractor's ground works. It seemed to comprise at least two north-south sections which articulated with a 17m-long frontage, extending from the inlet in the centre of the site to beyond the western limit of excavation. Ten earthfast posts were recorded in the frontage, set vertically into post pits dug into the foreshore at intervals of *c*.1m. The squared posts were up to 3.45m long and *c*.0.3m square in cross-section. Two posts which survived to their full length had pegged splayed scarf joints cut on their heads, suggesting that the revetment had been extended higher or that an additional structure, probably a parapet, but just possibly the southern wall of a building, had been superimposed upon it. There was some evidence of a light brown sandy mortar layer, possibly an internal surface, extending up to the north edge of the frontage.

The posts had 70mm-wide rebates up to 80mm deep cut into their east and west faces. These accommodated at least seven levels of radially-cleft planking up to 100mm thick set horizontally edge to edge. The planks were tapered to slot into the grooves, and wedges had sometimes been added to hold the planks in position.

The frontage was supported to the south by diagonally-set roundwood braces, the tapered head of each being housed in a splayed, tapered recess cut in the south face of the post. The foot was cut to butt against the shoulder of an east-west timber, laid on the foreshore some 1m to the south of the frontage and retained by beech piles. Two sections of this baseplate were recorded, joined with an unpegged stop-splayed scarf joint.

To the north, further support was provided by back braces, seven of which were observed. Each back brace seemed to comprise a diagonally-set squared timber over 4m long, the head of which articulated with the west face of the post in a pegged notched squint-lap joint. The foot rested on the foreshore, secured by a pile-retained bar passed through a squared mortise cut through the brace.

Archive reference: TEX88 Structure 496

Dating: The TX7 structure was stratigraphically later than a sequence of structures broadly contemporary with TX1 and TX2 (*ie* 10th and 11th-century in date), but earlier than the 13th-century TX8.

Dendrochronological summary: Of the 14 samples from the TX7 structure, eight were dated and four had sapwood. Of these, two had 35 sapwood rings and bark (Timbers 650, 655): felling dates of 1183 and 1184 are indicated (Figs 9, 39).

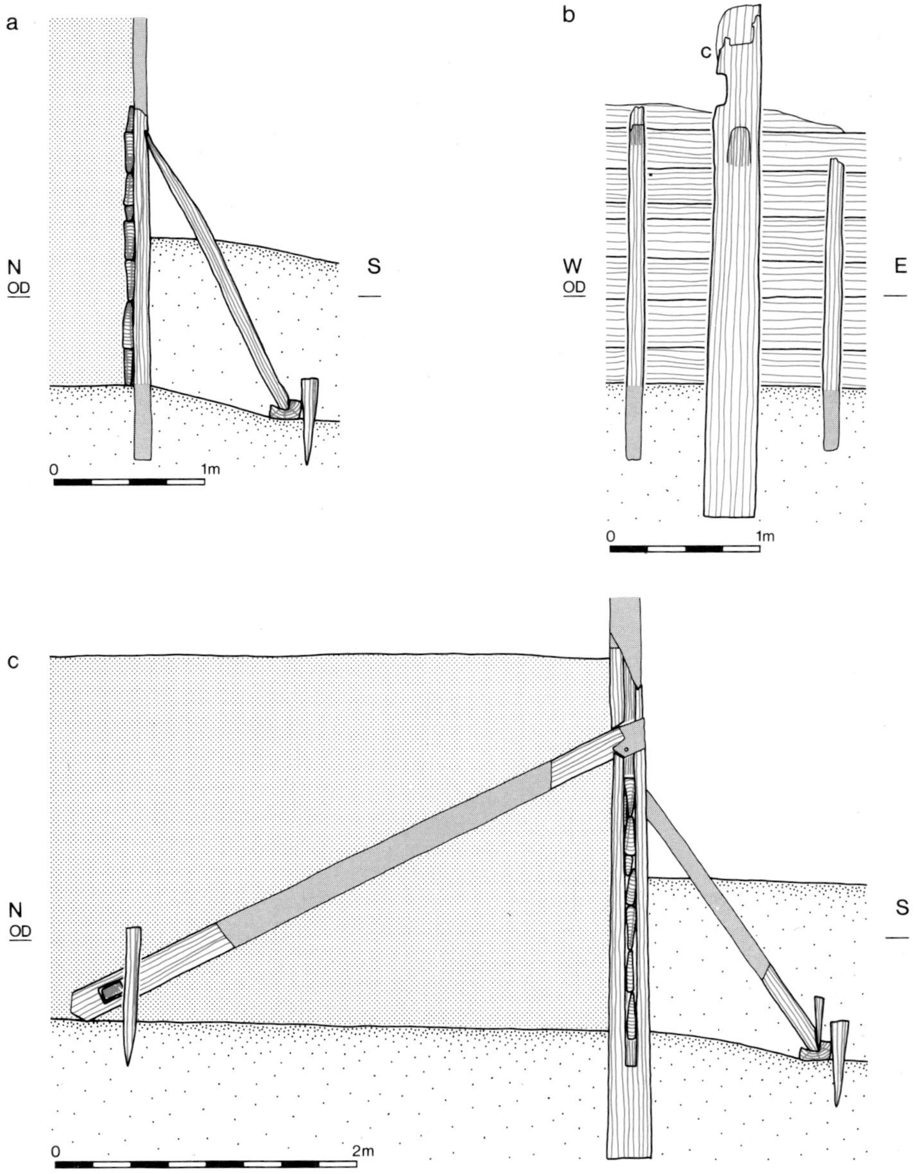

58. Left: Thames Exchange (see Fig 38e). Riverward face of late 12th-century TX7 *revetment looking north, exposed and hurriedly cleaned during contractors' ground reduction work. The 5 x 100mm scale stands on the primary foreshore into which the structure's earthfast posts were set.*

59. Above: Thames Exchange. Structure TX7*: a) side elevation of earthfast intermediate post (marked a on front elevation); b) south facing front elevation with front braces removed, showing earthfast posts set in the foreshore; c) side elevation of earthfast principal post (marked c on front elevation) showing radially-split cladding set in grooves, and arrangement of front and back braces. Note scarf joint on the head of the post.*

STRUCTURE TX8

The TX8 front- and back-braced post and plank revetment was observed on five separate occasions during the contractor's ground works. It directly succeeded the TX7 structure, lying 11m to the south, and was traced for a length of 21m east-west. Nine posts, six front braces and two back braces were recorded, from which a composite picture of the revetment has been built up (Fig 60). The first element laid seems to have been the squared baseplate for the north-south back brace, which was 0.2m x 0.2m in cross-section, with a rebate cut at its south end. Into this, the principal baseplate had been laid east-west, a timber 0.2m wide but only 0.1m deep with mortises cut in its upper face. These accommodated the pegged shouldered tenons cut on the feet of the squared vertical posts which stood up to 2.5m tall, and were 0.2m x 0.2m in cross-section. The posts were set 0.4m apart, and a cladding of at least five levels of sawn boards laid edge to edge was pegged to the north face.

Each post was supported to the south by a diagonally-set squared front brace, the head of which was cut to fit a splayed, tapered recess in the south face of the post. The foot of the brace was wedged in a chase mortise cut through a pile-retained north-south subsidiary baseplate. These plates seem to have been reused timbers, since features such as extra peg holes were recorded. Some of the front braces seem to have been repaired and replaced.

To the north, further support was provided by more widely-spaced back braces, of which none survived in sufficient detail to permit a definitive reconstruction. However, the brace must have incorporated a combination of vertical, horizontal and diagonal members. Evidence of pegged, diagonal lap joints was recovered, and it seems that a horizontal timber articulated with the vertical post in a shoulder cut some 1.8m above baseplate level.

Archive reference: TEX88 Structure 479

Dating: The TX8 structure was stratigraphically later than TX7 (1184), but earlier than TX9 (1239), and must be early to mid 13th-century in date.

Dendrochronological summary: One of the 11 samples from the structure was dated, but had no sapwood. The estimated felling date is after 1169 (Figs 9, 39).

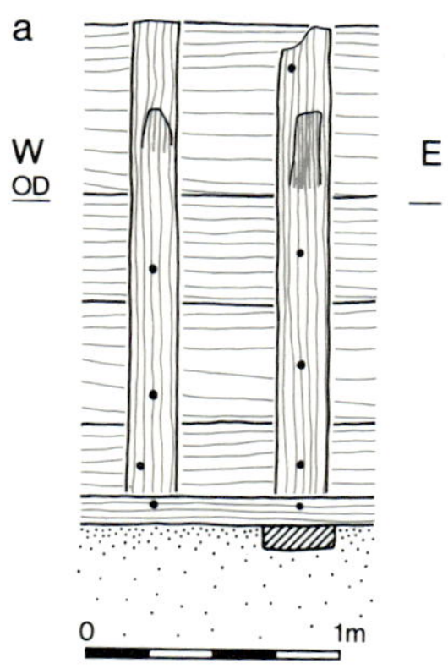

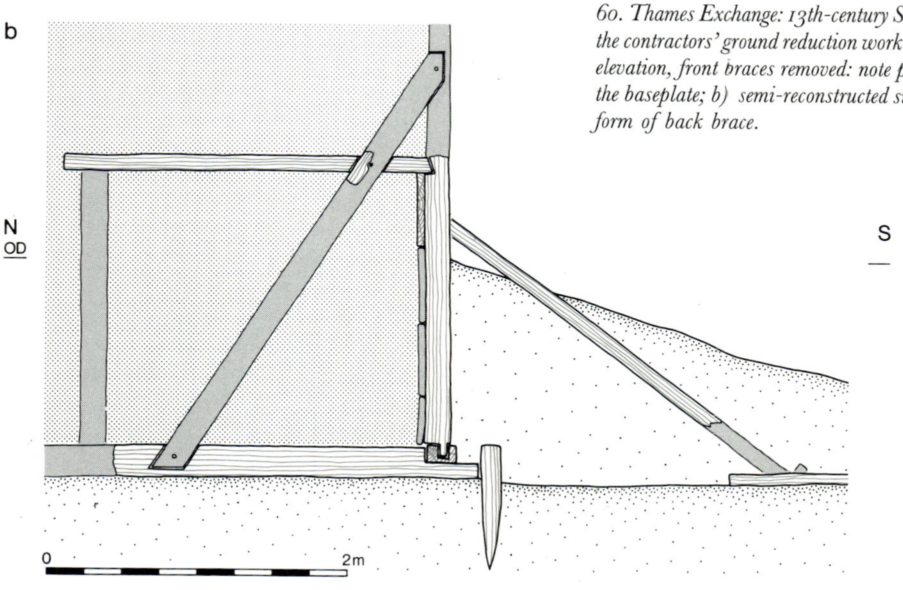

60. Thames Exchange: 13th-century Structure TX8, *recorded during the contractors' ground reduction work (see Fig 38f): a) south facing elevation, front braces removed: note posts tenoned and pegged into the baseplate; b) semi-reconstructed side elevation to show possible form of back brace.*

STRUCTURE TX9

This front and back-braced revetment, observed on four occasions during contractors' ground works, was traced for a length of 19.5m. Ten squared vertical posts were recorded, most of which were front-braced. Evidence for six back braces set 3m apart was also recovered. The reconstruction in Fig 61 is a composite of data from all the observations.

The north-south back-brace baseplate had a trench cut in its upper face at its south end for the subsidiary baseplate, while a second trench cut to the north accommodated the principal baseplate, also laid east-west. The principal baseplate was 0.25m wide by 0.20m deep, and comprised two timbers joined with a stop-splayed scarf joint with three face pegs. It was cut by rectangular mortises, into which central tenons on the feet of the vertical posts were pegged. The posts, *c.*0.3m square in cross-section, survived to a height of 2.2m, and were set at intervals of 0.5 to 0.7m. Pegged to their north face were three levels of tangentially-faced planks 0.6m wide, the lowest of which was set in a rebate 15mm deep cut along the edge of the baseplate.

The southern face of all but two of the posts was cut by a splayed recess to house the head of the squared front braces. The feet of these braces had been destroyed by later foundations. Presumably, they butted against the subsidiary baseplate, which comprised two timbers up to 6.3m long joined by a stop-splayed scarf joint with three face pegs; a continuous rebate 50mm deep and 110mm wide was cut along the north edge of the upper face.

The back braces had suffered considerable damage. However, each may have comprised a diagonal member running north from the head of the post to join the baseplate. An additional strut was lapped to the brace, the vertical post and to the south end of the brace baseplate. The plank cladding had been cut to accommodate this strut.

Archive reference: TEX88 Structure 410

Dating: The TX9 structure was stratigraphically later than the early 13th-century TX8.

Dendrochronological summary: Of the 16 TX9 samples, two were dated. The heartwood/sapwood zone survived on one (959), and a felling date range of 1228-73 is estimated. The other (649) had 14 sapwood rings and traces of bark: a felling date in 1239 is indicated (Figs 9, 39).

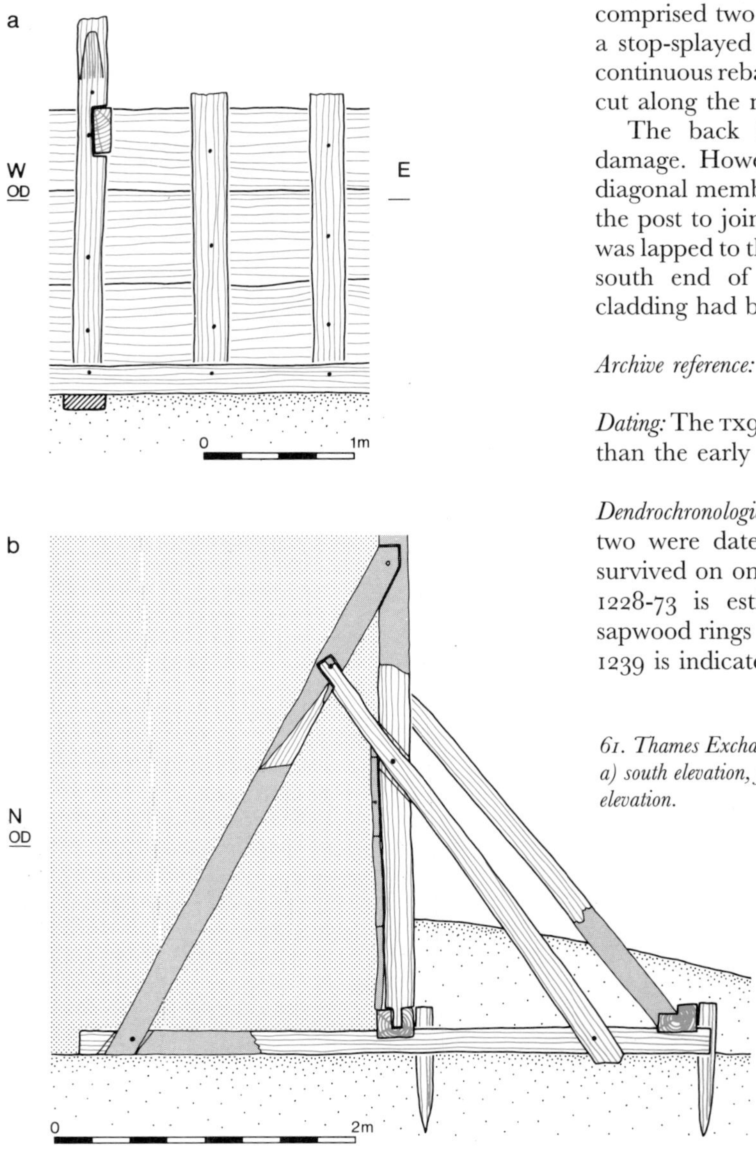

61. Thames Exchange: 13th-century Structure TX9 *(see Fig 38g): a) south elevation, front brace removed; b) semi-reconstructed side elevation.*

TRIG LANE AND SUNLIGHT WHARF SITES
1974-6; 1984; 1986-7
TQ32078083 Site codes: TL74; TIG84; SUN86

The Trig Lane/Sunlight Wharf site formed part of a series of contiguous recent redevelopments of the western end of the City waterfront between Blackfriars and Southwark Bridges (Fig 62). To the west was the Baynard's Castle site, which was excavated in 1972-3, 1975-6 and 1981, while the Broken Wharf site to the east was rebuilt in 1975-6, although no archaeologists were allowed to monitor the work there. In 1971, during the construction of a new river wall, the remains of three boats were recorded at the southern end of the site (Marsden 1979), while trenches dug for the realignment of Upper Thames Street exposed sections through medieval occupation and street levels (Haslam 1972).

The first major controlled excavations (site code: TL74) took place on a 450 square metre area in the south of the site from July 1974 to December 1976. Initially, the work was supervised by Mark Harrison, but direction of the project subsequently passed on to Gustav and Chrissie Milne. The structural sequence incorporated a series of riverfront revetments dated from the 13th to the 15th centuries, and has been published in detail (Milne & Milne 1978; 1981; 1982). Revetments recorded on the east side of the site included the G3, G7, G10 and G11 structures, summarised as TL3, TL7, TL10 and TL11 respectively in this catalogue; structures on the west side of the site are not described here.

Directly to the north of these excavations, the cutting of sewer trenches in January 1984 exposed an earlier structure, recorded under the site code TIG84, supervised by Brian Pye. Some two years later, work began on a 60m (north-south) by 100m (east-west) development, the Sunlight Wharf project (SUN86). Although the archaeological levels over much of the eastern part of the site had been destroyed when double basements were inserted below the Sunlight Wharf warehouse building, the west half included some of the area excavated by 1976, and also the area immediately to the north, extending *c*.10m south of the line of the Upper Thames Street underpass. Observations during the contractors' ground works programme facilitated the partial recording of some eight revetments, while fragments of twelve more were noted, together with many masonry foundations and other features (Hunting 1988; Spence 1989, 24-5). This phase of work ran principally from December 1986 to March 1987, and was supervised by Richard Bluer, who also compiled the archive report for structures TL1 and TL2.

As a result of all this work, parts of the reclamation sequence on at least five contiguous medieval properties were investigated, the most complete sequence, from the 12th century to the present day, coming from Property D (Hunting 1988, 18), which lay immediately west of Trig Lane. It is the sequence of revetments from that property which is described in the catalogue below, beginning with the TL1 revetment, a structure observed on the TIG84 site but recorded in more detail during the SUN86 project. However, it should be noted that the line of the natural river bank was not recorded on this site, and must therefore lie to the north, beneath or beyond the line of Upper Thames Street. As a consequence, the date at which medieval waterfront development began in this area must be earlier than the late 12th to early 13th-century date established for the earliest riverfront structure recorded.

New dendrochronological work
by Ian Tyers

The samples were originally examined by Dr Donald Brett at Bedford College, University of London. However, the publication of these results (Brett 1978; 1982) did not provide precise felling dates for the timbers used in the structures, since insufficient reference material was available at that time, although a substantial series of relative dates and an approximate radiocarbon date range were presented. Since then many more tree-ring chronologies have been produced. Working with this new material, some of the original Trig Lane samples have been re-examined in a comprehensive study of the site specifically for this report.

As many samples as possible were measured and dated against each other and appropriate reference chronologies. In the event, only 19 of the original 94 samples were dated: these are shown in Fig 63, which represents the definitive tree-ring analysis of the Trig Lane sequence. The samples are characterised by short sequences, fast growth rates and general lack of sapwood. The first two characteristics seem common to timber of this period within central London, while the last is at least partially a reflection of the length of time over which the samples had been handled and stored. Taken together, these are the reasons for the overall poor dendrochronological dating ratio for this site. More samples should have been taken from this extensive site to provide the necessary replication, as Dr Brett pointed out, but the necessary technical assistance was not forthcoming in 1975-6 (Brett 1982, 75).

62. Right: plan showing extent of controlled excavations on Trig Lane site (TL74) in relation to the area of watching brief on Sunlight Wharf site (SUN86: cf. Figs 1; 3), with alignments of medieval waterfront structures from late 12th to 15th century indicated: structures described in the catalogue (eg TL1, TL2) are marked. Scale 1:1250.

63. Below: bar diagram showing tree-ring results from waterfront structures from Trig Lane site (TL74).

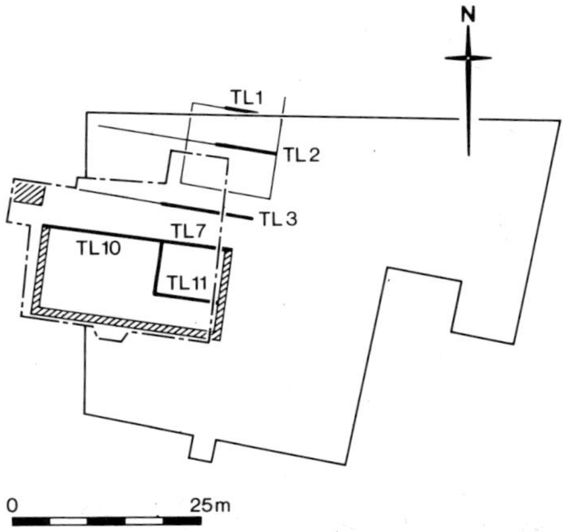

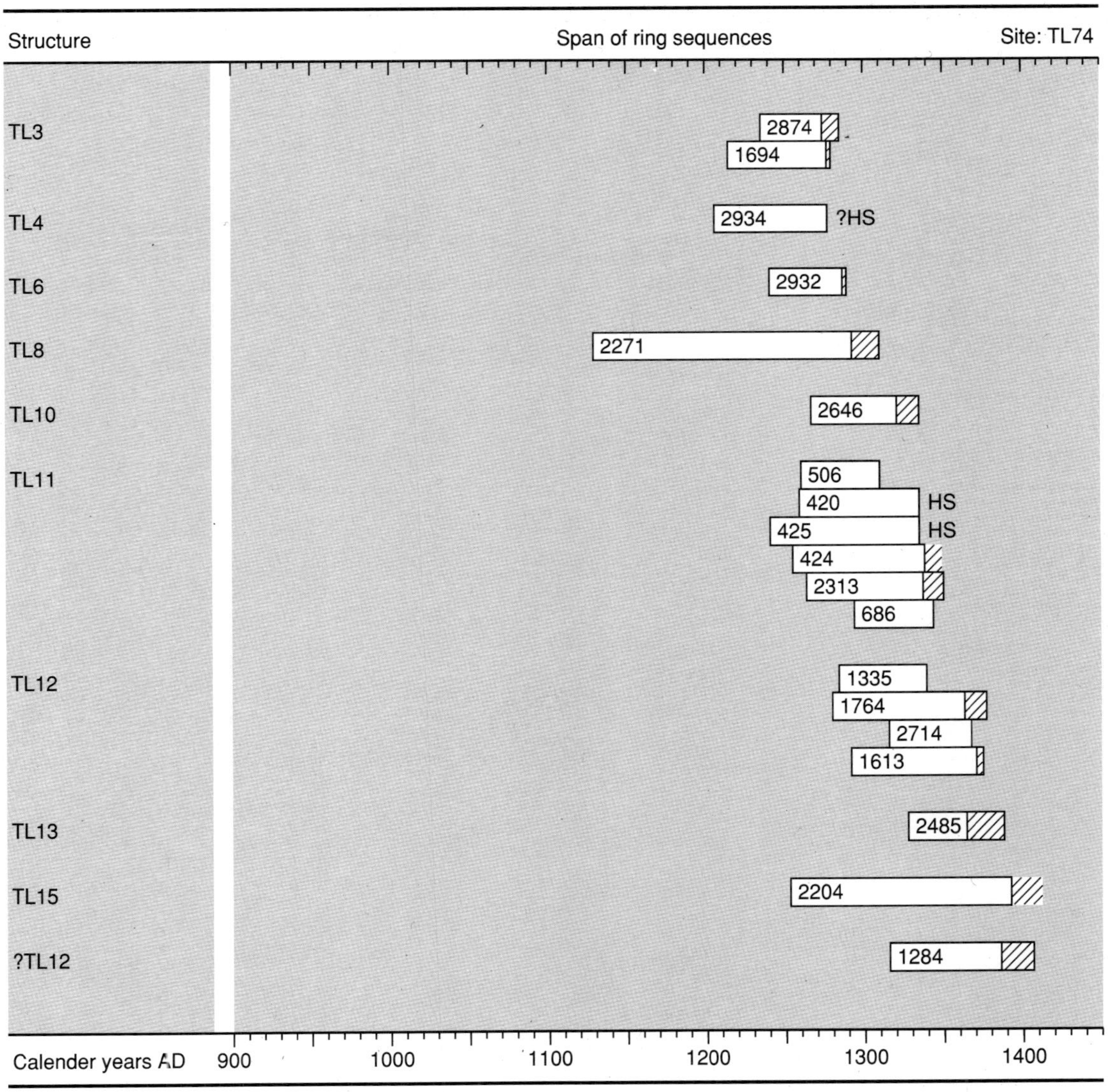

STRUCTURE TL1

(Figs 64-6)

Timbers from the stave-built front-braced TL1 revetment were first recorded in 1984. More extensive observations were made in 1987, when the structure was traced for a length of 9.3m east-west and a section some 5m long was recorded in detail. Earthfast posts 3m long and up to 0.4m x 0.45m in cross-section were vertically set in post pits 0.75m deep and 2.2m apart. Between each pair of posts was a baseplate 0.3m wide and 0.2m deep set horizontally on the foreshore, and tenoned into the edges of the posts to the east and west. A slot 80mm wide x 160mm deep accommodated the bare-faced tenons on the feet of a wall of staves. These timbers were arranged in groups of three, each one at least 2.5m tall and 0.25m x 0.12m in cross-section. Each group was separated by a more substantial member 0.25m x 0.25m in cross-section with a central tenon on its foot pegged into the slot in the baseplate. These timbers were supported by diagonally-set braces often cut from branches used in the round, the head of each being housed in a splayed recess in the southern face of the post. No evidence was recorded of longitudinal support for the stave wall in the form of free tenons or pegs in adjacent edges: all the members seemed simply to butt flush.

Archive reference: TIG 84; SUN86 G1

Dating: The TL1 structure was earlier than the 13th-century TL2, which was in turn earlier than TL3 (*c.*1290-1330). An early 13th-century date may be suggested for this structure.

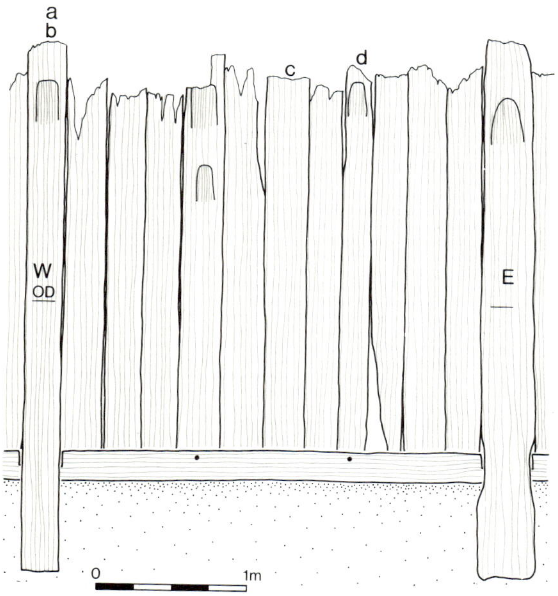

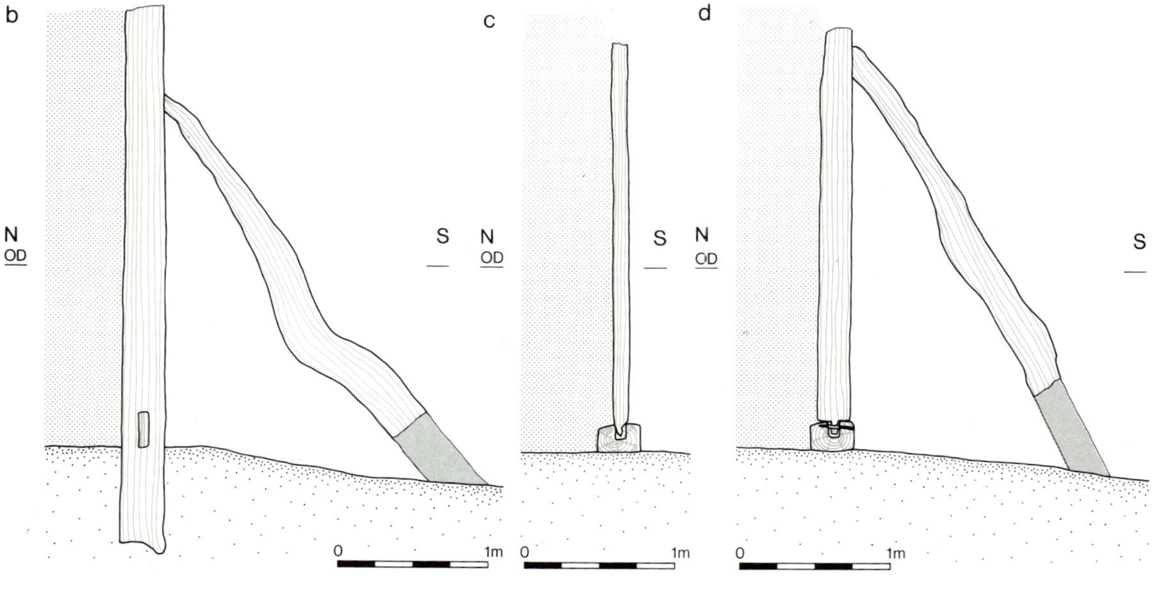

64. Sunlight Wharf, late 12th- early 13th-century Structure TL1: *a) south facing elevation with front braces removed, showing the stave wall set in baseplates between the earthfast posts; b) side elevation of post marked b on front elevation; c) side elevation of post marked c on front elevation; d) side elevation of post d on front elevation.*

65. Sunlight Wharf: south (riverward) face of stave-built TL1 *structure, against which the 10 x 100mm scale rests, exposed during contractors' ground reduction programme. The waterfront was subsequently advanced in the 13th century with the erection of* TL2, *the post and plank revetment partially exposed in the foreground, next to the submersible pump.*

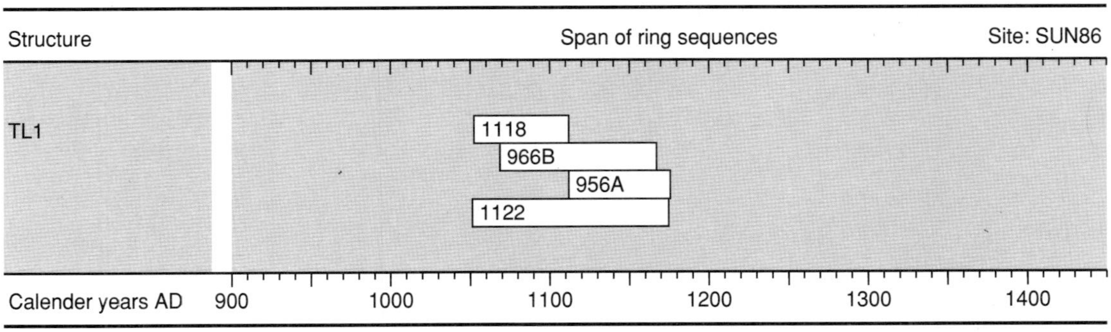

66. Bar diagram showing tree-ring results from TL1 *structure from Sunlight Wharf site* (SUN86).

Dendrochronological summary: Of the six samples examined so far from the TL1 structure, four were dated by Ian Tyers but none had sapwood: the estimated felling date is after 1186 (Figs 9, 66).

The front-braced post and plank TL2 revetment marked the riverward limit of an extension directly south of the TL1 structure. The new revetment ran southwards for 4.8m then returned west for at least 5m. The structure had partially collapsed in antiquity, timbers suffered machine-damage before recording could begin, and the lower levels were not exposed during the excavation. Nevertheless, plans and some individual timbers were recorded, and a reconstruction attempted (Fig 67).

The south return of the revetment comprised a squared baseplate into the upper face of which rectangular mortises had been cut between 0.4 and 0.5m apart. At least seven squared posts had been set in this plate, with pegged central tenons on their feet. The posts varied in cross-section from 0.13m x 0.14m to 0.2m x 0.18m, and were at least 1.75m tall. They were supported to the south by diagonal front braces 1.6m long and up to 0.16m x 0.17m in cross-section, although some of the members had been used in the round. The junction between post and brace was not recorded. However, a chase-tenon cut on the foot of each brace suggests that they were set in north-south subsidiary baseplates laid on the foreshore. The cladding comprised four levels of planking up to 45mm thick and 0.45m wide, laid horizontally edge to edge. It is not known if the planks were nailed or pegged to the posts.

Archive reference: SUN86 G3

Dating: The TL2 structure was stratigraphically later than TL1 (*c.*1186+), but earlier than TL3 (*c.*1290-1330).

67. Sunlight Wharf, 13th-century Structure TL2, *recorded during contractors' ground reduction programme: semi-reconstructed side elevation.*

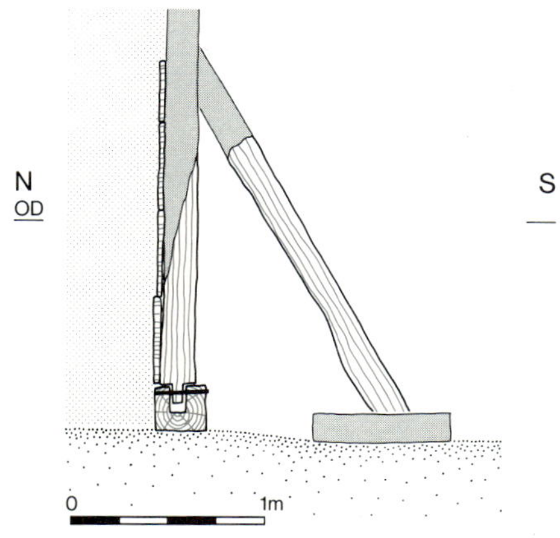

(Figs 68-70)

The front and back-braced TL3 revetment was traced for 16m east-west, and survived to a height of 2.4m (Milne & Milne 1982, 18-21). It comprised a pile-retained baseplate composed of several timbers joined with edge-halved scarfs with square vertical butts. It had been laid directly over the baseplate of an earlier revetment, the superstructure of which had been robbed out. Squared vertical posts, 0.2m in width and surviving to 2m in height, were set in the upper face of the plate, with a central tenon pegged into a standard mortise, at 0.7m centres. Up to six levels of horizontal planking were laid edge to edge against the north face of the posts, secured with round or oval-headed nails, or, in one instance, set into rebates cut down the north-east and north-west corners of the posts. Each post was supported to the south by a brace, to which it had been joined by a chase mortise and tenon. The brace itself ran diagonally southwards, its foot cut to form a bird's-mouth abutment wedged against the north shoulder of a subsidiary baseplate. The latter ran parallel to and 1.6m to the south of the principal plate, and was evidently a reused timber.

Three back braces were located at intervals of 3.4m, cut into the dumped deposits retained by the planking. Each comprised a horizontal tie-back 3m long, which had a central tenon pegged into the vertical post at its south end. To the north, stability was provided by a crosspiece trenched and pegged over the tie-back, and retained by piles. An additional strut, chase-tenoned into the face of the tie-back, ran diagonally upwards and southwards, but the actual junction of this member with the revetment facing did not survive.

Archive reference: TL74 G3

Dating: The TL3 revetment was a refacing of a structure which once retained reclamation dumps containing pottery dated to *c.*1270 (Vince 1985, 86) and an ampulla of *c.*1275. TL3 was stratigraphically later than the 13th-century TL2, but was earlier than the early 14th-century TL7.

Dendrochronological summary: Of the seven samples from the TL3 structure, two were dated and both had sapwood (Brett 1982): the estimated felling date range is 1290-1330 (Figs 9, 63).

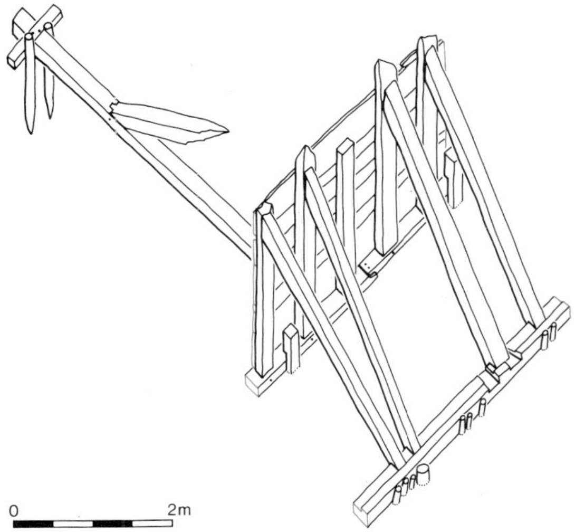

68. Above: Trig Lane, late 13th-century Structure TL3. *Axonometric projection of part of structure as found.*

70. Above: Trig Lane. Two squared front braces from TL3 *revetment, looking north-east. The 5 x 100mm scale rests on the foreshore upon which the principal baseplate was laid, just visible to left (north). Note the bird's-mouth abutment on the foot of the brace, where it meets the partially-exposed subsidiary baseplate.*

69. Below: Trig Lane, Structure TL3. *Semi-reconstructed side elevation showing back and front bracing.*

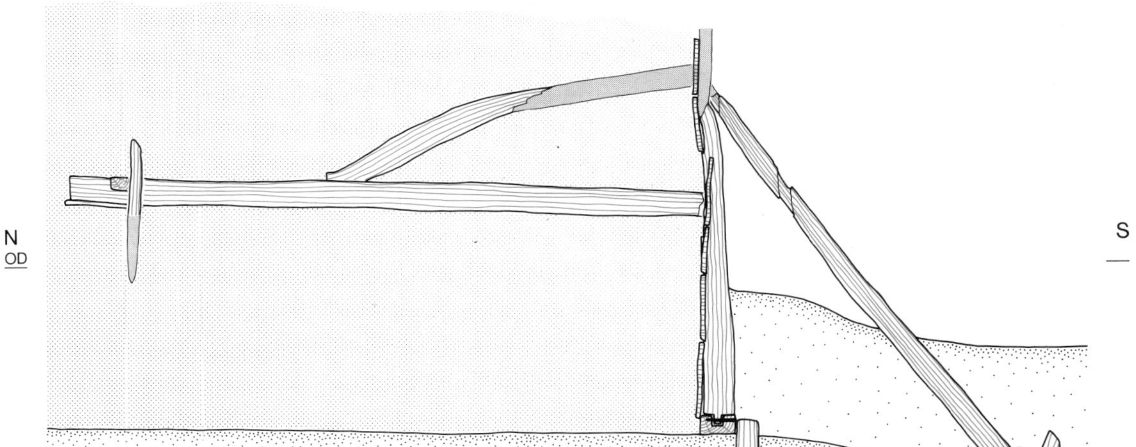

STRUCTURE TL7

(Figs 71-3)

The TL7 back-braced and horizontally-planked revetment ran east-west across the site 3m to the south of the TL3 structure (Milne & Milne 1982, 21-4). It had been robbed down to the level of the baseplate in the west but survived virtually intact in the east. Here it comprised at least two sections of pile-founded baseplate joined by an edge-halved scarf with square vertical butts. Into it, a series of squared vertical posts with full or half tenons on their feet had been pegged, usually at 0.4m intervals. However, where the horizontal back brace passed through the frontage, the posts were coupled and the adjacent edges of each pair had been trenched to accept the southern end of the tie-back. The brace, or anchor-beam, was itself edge-trenched, passing between the posts at a height of 1m above the baseplate; it was stabilised at its north end by a pile-retained crosspiece.

Evidence of a second and higher tier of tie-backs was recovered. The remains of two north-south back braces were recorded passing through the revetment face, at which point the ends of the braces were pierced by a long horizontal east-west bar. Up to five levels of horizontal planking laid edge to edge were nailed to the northern face of the posts to retain the dumped material, which a longitudinal section showed had been tipped from east to west.

Archive reference: TL74 G7

Dating: The TL7 structure was stratigraphically later than TL3 (*c.*1290-1330) and an early 14th-century structure which incorporated a timber felled between 1300 and 1345 (archive reference: TL74 G6), but earlier than TL10 (*c.*1336-75). It was associated with a large assemblage of early 14th-century pottery. A date of *c.*1340 is therefore suggested for the TL7 revetment.

Dendrochronological summary: Of the seven samples from the TL7 structure, none was dated (Brett 1982).

71. Trig Lane, mid 14th-century Structure TL7*: semi-reconstructed side elevation showing two levels of horizontally laid back braces with a lockbar on the upper level.*

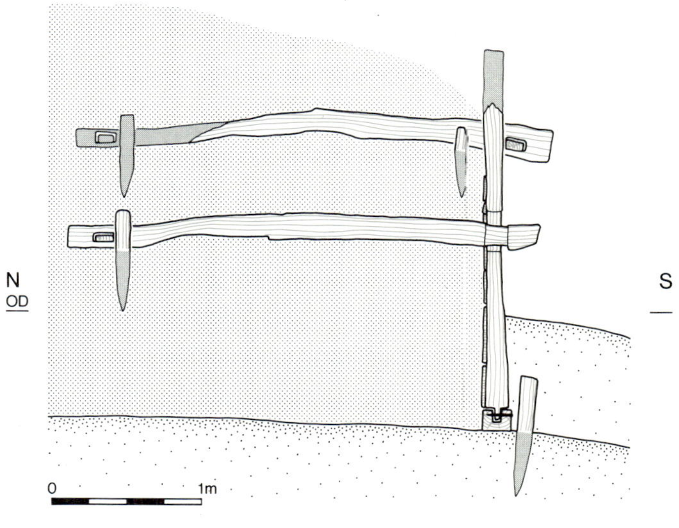

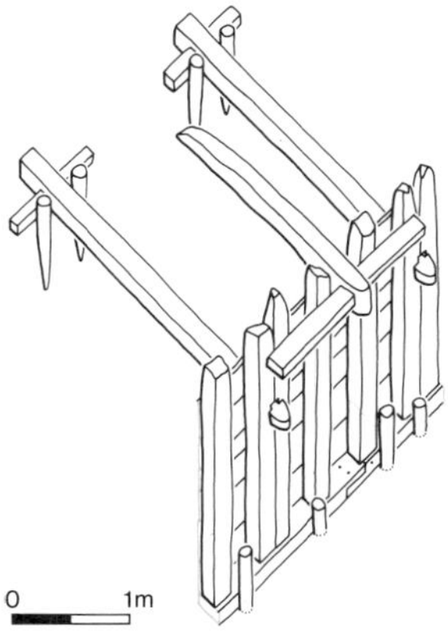

72. Left: Trig Lane, Structure TL7*. Axonometric projection of part of the structure as found.*

73. Below: Trig Lane, front (riverward) face of the post and plank TL7 *revetment, looking north-east, with triangular back braces of the later* TL11 *structure visible in foreground. The 4 x 500mm scale stands at the east end of the exposed section of the back-braced* TL7 *structure. This was supported with lockbars which passed through the protruding southern ends of the pile-retained anchor beams (cf. Fig 15).*

STRUCTURE TL10

(Figs 74-6)

The back-braced TL10 revetment ran east-west across the site on the same alignment as the TL7 structure (Milne & Milne 1982, 26-9). It incorporated six baseplates joined together with edge-halved scarfs with square vertical butts, into which 45 staves were set in a continuous squared groove.

The staves were *c.*1.4m high, 0.3 by 0.15m in cross-section, and the edges and southern face of each member butted flush with its neighbour. Most of the staves were cleft timbers and D-shaped in cross-section, although six staves at the west end of the revetment were sawn. Assembly marks were incised on the southern face of the staves (cf. Harris 1978, 15) and seven base motifs were identified in an accumulative sequence which developed from west to east.

Support for this structure was provided by five back braces. Each comprised a baseplate into which two timbers were chase-tenoned, one at either end, inclined towards each other. The southern strut was chase-tenoned into the underside of the north strut, but decay and later activity had severed all the braces at the junction with the stave wall. Many of the brace timbers were clearly reused.

Four of the brace baseplates were edge-trenched at their south ends, as anchor beams, where they passed between vertical members of the revetment wall. The relevant pair of staves was edge-trenched to accommodate the baseplate, while free tenons pegged into mortises cut in the abutting edges of these staves ensured that they could not move apart. A second level of timberwork had extended the revetment upwards by some 0.5m, but the original upper level was replaced in the 15th century by the G12 structure (Milne & Milne 1982, 36-7).

Archive reference: TL74 G10

Dating: The TL10 structure was stratigraphically later than the early 14th-century TL7, but earlier than TL11 (*c.*1351-90). It was associated with a large assemblage of artefacts, including much mid 14th-century pottery.

Dendrochronological summary: Of the 14 samples from the TL10 structure, only one was dated. However this had some sapwood rings surviving (Brett 1982) and a felling date range of 1336-75 is estimated (Figs 9, 63).

74. Trig Lane, mid 14th-century Structure TL10: *south facing elevation showing assembly marks.*

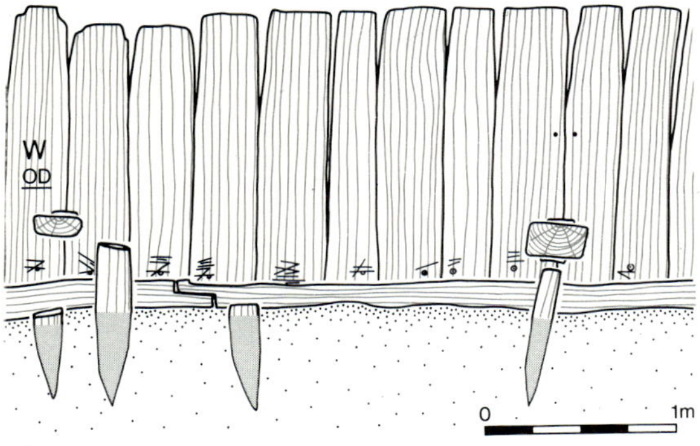

75. Trig Lane, Structure TL10: *semi-reconstructed side elevation of the back-braced stave wall with the second level of vertical cladding.*

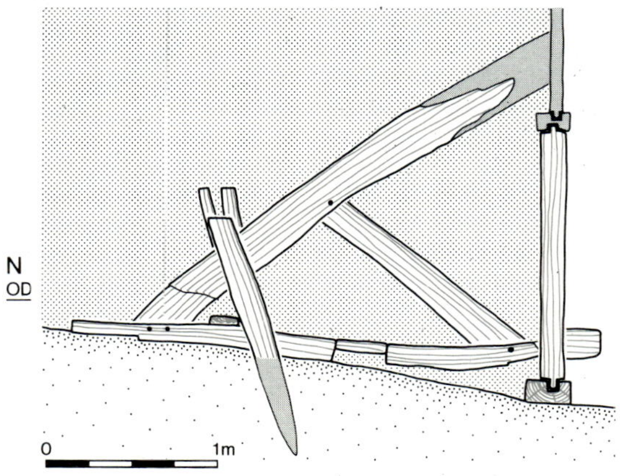

76. Trig Lane: north (landward) face of TL10 *revetment, looking east. The horizontal 5 x 100mm scale rests on the grooved baseplate into which the staves were set: three triangular back braces which supported the 16m-long stave wall from behind have been partially exposed in the trench cut through the infill deposits.*

STRUCTURE TL11

(Figs 77-8)

The back-braced stave wall TL11 revetment projected 6m south of the TL10 structure, then ran eastwards for at least 7m (Milne & Milne 1982, 29-36). The structure survived to a height of 1.7m and was supported by triangular back braces. The remains of a timber platform recorded in the south-west corner are interpreted as the base of a fish tank.

The two timbers which formed the pile-founded baseplate of the west wall were joined with an edge-halved bridle-butted scarf (Fig 8f). The mortise pattern cut in the upper face of the baseplate comprised a series of up to five short mortises 0.4m long interspersed with single longer mortises up to 0.9m long. The construction sequence saw the south wall erected from east to west, after which the west wall was constructed from south to north. Into these mortises the tenons on the feet of the plain-sawn vertical members were set. They were on average 0.45m x 0.07m in cross-section and stood up to 1.6m high. Each was joined to its neighbour by a 300mm-square dowel driven into circular holes bored into the adjacent edges of the vertical timbers. Tenons on their heads accepted a plate which also had mortises in its upper face, showing that the structure originally carried a second level of vertical planking, none of which survived. The corner post was an inverted jowled timber. Its foot extended below the level of the revetment baseplate to articulate with a platform on the foreshore.

a

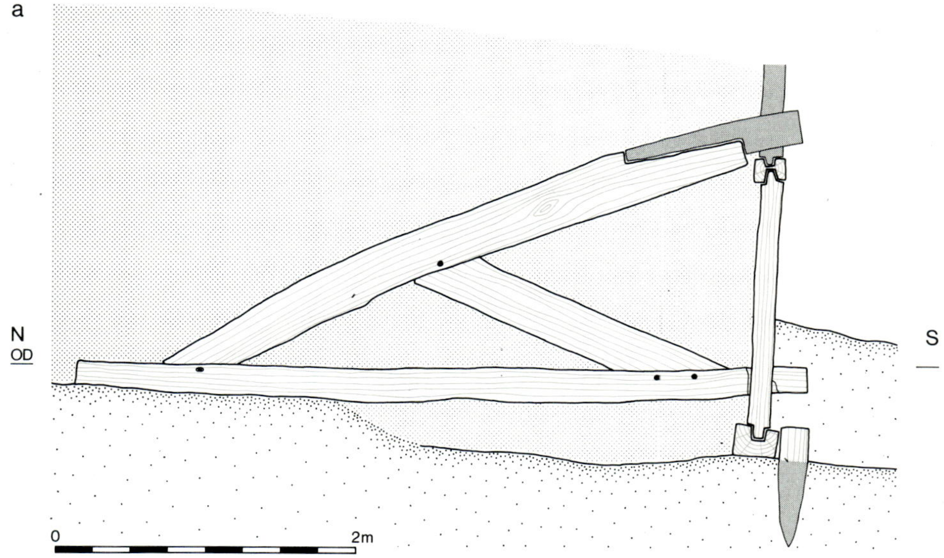

b

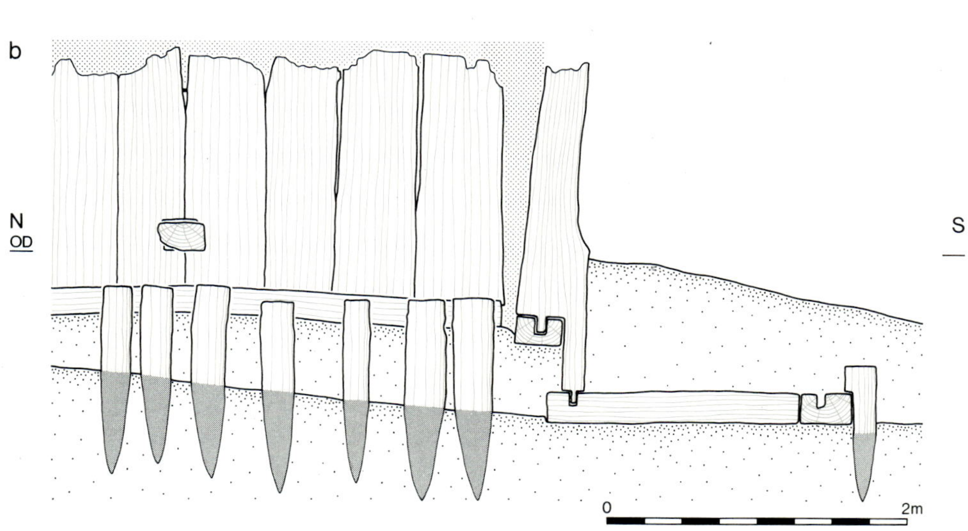

This platform extended 2m south of the revetment, and was 3.4m wide. It consisted of three squared plates, mortised and tenoned together at their south-east and south-west corners. The frame was an integral part of the TL11 structure since both the east and the west plates were joined to well-cut tenons on the feet of the jowled posts. Three joists were centrally tenoned into the two shorter plates, and well-fitted planking up to 0.04m thick was nailed to them, the edges set into rebates cut along the upper edge of the frame. Individual mortises in the upper face of the east and west frame members and a groove cut along the length of the south member presumably supported a tank-like superstructure.

Within the body of the revetment and sealed by the refuse dumps retained by the stave walls was a series of substantial back braces, four of which were recorded in detail. They were similar in design and joinery to those described for the TL10 revetment, but exhibited a higher standard of workmanship, and only utilised primary timber. The head of the shore, the longer of the two members which comprised the brace, was cut back to form an edge-halved scarf joint above the level of the upper plate.

At least six tie-back braces had been laid at the level of the upper plate, cut into the dumping behind the revetment. Although much decayed, they were clearly of cruciform type, aligned at right angles to the revetment wall, with a cross member passed directly through the northern end and retained by piles to the south. The lower of these tie-backs passed through the revetment face just below the upper plate, but the southern ends of the upper three had suffered from decay and subsequent disturbance (not illustrated).

Archive reference: TL74 G11

77. Left: Trig Lane, late14th-century Structure TL11. *a) semi-reconstructed side elevation of the brace in relation to the bipartite stave wall; b) west-facing elevation of part of the stave wall as found, in relation to the baseplates of a ?fish tank built into south-west corner (cf. Fig 78).*

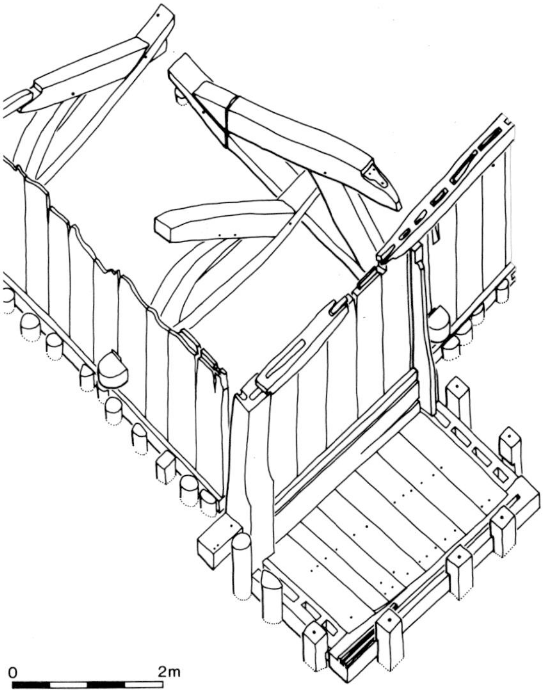

78. Trig Lane, Structure TL11: *axonometric projection of the south-west corner of the revetment, as found, but with upper level back braces not shown.*

Dating: The TL11 structure was stratigraphically later than the mid 14th-century TL10 (*c.*1336-75), but earlier than the mid 15th-century river wall constructed in 1430-40 (archive reference TL74 G15). TL11 was associated with a dump containing a large assemblage of late 14th-century pottery, as well as jettons and pilgrim souvenirs dated to *c.*1370-80.

Dendrochronological summary: Of the eight samples from the TL11 structure, six were dated and two had sapwood (Brett 1982): a felling date range of 1351-90 is estimated (Figs 9, 63).

CITY OF LONDON BOYS' SCHOOL SITE 1986-7
TQ31548092 Site code: BOY86

The late 17th-century riverfront structure recorded on this site has been included in the catalogue since it incorporates several features, such as imported softwoods and iron spike fastenings, which contrast significantly with the techniques described for the earlier revetments. This revetment may also be compared with surviving contracts for contemporary works, such as that for the dock at Blackwall constructed in 1659 (British Library, Addit Charter 13,686: Julian Munby, pers comm).

The site lay to the west of the River Fleet at its confluence with the Thames (Fig 1), and was directed by Craig Spence, who prepared the archive report from which this description was compiled. A north-south trench 58m long and 2m wide was excavated in the former school yard (Spence 1989, 28-9). Many features were recorded, including a late medieval masonry river wall, 16m to the south of which the 17th-century BY1 timber revetment was constructed. The area between the river wall and the revetment was infilled with deposits consolidated with piles, many of which were cut from reused ships timbers (Goodburn 1988).

STRUCTURE BY1

(Figs 79-80)

The BY1 riverfront revetment incorporated a sequence of oak levelling timbers laid beneath the principal softwood baseplate. These included a halved timber 0.25m x 0.15m in cross-section used as a bearer, over which were laid plain-sawn oak planks 0.2m wide by 0.1m thick and a reused oak baseplate at least 2.3m long and 0.3m x 0.2m in cross-section. There were five empty rectangular mortises cut in its upper face, which had once accommodated tenons secured with wooden pegs. This reused late medieval-style plate supported the revetment's principal baseplate, which was cut from an imported softwood and was at least 2.3m long and 0.25m x 0.25m in cross-section. It was secured to the underlying timbers not with wooden pegs but with iron spikes.

The cladding comprised at least five levels of sawn planks, up to 0.3m wide and 80mm thick, set horizontally on edge and secured with iron spikes. All these planks were of oak. Careful examination of treenail holes and other features showed that they had been reused from a substantial carvel-built vessel. Set vertically against the riverward face of the revetment were two plain-sawn softwood planks, also up to 0.3m wide by 80mm thick. The posts which supported the cladding had been removed in antiquity, and it is not known precisely how the structure was braced.

Archive reference: BOY86 G10

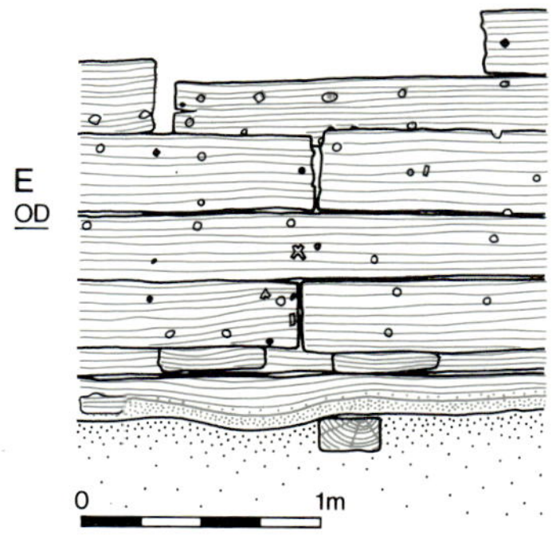

79. City of London Boys' School, late 17th-century Structure BY1*: north-facing elevation of revetment, from which the posts were removed in antiquity.*

80. City of London Boys' School: a 2m-length of BYI *revetment baseplate. Note the mortise pattern, wedges below the baseplate and retaining timbers to the south.*

Dating: The BYI revetment was erected on the foreshore to the south of a late medieval river wall, the area between the two structures being infilled with mixed rubble deposits which incorporated late 17th-century material. These deposits are thought to include debris cleared from buildings destroyed in the Great Fire of 1666. The evidence strongly suggests that the BYI structure was part of the programme of post-Fire redevelopment which began in *c.*1671 in this area.

4: STUDYING MEDIEVAL WATERFRONT INSTALLATIONS

Gustav Milne

The status of riverfront revetments

The most cursory examination of the catalogue shows that the design of riverfront structures underwent considerable change during the medieval period: the purpose of this chapter is to demonstrate the wider significance of these developments. It has already been argued that the medieval London waterfront installations were erected by the same persons responsible for timber building elsewhere in the City, and that the same general techniques used on dry land might be anticipated on the riverside. However, the separation of general attributes from those peculiar to this particular class of structure can only be achieved if the status, function and development of such installations are understood. The following discussion is designed to clarify this point, with regard to the structures described in the catalogue. The first and most obvious point to stress is that riverfront revetments cannot be sensibly described as high or low status structures without suitable qualification. That they were robustly functional features, rather than aesthetic exercises, can be readily accepted. However, the resources devoted to them would depend on the pocket of the occupier of the associated waterfront tenement. For example, revetments protecting the lands of a wealthy fishmonger might well have achieved standards and materials comparable with relatively high status housing. By contrast, structures erected for, or perhaps by, one of the more impoverished Thames-side tenants, might exhibit a greater use of reused material. So many revetments have been recorded that the variety of quality in their construction is clear. We have examples of the good, the bad and the ugly, and thus are in a position to attempt to differentiate the broadly representative from the unusually shoddy. Studying medieval buildings which have survived above ground on dry land is reliant upon a much narrower range of evidence, heavily biased towards the exceptionally well built.

Revetments and the river

Each City revetment comprised a framework designed to withstand the ebb and flow of the tidal Thames, while supporting a cladding which retained the earthern dumps thrown behind it. Such structures were therefore subject to pressure from both the landward and riverward sides. The size, spacing and position of the braces reflect these specific needs (as will be discussed below), whereas the *style* of brace and associated joinery adopted presumably mirrors contemporary construction practice in general. It will be noticed that the earliest medieval revetments are not as tall as the later structures, and also that the contemporary ground surface which they protected lay at a lower level. This implies that the river level relative to the land had risen during this period, an assumption borne out by the identification of river-laid flood deposits sealing waterfront features on several sites.

The study of river level change in London through the examination of Thames-side structures and related deposits is an important area of waterfront research. While it is of obvious relevance to our understanding of the ancient port, specific data concerned with the level of the tidal Thames is of importance to wider studies of sea level change (cf. Thompson 1980), such as those developed for the International Geological Correlation Programme (IGCP). Although by the end of 1987 the work in the United Kingdom on late Quaternary sea level change had amassed much material concerned with the last 10,000 years, somewhat surprisingly data for the most recent 3,000 years was less well represented (Tooley 1990, 5).

Clearly the London waterfront research has a significant contribution to make, and what follows is a summary of work that is still in progress. It has been possible to show that the Roman Thames was tidal in the 1st century and that the Mean High Water Spring tides may have reached *c.*+1.5m OD, substantially lower than present day values (Milne *et al* 1983). There is also evidence to suggest that the tidal level fell in the later Roman period, which implies that the tidal head of the river must have moved eastwards, away from Londinium, a situation which would have had a profound adverse effect upon the port (Brigham 1990, 143-9; Milne 1985, 84-6).

When the tides returned to London is now a focus of research: presumably it must have been before *c.*AD 600, when the settlement of Lundenwic was established just to the west of the abandoned Roman city (Cowie & Whytehead 1989; Vince 1990). Observations on the York Buildings site between the Strand and the Victoria Embankment in 1988 recorded wooden features incorporating timbers felled between 679 and 690, which had been erected on the contemporary river bank. This waterfront embankment had been sealed by a sandy deposit containing flint, ragstone rubble and reused Roman tile, the surface of which lay between +1.13 and 1.30m OD. It was sealed by waterlaid silts and clay up to a height of +1.60m OD, over which earth was subsequently dumped in the 12th century (Cowie 1989; Cowie, pers comm). It is possible, but by no means certain, that the level of the river relative to the land may have risen gradually in the 7th to 9th centuries, and this may have contributed to the decision to abandon the Aldwych site in favour of the Roman walled area.

A provisional assessment of data from the Thames Exchange and Vintry sites suggests that some of the occupation surfaces found at between +1.5m and 1.7m OD in the 10th century may have been subject to periodic flooding, while a revetment surface laid in 1030 on the Vintry site was at *c.* +1.7m OD (R Malt, pers comm). The mid 11th-century contemporary embankments at the Billingsgate Lorry Park site were surfaced at *c.*+1.9m OD, with internal surfaces of Building 1 laid just above +2m OD in the late 12th century (Steedman *et al* forthcoming), a level at which 14th-century occupation surfaces were recorded at Trig Lane (Milne & Milne 1982, 61).

A marked rise seems to have occurred by or, more likely, during the 11th century, perhaps represented by silt deposits and erosion levels on a number of recently excavated sites such as Thames Exchange, Bull Wharf and Vintry. The sea floods recorded in the Anglo-Saxon Chronicle for 1014 and 1099 (Garmonsway 1972, 145; 235) may be associated with such a general trend, while the later of these events may even be represented by a particularly thick silt overbank flood deposit identified on the London sites (R Malt, pers comm). The completion of the first stone London Bridge in 1209 would have artificially increased the level and depth of the water in London at certain states of the tide, while the effects of the documented floods of October 1294 have been identified on the Toppings Wharf site in Southwark (Sheldon 1974). In sum, the size and style of the contemporary revetments naturally reflected these fundamental changes in river level during the medieval period, with the development of taller and more robust structures, ultimately replaced by masonry river walls.

The top of each revetment can be assumed to have lain at or above the level of the highest anticipated tide and would have remained dry for most of its life. By contrast, the base of the structure would have been immersed by the twice-daily ebb and flow of the Thames, and the constant swelling and shrinking of the timberwork below the mean high water mark resulted in the degradation of the wood at that level (Milne & Milne 1982, 60-2; pl 72), which invariably caused the structure to fail within 25 to 50 years. This problem was appreciated by medieval riverfront revetment designers, and steps were taken to counteract it. In the 12th and 13th centuries, braces supported the vulnerable posts; the heads of front braces were set below the mean high water decay zone, whereas the heads of back braces were set above that level (*eg* TL3, Fig 68). There is even some evidence from the TX7 structure to suggest that the top of one of the posts was replaced by a later timber scarfed to it, perhaps in an attempt to prolong the life of the revetment (Fig 58): however, this particular instance may represent a repair or lengthening of the post before it was erected. Certainly by the 14th century, revetments were being constructed in two discrete levels, the upper of which was replaceable, as the TL10 and TL11 structures show (Figs 74, 77, 81).

The jetties (*eg* TX5, Fig 53) represent a different type of riverfront structure, usually free-standing openwork features built out over the foreshore into the river. They were designed not only to withstand the ebb and flow of the tidal Thames, but also to support timber decking laid above the level of the highest anticipated tide. Arguably, such open work structures may reflect contemporary house-building practice even more closely than do the contemporary riverfront revetments.

A further consideration relates to the nature of the river itself, that is, whether or not it was tidal: a fully-framed but prefabricated revetment could only be erected if the foreshore was exposed for a sufficiently long period at low tide. If the river was not tidal, there was little alternative but to build a pile and plank revetment, as was the case up-river

81. Trig Lane: general view of part of the bipartite TL10/G12 *revetment, looking south. The 5 x 100mm scale rests on an excavated horizon within infill deposits dumped to north of (behind) the stave-built 14th-century* TL10 *revetment. Over the top of the stave wall sits a grooved baseplate, part of the 15th-century* G12 *revetment, into which a line of vertical planks were set, of which the remains of three can be seen.*

at Kingston or in the less tidally-fluctuating creeks which ran between the Southwark islands. In such situations, piles would be driven and cladding applied, a technique little influenced by the subtleties of evolving carpentry practice. These deep-water revetments remain the simplest in style of this class of medieval structure: perhaps their chief interest lies in the material used for the sheathing, which often featured articulated sections of boat or ship's planking (Goodburn 1988), a cheap, quick and convenient method of building revetments on the banks of non-tidal waterways.

Timber building traditions represented on the London waterfront

An understanding of the developments and functions discussed above allows us to identify features of construction which are *particular* to revetment structures, and therefore to distinguish them from *general* attributes of medieval timber-working practice, of prime importance to this study. In addition, it demonstrates a desire to improve the efficiency, *ie* the longevity, of the structure being built, a motivation which led to considerable innovation in the medieval period. Some of these changes are of wide and considerable significance, and may be observed in the development of revetment construction, as will be shown. In matters of detail, for instance, the replacement of timber used in the round by squared timber can be readily traced, as can the gradual adoption of timbers of uniform scantling and the decrease in size of baseplates. Plank cladding was secured by wooden pegs in the 13th century, nails in the 14th and spikes in the 17th. The date for the introduction of new tools and techniques in medieval England can be suggested by showing that plain-sawn timber was unknown in the 11th century, but had appeared by the late 12th, for example.

Study of the general form of the medieval riverfront structures from London described in the catalogue shows that three main techniques or traditions are represented: *earthfast post, stave* and *frame-built*. For convenience, the ensuing discussion will be initially conducted under those headings, but how discrete the techniques actually were in practice is a question which will be considered later. What is clearly shown is that, in all five of the dated sequences discussed, structures with earthfast elements were superseded by framed structures incorporating baseplates at the beginning of the 13th century (TX4 to TX5; TX8 to TX9; BG12 &13 to BG14; SH2 to SH3; TL1 to TL2).

With *earthfast post building* (*eg* Fig 82), the principal posts of the structure are set or driven into the ground. The technique is recorded on the waterfront from the 10th century to the end of the 13th century. It is also represented in the desiccated remains of buildings constructed elsewhere in London in the same period (Horsman *et al* 1988): however, the evidence for such buildings usually only survives in the form of post holes.

On the waterfront, posts were initially used in the round (*eg* TX1), but by the 12th century squared posts are clearly in evidence (*eg* TX4, TX7). The planking was invariably cleft, and not sawn. Four

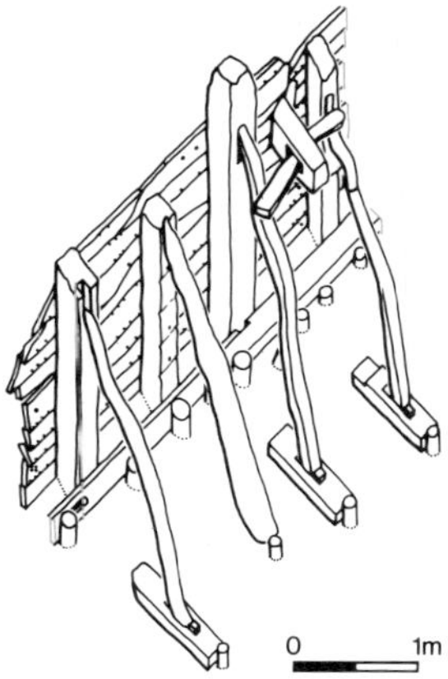

82. Old Custom House (CUS73): axonometric projection of revetment recorded in 1973: note the earthfast posts with splayed recesses which accommodate the heads of irregularly shaped front braces.

types of walling have been recorded on the waterfront: i) planks pegged (never nailed) onto the face of the upright posts; ii) planks set horizontally in grooves cut in the edges of the vertical posts; iii) planks set in rebates cut in the corner of upright posts when squared; iv) earthfast posts with wattlework, which was represented on the London waterfront on the Thames Exchange site as well as at Westminster (Green 1976, 62), and is known from contemporary domestic buildings in York (Addyman 1979, 69) and Dublin (Murray 1983), for example.

The term *stave building* is used here to refer to walls in which vertical timbers provide the rigidity for both the structural frame and the cladding. Examples of stave work on the London waterfront have been recorded in contexts ranging from at least as early as the 11th to the 15th century (Fig 4). Five wall types are represented: staves butted flush, edge to edge; staves joined with false or free tenons; staves joined with dowels; staves joined with rebates cut on the opposing faces of adjacent edges. The last method is reminiscent of that used in the construction of an 11th-century door at Westminster Abbey (Hewett 1980, 155 fig 149). The fifth form of vertical cladding, in which vee-edged boards were used, was recorded on the Baynard's Castle site (Fig 4e).

The earliest examples of stave walls found on the London waterfront were earthfast features (TX2; BG3). The other stave walls were set in baseplates, often in a running groove or slot, although individual mortises were recorded in the late 14th-century structure at Trig Lane (TL11).

It is suggested that the vernacular stave building tradition represented by these waterfront structures was one of considerable longevity and showed much variety in London, coexisting with both the earthfast post and framed building techniques. It has already been shown that the buildings incorporating baseplates which were constructed in London before the Norman Conquest were not fully-framed buildings but had stave walling (Horsman *et al* 1988).

In contrast to a structure incorporating earthfast structural elements, a *timber-framed* building 'relies on its site for no more than the support of its weight' (Hewett 1980, 57), since its principal posts are set in baseplates. This distinction, it has been argued, is fundamental, for an earthfast building is 'erected by a process of accretion, and each process is self-contained ... jointing is by half-lapping and scarfing. To compare these characteristics with those of timber-framing is to find we are dealing with opposites ...their design is wholly unified and construction interlocking by means of the mortise and tenon joint' (Charles 1982, 111). Structures exhibiting these essential characteristics, notably a principal baseplate into which vertical posts are tenoned, made their appearance on the London waterfront in the early 13th century (TX5; TX8; BG14; SH3; TL2), directly replacing revetments with earthfast elements in every case. Such a change can be observed on other London excavations, as at the Custom House site (Figs 82-3; Tatton-Brown 1974).

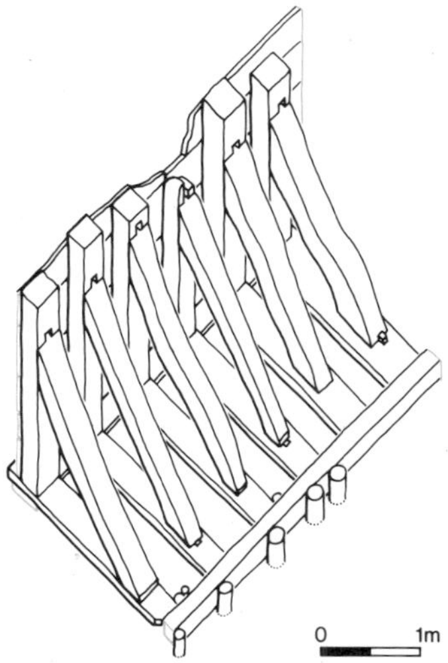

83. Old Custom House (CUS73): axonometric projection of the 14th-century revetment recorded in 1973: note the use of baseplates and chase tenons in both head and foot of braces.

'The study of *prefabrication* is of considerable importance, since its advent eventually produced a dramatic change in the cost of timber buildings, and, coupled with the use of clay, stone or brick footings, a great extension to their lifespan' (Smith 1982, 15). Clear evidence for prefabrication being practised by medieval City carpenters is provided by the incised marks on London revetments. Of especial interest here is that the earliest examples came from earthfast revetments (*eg* TX4), but framed (*eg* TX5; BG10) and stave structures (*eg* TL10) were also prefabricated.

84. Thames Exchange: detail of early 13th-century TX4 *revetment, showing the base of an earthfast post exposed in a trench cut through the foreshore deposits. The 2 x 100mm scale rests on a back brace which is joined to the post with a pegged notched lap joint.*

The transition from earthfast to timber-framed building

It is suggested in this report that the introduction of fully-framed structures could only occur after the development of a number of specific features: a) the use of timbers of squared, uniform scantling; b) the introduction of well-cut, closely-fitted joinery; c) the use of a baseplate; d) the development of the stone sill or dwarf stone wall upon which the baseplate rests; e) the adoption of the mortise and tenon with two shoulders to form the basic articulation at the head and foot of principal posts; f) the adoption of the chase tenon as the basic articulation for diagonally-set braces integral to the frame.

Since none of these elements are required of necessity in an earthfast structure, it could be argued that framed building represents a new building tradition imported into London fully developed, some time after the Norman Conquest. However, study of the well-preserved riverfront structures allows a different interpretation. It is now suggested that the technique of framed building was gradually developed following a fusion of attributes taken from the otherwise quite separate stave and earthfast traditions, which were themselves developing independently.

Working from the list above, it seems that a) and b), squared timber of uniform scantling and well-cut joinery, were being developed and used in earthfast structures (Fig 84) by the 12th century, while c), the introduction of the baseplate, has already been shown to be a product of the stave-building tradition by the 11th century. A study of the development of foundations in Saxo-Norman buildings excavated on inland sites in London has revealed the process whereby d), the stone sills evolved to support such baseplates (Horsman *et al* 1988). In origin, the mortise and tenon joint, the other crucial attribute of framed building, seems to owe something to both earlier traditions, but did not come into its own in the forms with which we are most familiar until the late 12th to early 13th century.

Thus the introduction of the baseplate, squared timbers, well-cut joinery and the long (*ie* rectangular rather than square) mortise in waterfront structures can be taken as indicating the establishment of the technology and the tool kit necessary for fully framed building in London as a whole. The date for this transition from earthfast techniques can now be assigned to the last decades of the 12th century, with the introduction of framed structures in the early 13th century.

Stuart Rigold's examination of timber bridge trestles offers a close parallel, for the type II trestle is seen as 'the essential component of the box-frame, and bridges provide its oldest remaining exemplars' (Rigold 1975, 84). 'Square or near-square mortises occur at Hen Domen, West Derby and Cashen Estuary Bridge, and at Penhallam (the last after 1200) ... but ... the long mortise, far more efficient in both directions and the very foundation of framed buildings as we know it, is attested in bridges from the middle of the 12th century' (Rigold 1975, 88). He goes on to show that 'the mature symmetrical frame (with a long sole plate to take shores external to both posts) cannot be traced before the later 13th century, but thereafter becomes almost universal' (Rigold 1975, 85). Evidence from the London waterfront shows that pre-Conquest baseplates with square mortises are known (Figs 5, 88), while the late 12th-century TLI revetment incorporates a well-cut mortise and tenon where the baseplate articulates with the edge of the earthfast post. However, the earliest structures using baseplates with long mortises penetrated by standard tenons cut on the feet of vertical posts seem to date to the early 13th century.

The development of the mortise and tenon, and through it the origins of timber-framing, can also be traced through the study of other types of structure, both above and below the ground, and through the careful examination of dated, reused timbers, such as the group of baseplates recovered from the Billingsgate Lorry Park site. This theme will be considered in detail in Chapter 5, and so need only be summarised here. Although square through-mortises were recorded on the basal members of the 9th-century millpool revetment at Tamworth, where they articulated with tusk tenons (Rahtz & Sheridan 1972, fig 2, joint B), this structure was not part of a timber-framed building (as defined above) since no principal posts were tenoned into the plates. No mortises and tenons were used to joint the feet of the posts to the baseplates of the 10th-century buildings at Coppergate, York (Hall 1982, 238-9), neither were central tenons cut on the heads of the posts (Hall 1984, 72-3, figs 1, 3). Tenons were also absent in the

85. Mermaid Theatre (THE79), looking north: all that survived from the south-west corner of this 13th-century revetment were these baseplates, exposed on the foreshore, and enclosing a rising bank of London Clay. To north of the 10 x 100mm scale to the left of the picture, the structure's western return wall is represented by part of the principal baseplate, running north-south in the top north-west corner, with subsidiary baseplates for front braces to west. The structure was supported by front and back braces, the latter represented by the five longest baseplates. Only broken fragments of the braces are visible at the northern ends of the baseplates, but these were joined with notched lap joints. Although the principal baseplate for the south wall was removed, its position is marked by the trench cut in the upper face of the brace baseplates.

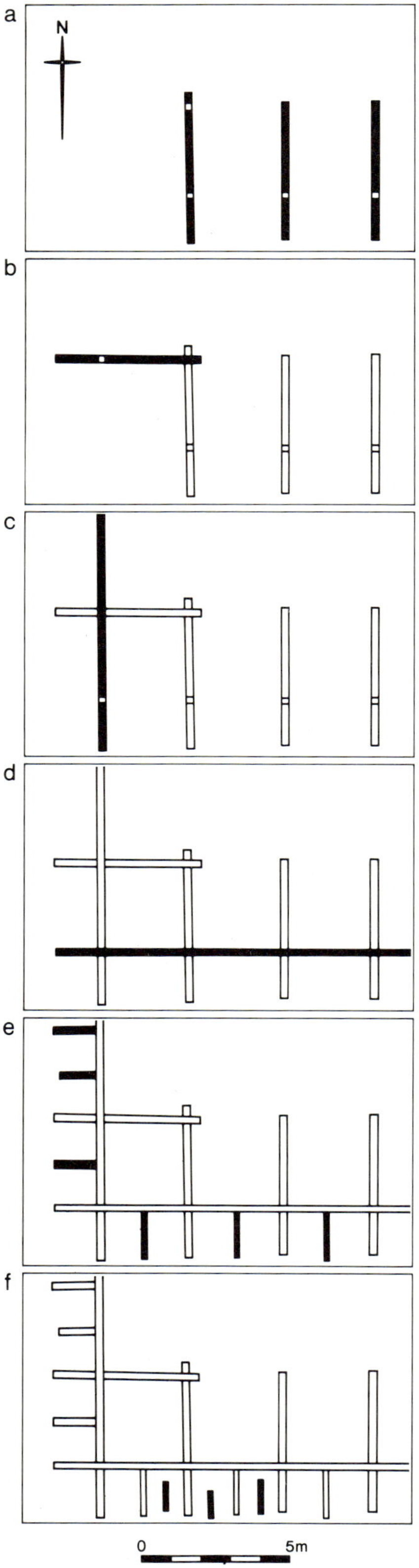

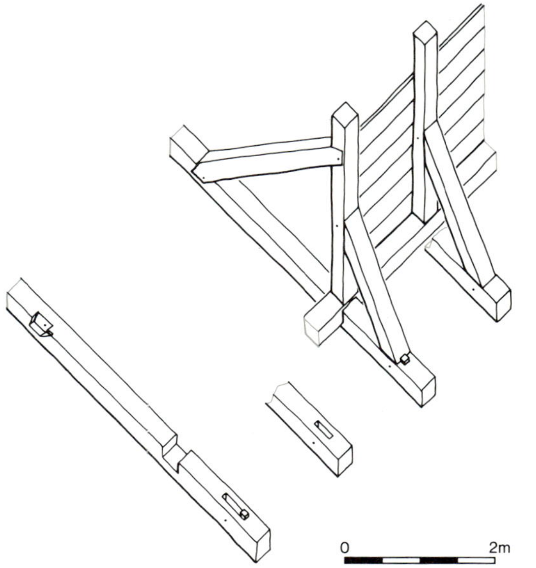

86. Left: Mermaid Theatre (THE79). Plan series showing construction sequence of baseplates for this framed mid 13th-century revetment.

87. Above: Mermaid Theatre (THE79). Semi-reconstructed axonometric projection of the mid 13th-century revetment: back braces are lapped to the posts, front braces are chase-tenoned.

pre-Conquest buildings at Dublin (Wallace 1982, 271), and in the roof of St Martin of Tours, Chipping Ongar, Essex, thought to date to the closing decade of the 11th century (Hewett 1980, 35, fig 30). The one apparent exception to this rule, the Rhenish helm at St Mary's church, Sompting, Sussex, which was once thought to be Saxon (Hewett 1980, 14-20), has now been shown to be of early 14th-century date (Tyers 1990; Aldsworth & Harris 1988).

To sum up, there is little evidence for the mature mortise and tenon or for fully-framed buildings in medieval Britain before the 12th century. Hewett's analysis of standing buildings in England suggests that the crucial point of transition from post to framed building was reached in the mid to late 12th to early 13th century, *ie* after the erection of the Grange Barn at Coggeshall - the main posts of which were set on stone stylobates - but before the introduction of the ground-silling system used in the Barley Barn at Cressing (Hewett 1980, fig 60), which was erected between 1200 and 1240 (Tyers 1990). It is of some significance that the date for the introduction of timber-framing in such high status structures as are described by Hewett is precisely the same as that of the introduction of those same techniques to the vernacular riverfront revetments.

Looking in more detail at the *range* of joints used on the London waterfront structures, some other general observations of possible wider relevance can be made. A recent study of medieval roofs in Herefordshire and Worcestershire showed that plain halving was common before 1150, after which various forms of notched lap joint were often used. Mortised end joints first occurred in some positions in the roof trusses in the later 12th century, but did not become normal in all positions until the late 13th century (Currie 1990, 19-20).

This sequence is paralled by the development of the waterfront braces, where notched laps were used in some of the earlier structures such as the Mermaid Theatre revetment (Figs 85-7) in the position where chase mortises would have been used later. Chase mortises were used only on the foot of front braces in the early 13th century, but on both head and foot by the end of that century.

Given a general affinity of revetment bracing with roof structures, it may be worth considering some of the possible wider implications of the anchor-beam-style braces used on the 11th and 12th-century stave structures (*eg* BG10, Figs 14-5). The closest parallel for such a scheme could be argued to be the anchor-beams (*Ankerbalken; entrait d'ancrage*) which are common in continental medieval roof structures from northern Poland to north-west Spain: the authors of a study of this technique note with astonishment that it is not represented in Britain or Ireland (Bans & Gaillard-Bans 1984, 58-9). It is pressing the evidence from the London waterfront too far to suggest that such roofs were once used here, but had been superseded by the 13th century, together with the earthfast post and stave-building techniques: nevertheless, it serves as a reminder that the study of 10th to 12th-century timber buildings is in its infancy, and that the riverfront revetments are rare examples of the contemporary traditions, from which much of wider interest may be learned.

5: REUSED HOUSE TIMBERS FROM THE BILLINGSGATE SITE, 1982-3

Trevor Brigham

INTRODUCTION

In the previous chapter, an attempt was made to identify significant developments in medieval timber building techniques through consideration of changes in the design of waterfront structures: this new chapter shares that aim, but makes use of a different class of evidence, fragments of medieval timber buildings found reused or discarded on the waterfront. The house timbers discussed here are part of a group from the Billingsgate Lorry Park site (BIG82: see p.24). Among the structures excavated was a series of early 11th to early 12th-century embankments, constructed largely of clay and gravel with timber lacing. These were succeeded by stave revetments (*eg* BG3, BG10) and in the 13th century by post and plank structures (*eg* BG14). Although many of the timbers in the embankments were unworked branches, a significant proportion were reused, and in common with material from the revetments, included boat and house timbers and parts of barrels. This catalogue deals solely with the house timbers, which are related to contemporary building construction, with particular regard to the development of timber framing. In an attempt to complete the picture, it draws on relevant data from sites where organic remains have survived, and from sites where they have not.

These 11th and 12th-century house timbers are of importance both because of the lack of preserved contemporary material and because they survived in sufficient quantity to provide a useful database. The development of carpentry in England is a subject of concern to archaeologists and to specialists in the field of vernacular architecture alike, and the reconstruction of ancient timber buildings from archaeological remains, both on paper and in replica, has become increasingly popular (*eg* Drury 1982). However, the resulting reconstructions for the early medieval period are often based on very limited archaeological information, which in the majority of cases is confined to what may be termed 'non-organic' evidence such as post holes, post trenches, beam slots or padstones. Where structural timbers survive therefore, either *in situ* or displaced as in this group, they are a crucial aid to such reconstructions.

CATALOGUE OF HOUSE TIMBERS FROM THE BILLINGSGATE LORRY PARK SITE

The house timbers presented in this catalogue form two distinct groups, *baseplates* and *posts or studs,* and are described chronologically. Although the date of the contexts in which they were found is known, only two house timbers have as yet been dated absolutely: 5531 and 4999 were cut from trees felled between 944-1026 and 1036-1152 respectively. In addition, some matching fragments were recovered from widely-separated contexts, which implies that there was considerable disturbance of old material. This creates some problems in determining relative dating, and hence chronological development, within the group. However, if a timber cannot be shown to have been reused more than once, then it is suggested that a nominal 30-year period be allowed from its primary use to its reuse: this reflects the projected lifespan of the original building, based on the average replacement rate of timber structures in the early medieval period. A reference such as W7 or BG12 with the four-figure context numbers refers to the structure from which each timber was obtained.

11th & 12th-century baseplates

Mortised baseplates

The chief characteristics of this group were: rectangular or wedge-shaped cross-sections; rect-angular or sub-rectangular unpegged mortises cut through the timber at intervals; tangential (occasionally, radial) splitting. Pegholes and smaller mortises were often present (Fig 88).

Although the baseplates were damaged and many had been deliberately split along the central axis, it was possible to reconstruct some of the missing information by correlation with similar examples. Several had dimensions or attributes in common with other fragments, and therefore may originally have been sections from larger timbers. In one salutary instance, a building timber, 5347, produced in *c.*1020-30 was presumably redeposited with 6672 and 8124 in Structure W1 in *c.*1055. Part of it was then removed for reuse in the early 13th century with Structure BG12, almost two centuries after its original use. Other fragments with features in common included: 6302 and 6304 (W1); 4771 (W6), 7904 and 7917 (W7); 6069A and 6069B (W8); 6861 (W9) and 6324 (W11).

Most of the (restored) timbers had an average depth-to-width ratio of *c.*1:3, and it is possible that some of these were actually *top-plates*, where a relatively compact form would have been of advantage *eg*, 6301, 6304, 6672 (BG3); 6069A (W8), 6862 (W9), 5347 (BG12). There were, however, several examples with a ratio of *c.* 1:6 *eg*, 6972 (BG3), 7088/8175 (BG3), 6784 (W6), 6072 (W8): evidence from excavations suggests that relatively wide baseplates were not uncommon, and traces of foundations of considerable width were recorded at Bargate Street, Southampton (Wacher 1975), Waltham Abbey, Essex (Huggins 1976) and from buildings in London (Horsman *et al* 1988).

The mortises were often crudely cut and were not pegged, in contrast to later examples (cf. Fig 91), which suggests that the joints provided little support for structural posts, and probably served to retain studs. Tusk tenons protruding a little way into the underlying soil would have provided a degree of stability, however, and the close spacing of the mortises (*c.*0.2-0.4m from edge to edge, an average of 0.3m) would have allowed the studs to act as adequate props for the top-plates. The task of providing a rigid frame and a solid base for the roof structure, in the absence of later developments such as secure jointing, rails and angle braces, must have fallen largely on either earthfast internal posts or wall posts with interrupted baseplates. In addition, top-plates and tie-beams would have been supported by the wall posts and/or studs.

The mortises in several baseplates were evenly spaced for regular close-studding comparable in appearance to that of later medieval buildings in eastern England (BG3: 6302, 6304, 6672; W8: 6069B; W9: 6861; BG3: 6932, 6972, 8124; W7: 7902). By contrast, two (W8: 6072; W9: 6862) were characterised by alternate large mortises for wider-spaced studs and smaller auger holes for light intermediate elements. On 6072 the presence of a doorway is implied by a 0.7m gap between two of the larger mortises. Both 6862 and 6303 may have had crude pegged scarfs.

Another type of baseplate (*eg* W6: 6784) was characterised by a single large mortise for the location of a principal post. One or possibly two smaller mortises followed the centre line, presumably for intermediate studs, with an auger hole and a peghole offset along one edge. These may have retained either the planks of a wooden floor or an internal screen forming a cavity wall, since they were aligned with the inner edge of the principal post.

A fourth type of baseplate (BG3: 6315, 6879) had one large mortise cut 0.5m from one end, which suggests that it had functioned as a pad supporting the base of a large principal post, possibly in an aisled hall. An identical timber (2305) has recently been recorded at the Thames Exchange excavation (Fig 95b). The ends were finished in a neat curve, partly chamfered on the presumed upper surface, suggesting that the timbers may have been exposed above ground. The timbers were tangentially split from planks selected from the centre of the tree, and required little trimming on the edges.

The quality of the carpentry was poor compared with similar elements from the 13th-century revetments; nonetheless, the variation within the group is indicative of developing technology. Some details of tool-working were recorded, despite the decayed condition of most of the timbers; pegholes suggest the use of a range of augers, mainly between 10 and 25mm, and it is also likely that mortises were started by drilling four corner holes. This could be seen in the recurved shape of the ends of examples where the drilled outlines partly survived (*eg* 6302), and also possibly in surviving auger holes near the corners of mortises, where the bit may have been wrongly positioned to begin with (*eg* 6301). A better example of this process has been recorded at the Thames Exchange site (Fig 95b: 2741). The remaining wood was removed with an axe, adze or twybill; normally the mortises were splayed from one face, suggesting that the cutting tool was held at an angle, although some mortises were splayed on both sides.

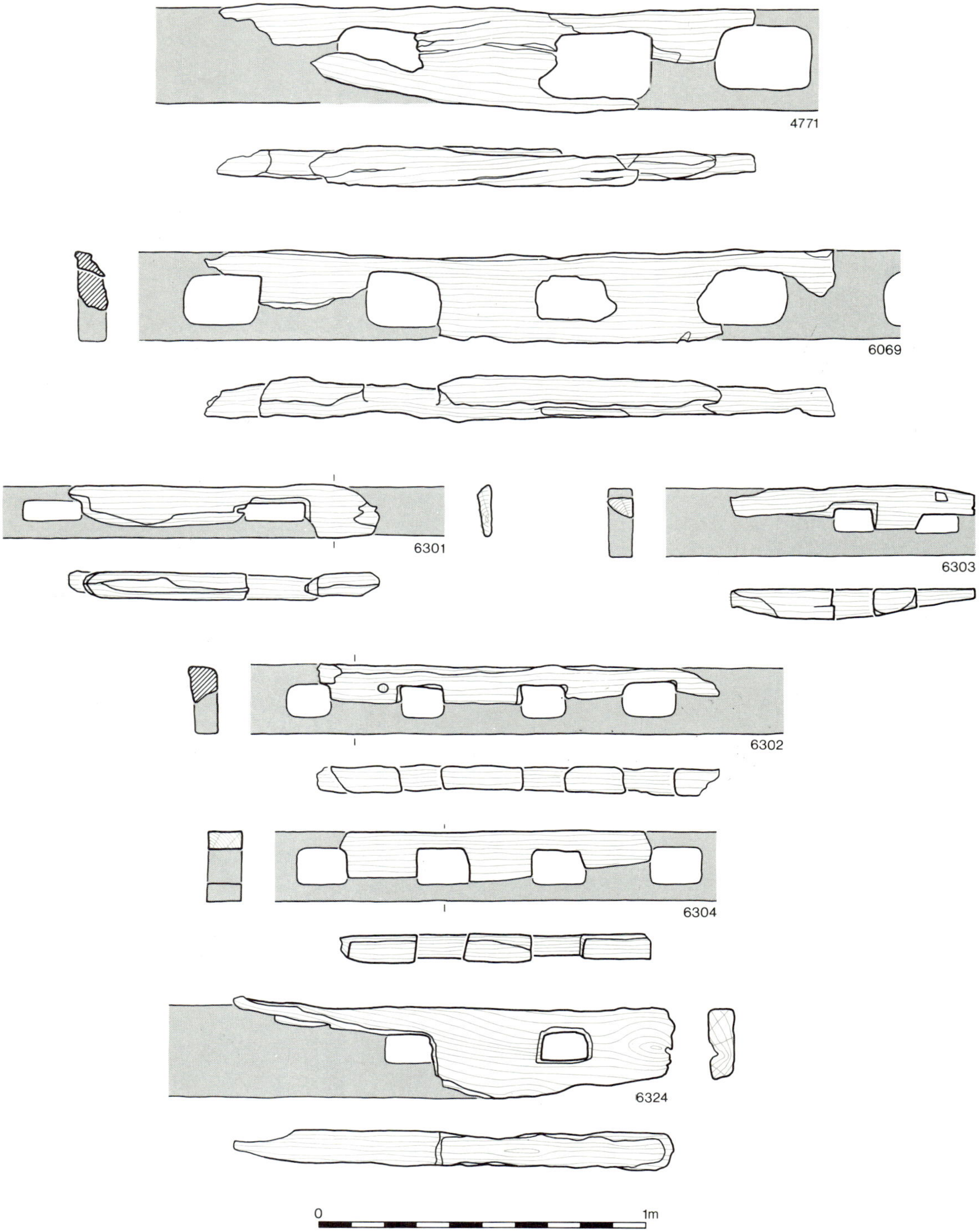

88a. Mortised baseplates from Billingsgate Lorry Park site.

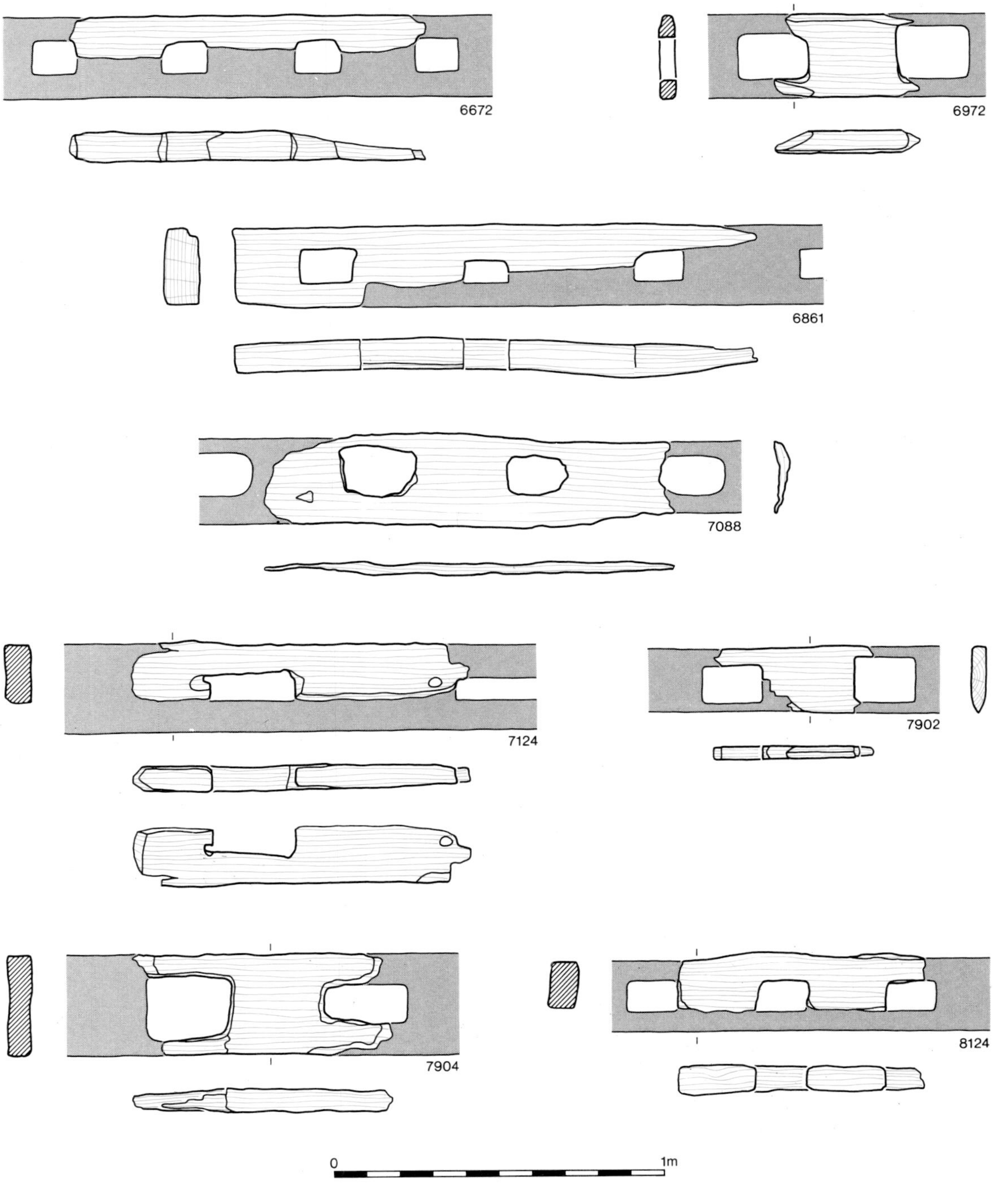

88b. Mortised baseplates from Billingsgate Lorry Park site.

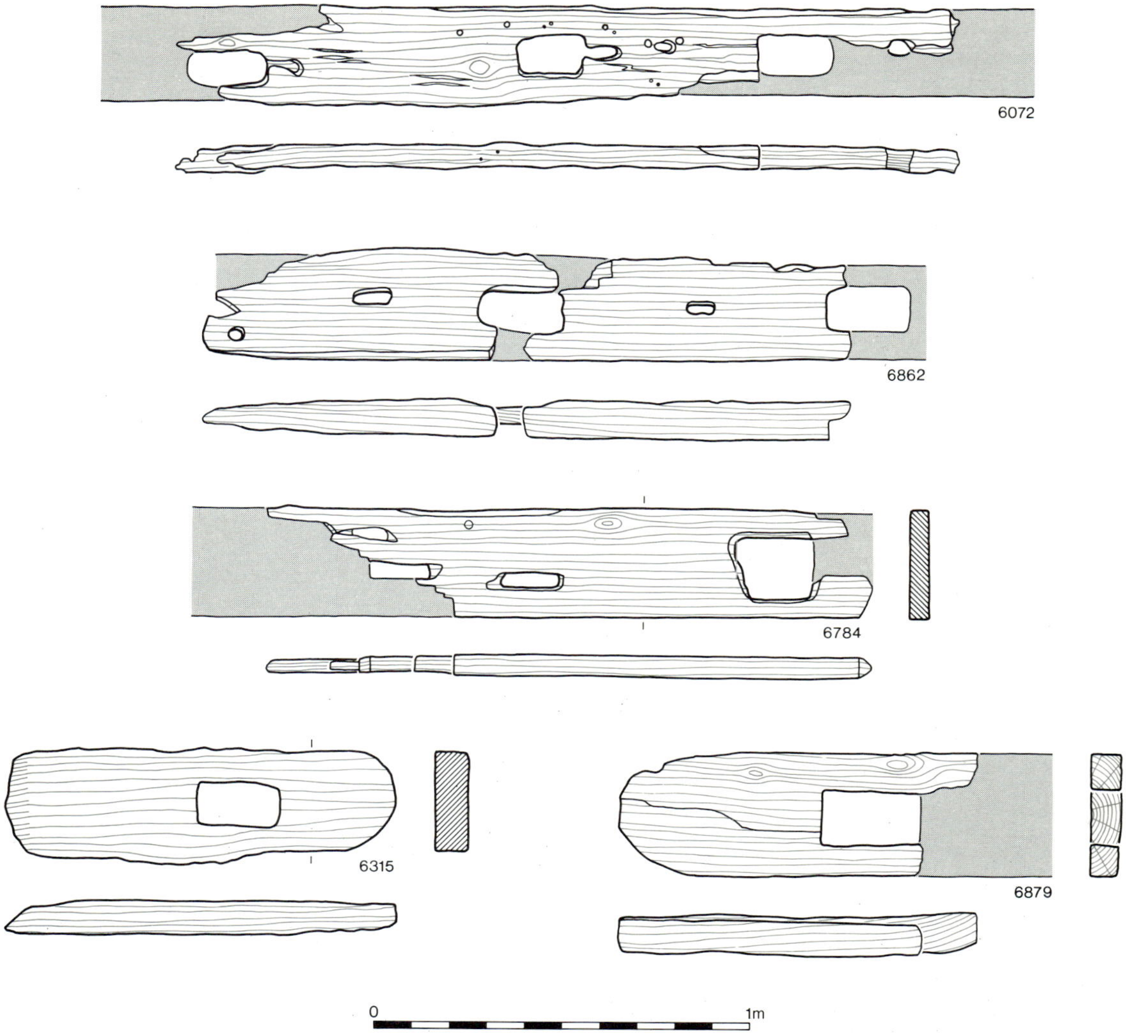

88c. Mortised baseplates from Billingsgate Lorry Park site.

Grooved baseplates

This group of timbers was characterised not by mortises but by a central groove, and would mostly have been used in stave buildings (Fig 89a). All were squared with the exception of two which were roundwood (6825, 6382), a feature shared with baseplates from Christchurch Place, Dublin (Murray 1983). Most were obtained from stave revetments of this date, although dendrochronological analysis suggested that one of the three early 12th-century W8 baseplates (5416, 6016) was cut from a tree felled some time after AD981. Two other timbers of a similar size (BG10: 6825; W11: 6382) which were reused in 12th-century contexts may be of a similar date. Another timber (W2: 7556) was probably derived from a Roman quay, since in photographs taken during excavation the characteristic small mortises for free tenons appear alongside the groove.

Four timbers (5416, 6016, 6382, 6825) had face-halved lap joints at one end only, which by analogy with baseplates from an 11th-century stave-built house from Buderich in Germany (Chapelot & Fossier 1985), and the 13th-century kitchen at Weoley Castle, Birmingham (Oswald 1962/3), were employed to lap them around principal wall posts (Smith 1965). Since no such posts were present in any of the stave revetments, it is clear that the baseplates

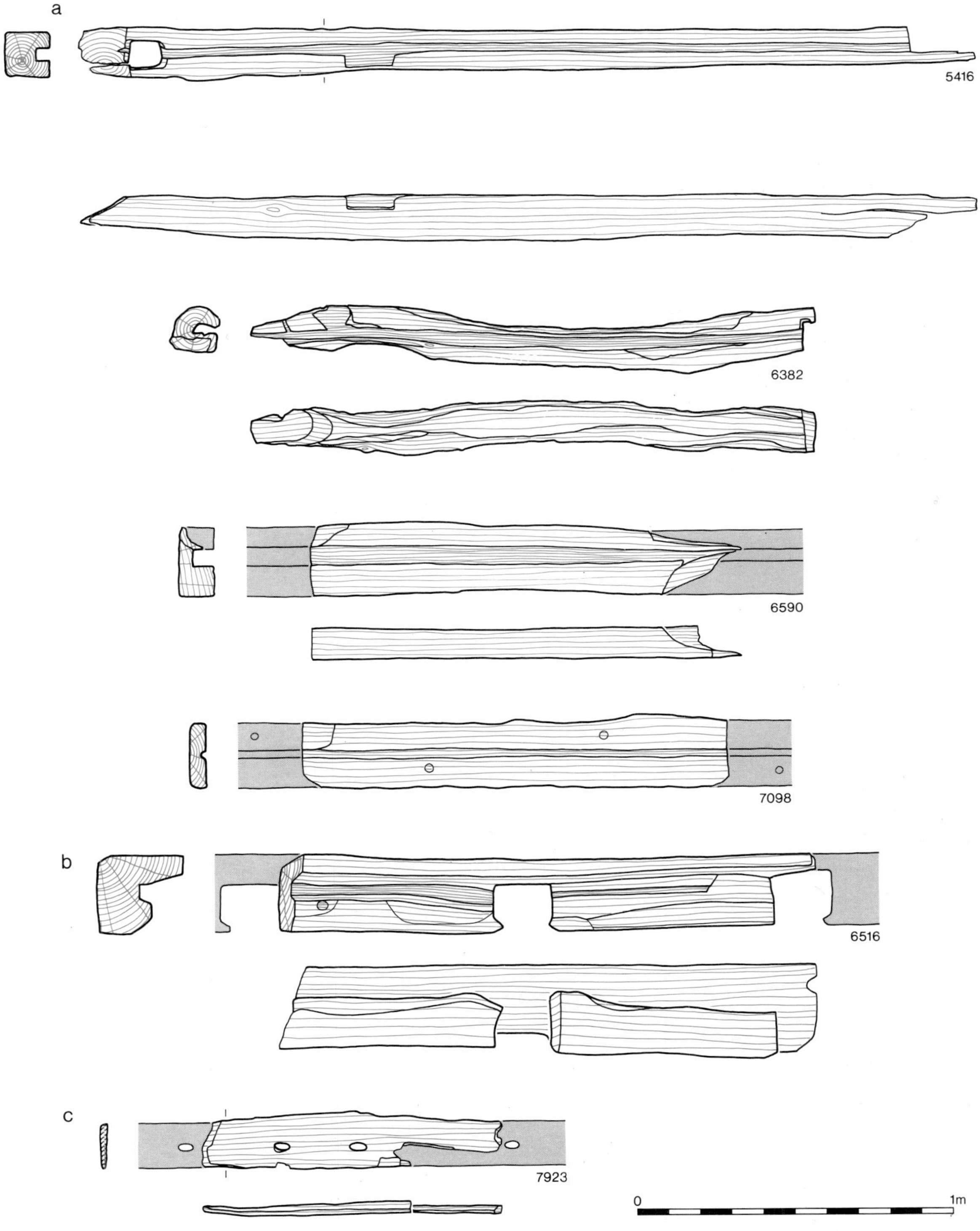

89. Baseplates from Billingsgate Lorry Park site. Scale: 1:20 unless otherwise indicated. a) Grooved baseplates (5416, 6382 scale 1:40); b) lipped baseplates; c) pegged baseplate.

were reused, and probably originated in a stave building akin to the Buderich structure. On one (5416) the opposite end to the lap joint had been cut obliquely to form a through-splayed scarf or finished end, and a large mortise inserted to accommodate a second wall post. The groove did not continue beyond the mortise and it is suggested therefore that the timber was originally lapped around a corner post, with an intermediate post (possibly flanking a doorway) retained by the mortise.

In these timbers, the position of the groove in relation to the posts varied from the centre to the outer face. This suggests that the posts could be either grooved down the edge or rebated on the outer face to retain the end staves of each wall section: both methods would ensure a weatherproof overlap. However, the presence of the posts would have prevented the staves from being inserted from the ends of the baseplate after the principal posts and top-plates had been erected. A solution to this problem of assembly seems to lie in the housing cut from one edge of 5416 and 6382 to the central groove, the depth of both groove and housing being equal. The housing had no function in the waterfront structure, but identical features were recorded in a building from Buderich (Chapelot & Fossier 1985). It is suggested that these additional housings enabled staves to be slotted into position, facilitating wall assembly and allowing for subsequent replacement or repair without wholesale dismantling of the wall.

A less substantial timber (w6: 7098/8057) with a shallow central groove flanked by small holes drilled alternately on either side was probably designed to retain the foot of a light plank or wattle-panelled partition, supported by thin rods. In its secondary use it appears to have formed part of a foreshore platform, the superstructure of which had been removed. Timber 6590 (w11) had a relatively shallow groove, and no other diagnostic features.

Other baseplates

One baseplate, a hybrid between mortised and grooved types (w11: 6516; Fig 89b), had an 'L'-shaped cross-section formed by a raised edge, presumably to retain wall planking. The discovery of similar timbers elsewhere suggests that they were not uncommon, despite the amount of timber which must have been wasted in their production. The Billingsgate timber differed in the provision of two cut-outs set 0.7m apart along one edge of the face for the location of posts. To retain the wall cladding, shallow grooves were cut between the centres of the posts, which must also have been grooved. Timber 4647 (w6) was outwardly similar, although in this case the lip may have been caused by later distortion. Baseplate 7923 (w7; Fig 89c) was a thin split board with a line of small oval holes along the surface, probably for the stakes of a wattled wall or screen.

11th & 12th-century posts and studs

Two wall posts (w4: 7570, 7654; Fig 90a) were identified by the presence of a line of pegholes. Since pegged planking was rarely used in riverfront revetments at this date, the timbers were probably obtained from a weatherboarded building. Both posts had a single row of regularly spaced pegholes which were drilled down one side only, terminating *c.*0.5m from what may be considered the lower, earthfast end. The dimensions suggest that they were load-bearing, with their flat bases resting in trenches or post pits.

The scantling of one timber (w11: 6381; Fig 90b) suggests that it was a stud rather than a principal post. It was rectangular in section with a groove cut down either edge which stopped short of both ends: these grooves may have retained panelling for a wall *c.*1.5m high. The tapered head of the timber was pegged, possibly for attachment to a top-plate. The flat base suggests that it had been set in a trench or post pit, or on a dwarf wall, rather than forming part of a fully framed structure.

A smaller fragment (w2: 7232; Fig 90c) which tapered towards one edge and had a groove on the other was probably not a stud and may have been an element from a tongued and grooved stave wall. Similar timbers have been found in excavated buildings from the Husterknupp and Buderich, in Germany, and in surviving Scandinavian stave churches, such as the example at Hedared, Sweden (Chapelot & Fossier 1985).

No internal principal posts were identified from this period. However, several posts from the 11th and early 12th-century revetments which lined the inlet were squared, in contrast to the majority which were normally either used in the round or cleft. Some of the squared timbers may have been reused, but are difficult to identify with so few diagnostic features.

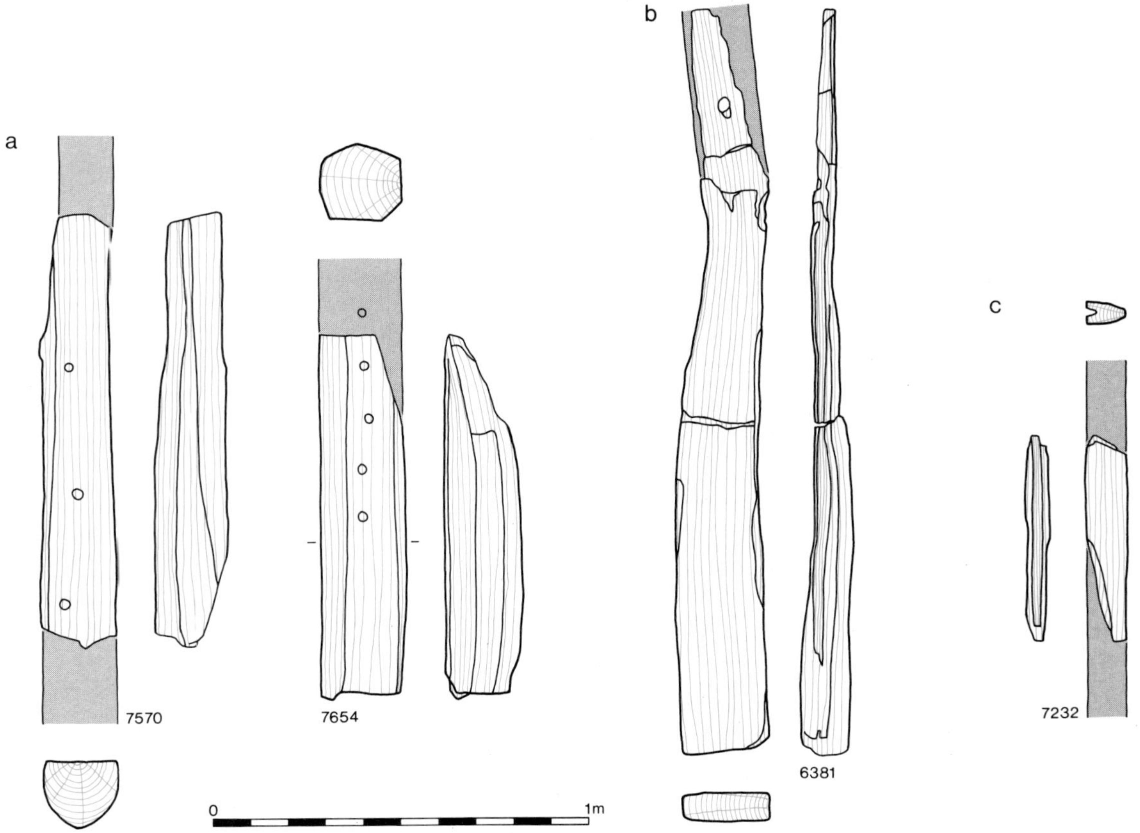

90. Posts and studs from Billingsgate Lorry Park site.

Summary

From the groups of timbers discussed in this section, we can postulate the existence in the first half of the 11th century of a type of domestic carpentry with particular characteristics, including the use of cleft timber baseplates, earthfast principals and unpegged mortises, which persisted into the 12th century. The nature of the carpentry, coupled with the independence of many of the elements, means that there had been no radical shift away from the preceding post-built tradition towards one using more fully integrated timbers.

13th-century baseplates

Although mortised baseplates were found at Billingsgate in mid 11th-century deposits, all had been discarded in secondary contexts. The earliest example recorded as a structural element in a riverfront revetment appears in the early 13th-century BG13 structure, although this baseplate (5721; Fig 91a) was itself reused and may have come from a building or an earlier revetment. It is an important late 12th to early 13th-century timber with attributes of both earlier and later carpentry traditions. By comparison with later timbers, the mortises were poorly aligned, differed in size, and their spacing varied between 0.1m and 0.4m, comparable with earlier types (cf. 0.7m for later waterfront baseplates 6248, 3865, 3866). Some of the mortises were now pegged, although in contrast to fully developed later examples, the pegholes were not drilled fully edge to edge: such 'blind' pegholes were apparently characteristic of 11th-century carpentry (*eg* 7570, 7654, 6302). The timber was halved and had a depth/width ratio of 1:1.2. The mortises, like those of later baseplates, did not penetrate through the timber, proving beyond doubt that the posts of contemporary structures were no longer earthfast. The onus of holding the posts and frame rigidly in position now depended

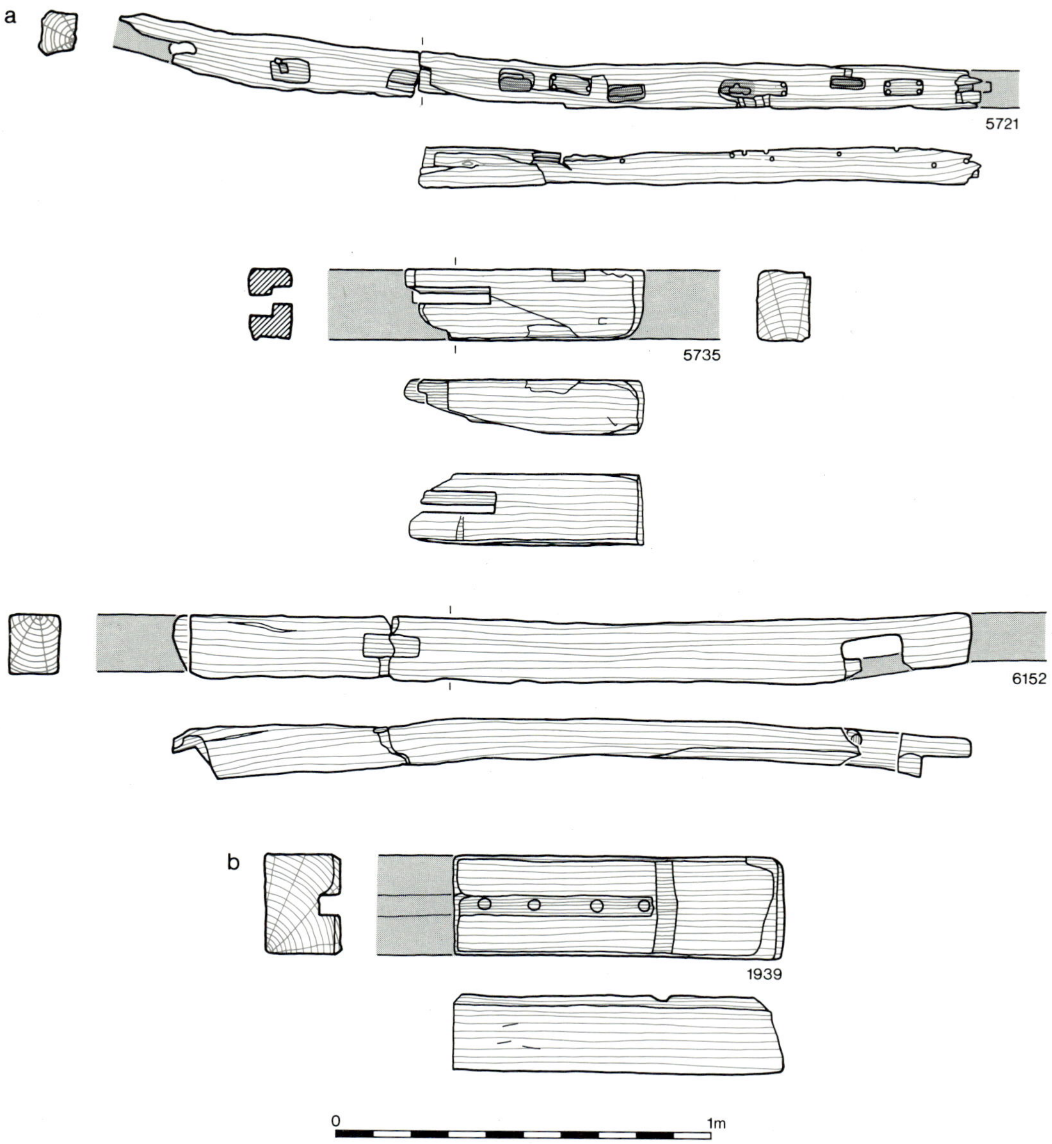

91. Baseplates from Billingsgate Lorry Park site. Scale: 1:20 for all timbers except for 5721 (scale 1:40).

on the strength of the jointing and the interdependence of the various elements. The mortises of this baseplate were still marked out using auger holes at the corners, which would also have acted as guides to the required depth. The impressions of auger bits and other tools on the bases of some mortises implies that the intervening wood was then drilled out and the remainder removed with a bladed tool, such as a chisel, adze or twybill.

Some of these details were confirmed by a section from a second mortised baseplate (5735; Fig 91a) which had been reused as a wedge beneath 5721: this had two half mortises cut from opposing faces, but in almost the same position, so that they met and overlapped slightly. One of the mortises was pegged, although again the peg did not penetrate from edge to edge. The presence of two mortises suggests that the timber was a mid rail in a timber-framed wall. A narrow rebate along one edge next to the pegged mortise may have retained panels, window shutters or weatherboards. A smaller angled rebate was cut into the opposing face near the second mortise, although it was not pegged or nailed. The purpose of this feature cannot be determined, beyond noting that if the timber had been sawn away at the end of a second mortise, the rebate would have been exactly midway between the two; the mortises themselves in that case would have been 0.4m apart.

Although the baseplates of subsequent revetments (*eg* BG14 to BG16) were produced specifically for the waterfront, they also reflected further developments in domestic carpentry. This can be seen from a number of very similar late 13th to early 14th-century timbers employed in two cellar structures (HS3/4 and CP13/2) from the High Street and Christchurch Place sites in Dublin, the only difference between these and the London examples being the use of pegged through-splayed as opposed to edge-halved scarfs, and the adoption of angled-down braces in the High Street structure. The mortises were evenly spaced and pegged, and the standard of carpentry was relatively high. Assembly marks on the Billingsgate baseplates matched others on the posts, showing the degree to which prefabrication had been adopted.

A wattle and daub building constructed behind the BG14 structure employed lengths of reused timber as baseplates, although one corner was marked by a post pad. All the timbers were simply pegged together, with no scarfing, and the uprights retained in small square mortises set 1m apart. None were pegged and only one penetrated the depth of the timber. The feet of the posts which survived were not cut into tenons, but simply rammed into position. The small size of the posts and the lack of adequate jointing suggests that the roof was carried largely by internal principals, as was the practice in preceding centuries.

Grooved baseplates did not appear in the later revetments at Billingsgate, although elsewhere they were employed into the 14th century (*eg* TL10, Figs 74-6). One short section of grooved baseplate (1939; Fig 91b) was however reused in repairs to the BG16 revetment. Dowel holes had been drilled into the groove at 0.10 to 0.13m intervals, presumably to hold a wattle panel. The groove terminated 0.35m from the end of the timber, and a second shallower cut passed across the face at this point. This divided off the remainder of the timber, which was featureless and may therefore have marked a doorway.

13th-century posts and studs

(Figs 92-4)

This category includes a large group of posts obtained from structures BG14 (Fig 92) and W15 (2655 2656, 2658, 2663, 2664, 2669 to 2672, 2674, 2675). In addition, a short offcut (6249) was used as underpinning beneath the BG14 baseplate. Eight of the posts had two longitudinal rebates, and were therefore 'T'- sectioned. The remainder, although rectangular in section, showed signs that they also had been rebated, and it became clear on closer inspection that all 16 posts were produced by sawing eight grooved 'H'- sectioned timbers into unequal halves down their narrow central spine.

Reconstructed, a typical grooved post would have been 3m long, *c*.0.35m wide at the base, tapering to 0.25m at the head. The edges were 0.25m wide, again tapering slightly, each with a central groove stopping 0.7m from the base. Like timber 6381, the base was probably flat for setting into a post pit. Some 2.3m above the base, a roughly rectangular chase mortise was cut into the outer face to retain a brace or buttress. The form of the head is unknown, but the grooves may have continued to the end. Similar timbers from revetments SH2 and TX7 retained horizontal boards (Figs 32, 58).

At the east end of the BG14 revetment was a reused post (6210) with a single groove identical in size to those of the other timbers. It was exactly half the width but the same thickness as those with double grooves, and the presence of an identical chase mortise suggests that it served as the end post of the same structure.

When the grooved timbers were converted, the rear face was cut away to form a rectangular timber in which the outer face appeared 'rebated'. Usually the timbers were found inverted, the earthfast sections cut away and new splayed chase mortises added, sometimes on the former inner face. Pegged tenons were cut as on the adjacent BG13 revetment. In this secondary use, the posts were numbered with a series of knife cuts which corresponded with similar marks on the baseplates.

The form of these timbers (earthfast and braced) matched those of the missing posts from the BG12 revetment which had formed an earlier frontage of the same tenement (Figs 10, 17). Although these posts therefore probably came from a revetment rather than a house, it is likely that they were modelled on types developed for use in land structures; buttresses are known from buildings of early and mid Saxon date (*eg* Millett 1983, fig 64;

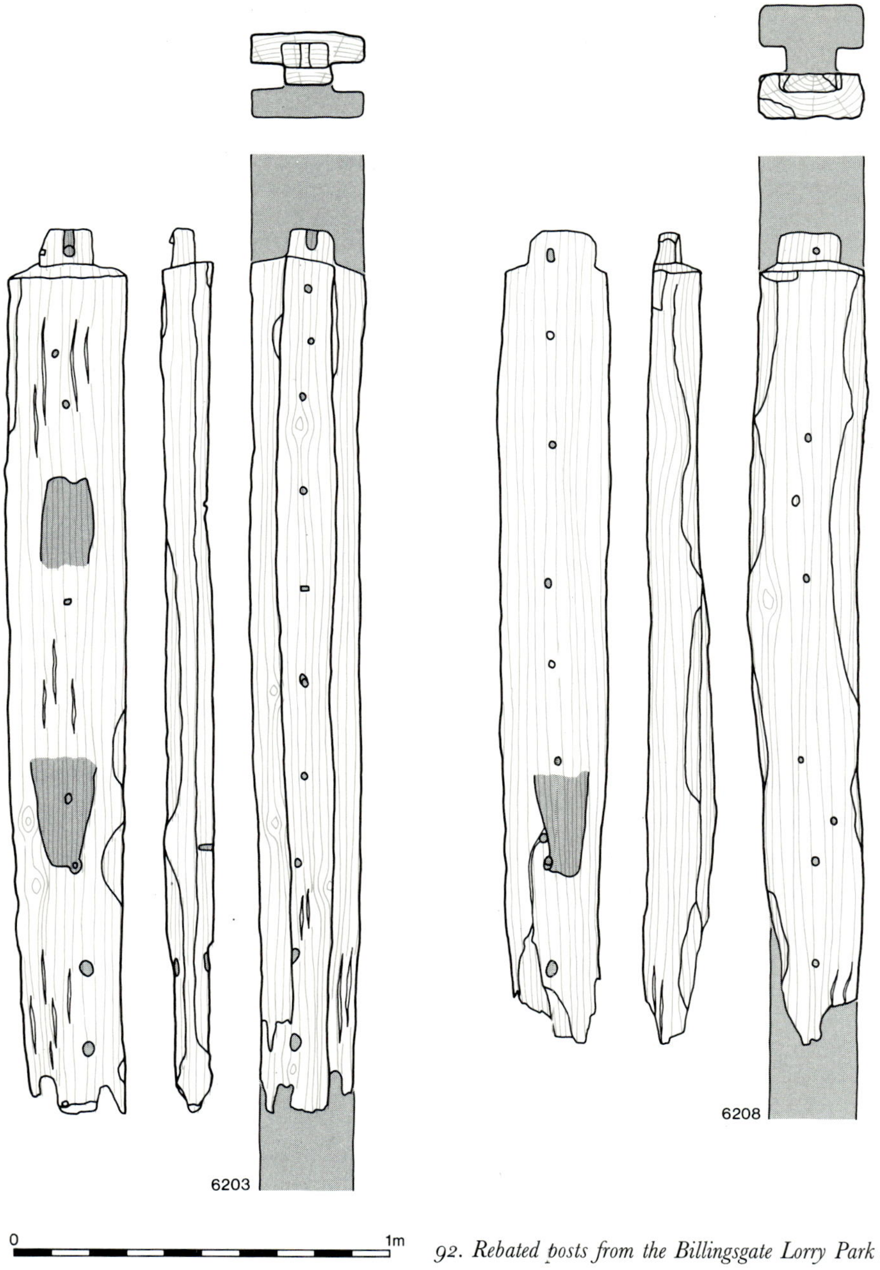

92. Rebated posts from the Billingsgate Lorry Park site.

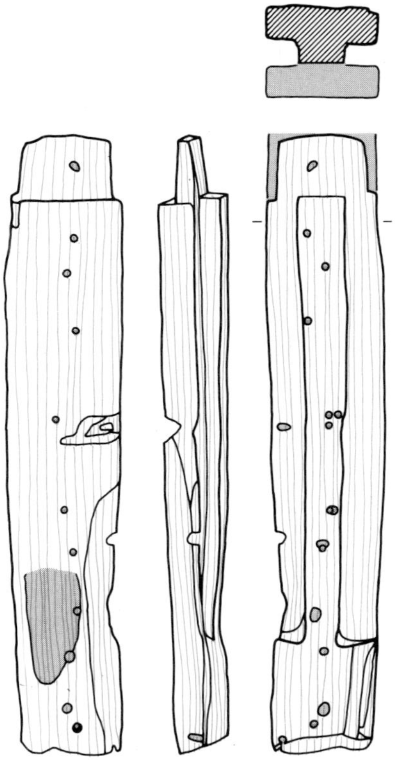

2656

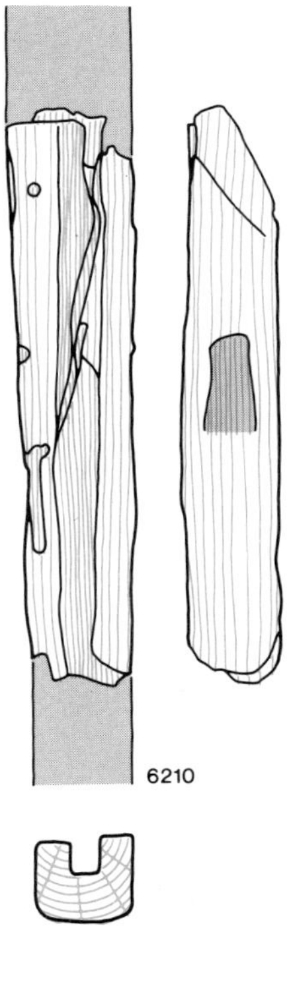

6210

James *et al* 1984) in the late aristocratic complex from the *burh* at Portchester, and in Saxo-Norman aisled barns (Hewett 1980). These were earthfast and left a distinct archaeological trace, whereas the later BG12 front braces rested on the surface and were prevented from slipping by a continuous rail (Fig 17); if this and its retaining piles had been robbed with the remainder of the revetment, it is doubtful whether the use of front braces would have been suspected. Buttresses retained by a similar rail, or by individual baseplates such as were used in 11th-century Hedeby and the 13th-century London waterfront, may have provided support for timber buildings of the period.

A triple-grooved post (Fig 93a; BG13: 5530) was similar to several from the TX7 revetment (Fig 58). However, since it was recovered from a reclamation deposit of building debris, it probably came from a building on land. The presence of three grooves suggests that it stood in the external wall of a building, at the junction with an internal partition. An unpegged half lap joint was cut at the head, facing inwards, which suggests that a top-plate was attached. The grooves for the outer walls continued above the joint, indicating that the soffit of the top-plate was also grooved to retain the upper edges of the wall panels. Some 0.75m below the lap joint, a mortise was cut into the central (partition) groove to retain a horizontal member, such as a subsidiary rail, although a similar joint held a grooved baseplate on the TX7 revetment (p.60).

Two redeposited wall posts (Fig 93b: 5529, 5531) from the same deposits may have been related to the original use of baseplate 5721. Both posts had pegholes drilled at *c*.0.22m intervals and pegged shouldered tenons. They also seem to have had barefaced tenons or half lap joints cut at the opposite end for a secondary use, the intervening length of post being only *c*.0.7m. The purpose of this is unclear, but the timbers may have been used to line a shallow cellar. A third pegged upright (5736) was used as a wedge beneath baseplate 5721, along with baseplate fragment 5735 (see above). Pegholes were spaced at just 0.1-0.13m intervals, and there was no second tenon. All three posts differed from the two earlier examples (7570, 7564) in not being earthfast, and by the pegholes being bored face to face.

Corner post 4986 was reused in a poor quality timber-framed building behind the north end of BG13. Two grooves were its only important features. A second building constructed behind the BG14 revetment produced two sections of studding reused as baseplates. The first (4759) had a narrow rebate

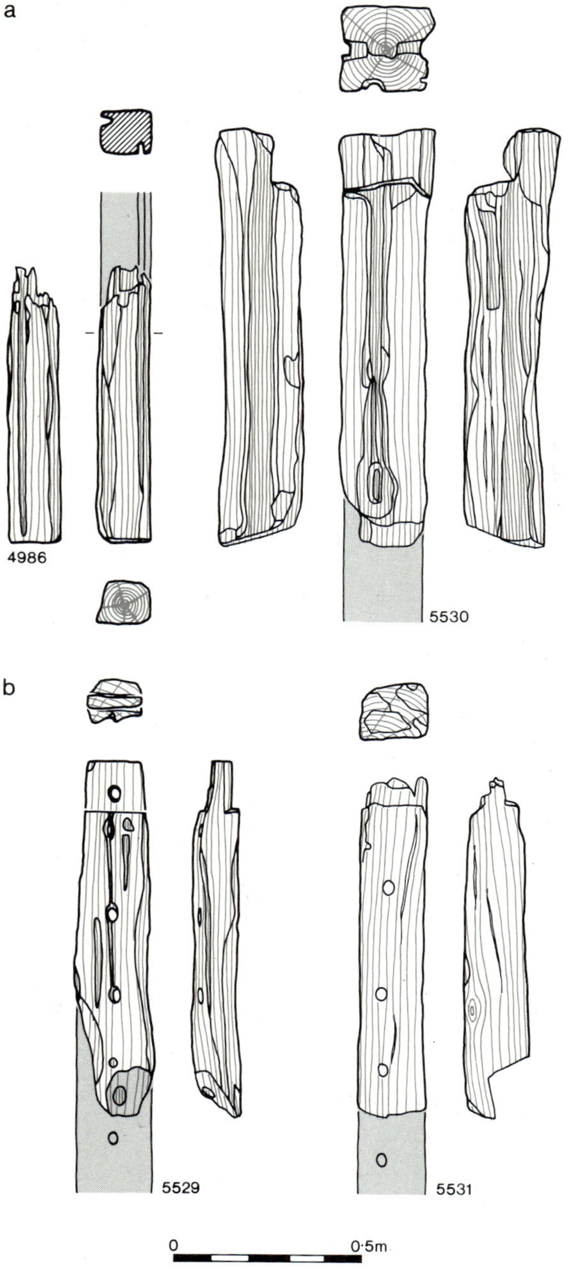

93. Posts from the Billingsgate Lorry Park site: a) grooved posts; b) pegged posts.

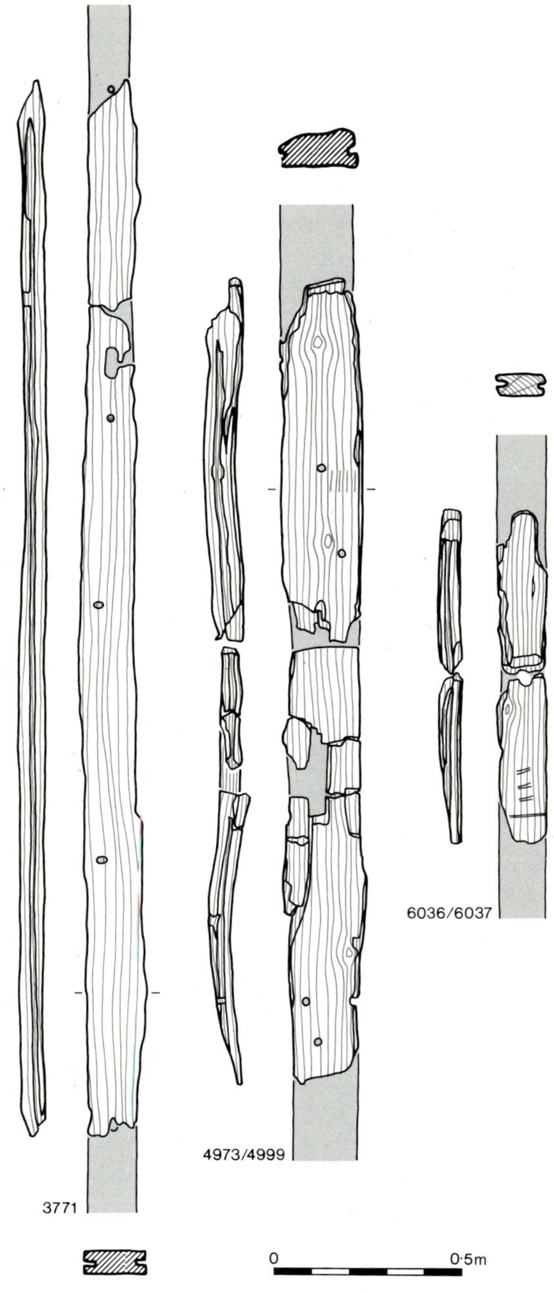

94. Studs from the Billingsgate Lorry Park site.

on both faces, adjoining a grooved edge, with a second groove on one of the faces, but the purpose of these features is unclear. The second timber (5203) bore a groove along both edges, with regular saw marks at 60mm intervals on the faces.

The BG16 revetment contained several fragments of grooved stud and rail (Fig 94). The first of these (3771), although cut down, was 2.8m long, and if it was from a side wall rather than a gable, a tall building must be envisaged. Secondary pegholes were drilled through the faces at 0.68m intervals to attach the timber to the revetment uprights for reuse as a piece of cladding. A much smaller fragment from a less substantial timber (4892) was possibly a rail. The grooves were of similar dimensions to those of 3771, but had been largely trimmed away for reuse in the cladding. Pegs near both ends may have been original features.

Two fragments (6036, 6037) joined to form part of a timber of similar scantling to stud 3771, although the surviving section was only 0.9m in length. There was a central peghole where the timber had been broken. At one end was an incised line running across the timber, with three chisel marks side by side next to it. This was an assembly mark, of the same type as examples seen on three planks from the same waterfront. The marks suggest that one end at least was original, and the full length of the timber may have survived. If this is the case, the timber was probably a rail, although it is not clear how it would have been attached.

Two more fragments (4999, 4973) joined to form a substantial stud 2.15m long. One fragment had been converted into a baseplate with a single mortise, into which the other fragment was tenoned. Pegholes were drilled through the timbers, possibly for the attachment of cladding. There were no other diagnostic features apart from a compression mark along one edge, which may have been caused by a wedge during the initial conversion process. Again, the length of the timber argues for a substantial wall height.

Summary

Late 12th and early 13th-century carpentry was quite different from that just discussed, and can be recognised as belonging to the early stages of full framing. The transition was represented by the BG12 structure which, although largely robbed, was a front-braced revetment with earthfast posts. It may have been the origin of the posts reused in the BG13 and BG14 structures.

By the 13th century, fully framed structures were employed on the waterfront, and had clearly been adopted in land building. This type of construction was typified by substantial squared timbers, interdependent elements, and pegged, closely-fitting mortise and tenon joints.

COMPARATIVE DATA

Building development from the 10th to 13th centuries: evidence from 'wet' sites

There are few sites where evidence for structural carpentry has been preserved organically from the period under discussion. At Coppergate, York (Hall 1984) the earliest wattle-walled structures were replaced in the 10th century by sunken featured buildings, which employed lipped baseplates to support the horizontally planked walls of the cellar area (cf. 6516). The 1.75m posts were retained by the lips, and set at 0.3m intervals with floor planking carefully fitted around their bases. The surviving tops of the posts had pegged bare-faced tenons, which suggests that they articulated with a plate just above the contemporary ground level. The plate would either have acted as the base for a superstructure, or if the buildings did not have a second storey, to support the roof rafters; there was no reason to suppose that it would have been mortised. Similar lipped baseplates were employed in an 11th-century cellared building from Watling Court, London (Horsman *et al* 1988), and a late 11th to early 12th-century 'platform' from Christchurch Place, Dublin (Murray 1983; CP11/1). The Dublin example differed from the others by countering pressure from inside rather than outside the structure. These examples give some indication of how the Billingsgate timber 6516 was used, although in that case, the posts passed through edge trenches and presumably rested on the underlying soil.

At Christchurch Place, a building constructed *c.*1059 (Murray 1983; CP85/1) used grooved baseplates to support stud and plank walls. The layout was otherwise the same as the more normal wattle-walled buildings on that site and elsewhere in the Viking town, with four internal posts supporting the roof. The baseplates were roughly-dressed trunks 0.1 to 0.26 wide, with grooves 40-70mm wide by 30-60mm deep (cf. Fig 89a: 6382). Mortised baseplates are not known in Dublin at this period, and the earliest examples date from the late 12th century (see below). The common use both of wattled wall and of stave construction in Scandinavian-controlled areas suggests that these techniques were introduced by them, although both were largely supplanted by timber-framing based on post construction by the end of the 13th century.

At Westgate Street, Gloucester (Heighway *et al* 1979), the 9th to 11th-century sequence was similar to that at Coppergate: mixed post and plank and post and wattle buildings were replaced by a sunken-featured structure, which used baseplates of unknown type to support the timber lining. In the early 12th century, stone was introduced, probably restricted to the construction of dwarf walls. Two timbers from a contemporary mixed pit assemblage can now be identified as parts of a mortised baseplate, which may have rested on such walls; it had been suggested previously that they were part of a piece of furniture (Morris 1979). Reinterpretation was possible because of the marked resemblance of the larger fragment (WS23) to Billingsgate timbers 6072 and 6784 both in features and in depth to width ratio. Dendrochronological analysis dated the smaller piece (WS26) to 1110+, contemporary with the Billingsgate structures W8 and W9.

Two mortises were cut through WS23 close to the probable outer edge (Fig 95a), one still retaining a broken tenon. The mortises were 0.3m apart, equivalent to the average spacing noted at Billingsgate, and it is suggested that they held light studs rather than large principal posts. Mortises were absent from WS26, which suggests that this section of the baseplate spanned a doorway. A total of six pegholes were drilled along the outer edge of the timbers, possibly to retain the base of weatherboard cladding where the lowest plank overlapped to protect the junction between dwarf wall and superstructure. The weatherboarding must have continued across the threshold, as was the case in some of the Dublin buildings (Wallace 1982). The use of weatherboards in Dublin was a continuation of a local tradition, since the remains of pegged planks, still retaining some willow trenails, were found in a 9th-century building from the same site. Five pegholes on the face of the Gloucester timbers may have been for the attachment of fitted planking for a raised internal floor.

A cellar structure excavated at High Street, Dublin (HS1/2) consisted of three reused mortised baseplates, one of which was dated by dendrochronology to 1194-5 (Murray 1983, 175-6, fig 79); the structure itself is more likely to have belonged to the first half of the 13th century. The resemblance of the eastern and western timbers to the earlier Gloucester WS23 and Billingsgate 6784 is striking, although they were broader and thinner. The western timber had one larger mortise which was out of sequence with the rest, and this may have held an extra post supporting a tie-beam; a similar mortise was observed on a later baseplate from Christchurch Place (see below). Smaller pegholes along the inner edges may have retained the baseplates of partitions, or possibly floor planks. The depth to width ratio of the third timber lay between that of the early types and that of later baseplates. As might be expected, the timber showed attributes of both groups; the mortises were unpegged, but were between 0.40m and 0.85m apart.

The timber-framed kitchen at Weoley Castle, Birmingham was constructed in *c.*1200, with six phases of reconstruction before 1260, and combined both mortised and grooved types of construction (Oswald 1962/3; Smith 1965). Earthfast principals were positioned at each corner of the building, with several more set intermediately, and there were in addition three pairs of internal posts to help carry

95. Baseplates from a) Gloucester (Heighway et al 1979); b) Thames Exchange, London.

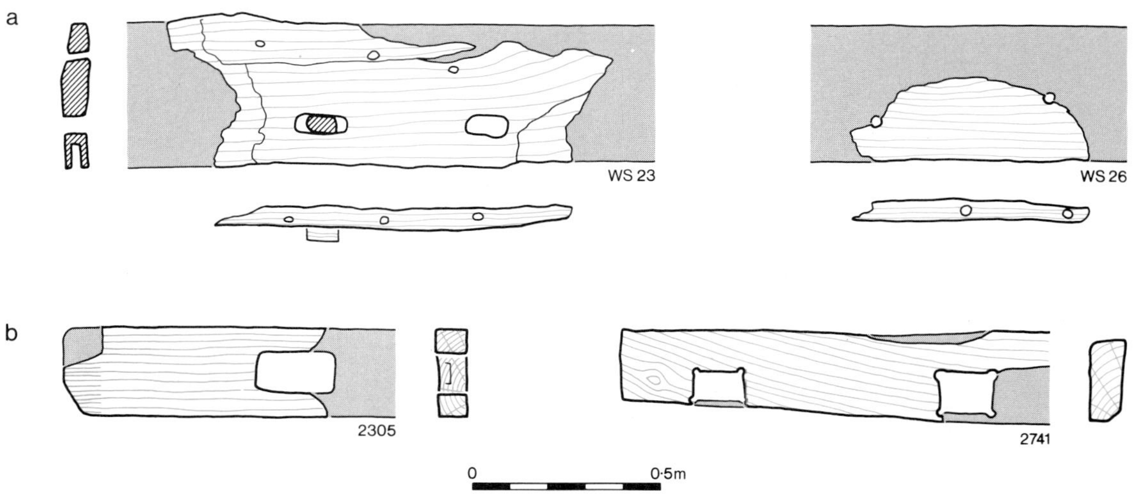

the load of the roof. Between, and unconnected, were lengths of mortised and grooved baseplate, with studs attached at 0.9 to 1.2m intervals (cf. 0.83m at Dublin). The studs were also grooved to accept horizontal planking. In later phases, vertical planking was pegged to rebates in the outer edges of the baseplates. The planking consisted of alternate wide and narrow boards, the narrower being set behind the wider, creating an external appearance resembling stud and plank construction. The kitchen therefore had much in common with the Pudding Lane 3 (see below) and Christchurch Place buildings, although it was rather later. Similar interrupted baseplates have been found in contemporary revetments, such as the TL1 structure (Figs 64-5).

The next development can be seen in two late 13th to early 14th-century cellar revetments from Dublin, from the High Street site (H53/4) and from Christchurch Place (CP13/2). Both structures utilised pegged mortise baseplates, identical to those from the later revetments at Billingsgate, except in the use of edge-halved, as opposed to through-splayed scarfs. Also recorded were surviving uprights, planking, and at Christchurch Place, angled braces attached with pegged notched lap joints (Murray 1983, 67-9; 176-9, figs 80-1: cf. Fig 85). One of the baseplates from Christchurch Place also had an additional large mortise similar to H51/2. The spacing of the mortises of the two structures was 0.55m (HS3/4) and 0.7m (CP13/2), although it is not clear whether this continued above ground level, or whether the panel width was reduced to 0.3m as at Billingsgate, Coppergate and Gloucester. Wide spacing was also characteristic of waterfront revetments: since posts in such structures were of relatively heavy scantling and contributed equally to the strength of the revetment, fewer were required.

Building development from the 10th to 13th centuries: evidence from 'dry' sites

Study of sites with no organic preservation also suggests that buildings made increasing use of baseplates in the later 10th and 11th centuries. Unfortunately, the evidence is often negative, as at the Queen Street site in Oxford, where no postholes were recorded at the foot of the wall of a late Saxon timber-lined cellar (Sturdy & Munby 1985, 92-4). Such sites also furnish little evidence for the use of mortise and tenon joints in the form of tenon impressions in the underlying soil, and it seems likely that most baseplates in the early period were either grooved or lipped or were simple planks supporting the bases of studs. This can be partially confirmed by the published evidence from several 9th to 11th-century sites in London (Horsman *et al* 1988). This *corpus* includes both sunken-floored and surface-laid buildings, both of which made occasional use of baseplates, although there was no evidence for the use of mortises. Indeed, the outlines of grooved baseplates from Building PDN3 at Pudding Lane were preserved in organic silts. The walls of such a building were probably continuous stave walls similar to the BG10 revetment (Fig 14).

The 11th-century bow-sided halls from Sulgrave (Northamptonshire), Goltho (Lincolnshire) and Buckden (Huntingdonshire) made use of baseplates; their location in areas of Scandinavian occupation suggests that the timbers were grooved, and supported stave walls. The Goltho hall certainly replaced an earthfast stave building (Beresford 1987). A rectangular post-built hall (Building E) of comparable size from Thetford (Norfolk) had an external framed staircase which employed interrupted baseplates.

Clear evidence for the 11th to 12th-century transition from the earthfast post to the framed tradition comes from Bargate Street, Southampton (Wacher 1975), where a post-built hall was replaced by a merchant's house just after the Norman Conquest. That building was demolished by 1150, when a strip building of typical later medieval plan was constructed. The building was founded on baseplates of subrectangular and triangular cross-section, represented by a mid brown soil set in rubble-filled trenches. Wacher concluded that the cross-sections of the timbers identified them as cleft timber; the use of radially and tangentially-split timbers can now be confirmed by the Billingsgate evidence. The trenches varied in size from 0.15m for a light partition to 0.61m for an outer wall, with a depth of *c*.0.3m. Several overlapped at the corners, and the baseplates had clearly been placed one over the other without jointing as in Building PDN3 from Pudding Lane. Most significant was the presence of small squarish impressions left by the ends of posts which had protruded through the baseplate into the underlying soil at 0.5m intervals. This demonstrated conclusively that the building was not constructed in the stave tradition, but employed mortised baseplates. The principal posts were set earthfast, in pits up to 0.4m deep, at the corners of walls and flanking doorways. The posts were 0.23 to 0.41m square, comparable to examples from Billingsgate. Doorways in the building were sometimes marked as gaps between posts, but generally the baseplates continued across to form a threshold (cf. Fig 88: 6072; Fig 95a: ws26). Each wall comprised a number of interrupted baseplates, marked by changes in width and alignment. Building 4 from the Old Gasworks Site VIII in Southampton also reflects the 11th-century transition from post trench construction to framing using baseplate trenches and separate structural posts, although the evidence is less compelling (Holdsworth 1980).

TIMBER CONSTRUCTION IN THE 11TH TO 13TH CENTURIES

The origins of Saxo-Norman timber building construction will not be discussed here (see *eg* James *et al* 1984). The relationship between early medieval building technology and that of the later Saxon period is in any case unclear, and many early techniques disappeared, with new types making an appearance, particularly in urban areas.

The importance of unique survivals such as the Tamworth mill to the study of English carpentry can be overstated, since this type of structure was not necessarily indigenous. Horizontal mills, common in Ireland from the 7th to 11th centuries, had a range of joints including mortise and tenon, chase mortise, tongue and groove, and dovetail (Wallace 1982). The similarity of Irish and Roman work may imply that Irish millwrights owed something to Roman traditions, possibly introduced through the church. Similar influences may have helped the spread of Romanesque architecture in 11th and 12th-century England.

The Billingsgate material represents elements of three main traditions known to the English carpenter in the Saxo-Norman period: wattle, stave and post wall construction. The first two were apparently characteristic of Scandinavian-dominated areas, both in England and in the Viking-founded Irish towns, and the hegemony of Scandinavian kings in the 11th century, particularly Cnut, may well have led to the extension of their influence on building design beyond the areas of immediate settlement. The use of wattled walls with internal roof supports similar to those of the early Germanic coastal settlements on the continent, can best be seen in York (Addyman 1979; Hall 1982) and Dublin (Murray 1983). Door jambs were often grooved to accept the exposed edges of woven panels, but otherwise there was little carpentry involved in the walls at ground level. This style proved popular, particularly for lower status urban buildings, and was still common in Durham (Carver 1979), Perth and Aberdeen (Murray 1982) in the 13th century.

Stave construction appeared relatively early in the Scandinavian areas, but was initially earthfast and limited to higher status structures. Grooved baseplates were introduced in the later 10th century at Skeldergate (Addyman 1979) and Coppergate, York (Hall 1982); in the mid 11th century at Christchurch Place (Murray 1983), Fishamble Street III, Dublin (Wallace 1982) and London (Horsman *et al* 1988). The surviving stave church at Greensted-juxta-Ongar (Essex) is thought to belong to this period (Hewett 1980); the walls are of filletted half-logs tenoned into grooved base and top-plates. Baseplates were therefore introduced in stave-built buildings and waterfront structures several decades before mortised examples first appeared. In Scandinavia, stave construction developed into a diversity of forms, and reached its apogee in churches such as at Urnes (Norway) and Hanger (Sweden), whereas in England it gave way to other types of building towards the end of the 11th century (Beresford 1982, 114), and in medieval London its use was confined to substantial waterfront structures.

Early framing

Although buildings constructed in the stave tradition were often self supporting, they were not 'framed' in the accepted sense, and relied not on jointing for rigidity, but on the interdependence of contiguous wall elements; 'true' timber framing was the ultimate development of post construction. It is clear from excavated plans and the Billingsgate timbers themselves that 'the structural stability of the (Saxon and Norman) buildings was dependent upon earthfast foundations and the buildings were constructed without the complex framework generally known as timber framing' (Beresford 1982, 113). The function of the mortised baseplates was therefore primarily to hold intermediate studs and wall posts which were retained by simple tusked tenons. These supported the cladding and the top-plates between the load-bearing uprights, and hence took some of the roof load indirectly, but the buildings otherwise relied on earthfast posts. It may be argued that if buildings still relied on earthfast posts for stability, there was no structural reason to introduce baseplates, and it must be assumed that were other reasons for their introduction.

Although the use of post trenches has been cited as an attempt to correct post alignment prior to the introduction of baseplates, in practice it should have been just as simple to erect a line of posts accurately as it was to cut a trench; it is more likely that post trenches were developed to embed the base of the walling material, in order to produce a vermin- and weatherproof join. Baseplates allowed posts to be spaced and aligned as accurately as the mortises could be cut, which was important only if the intention was to match the posts to mortised top-plates. That this had not been done previously implies that mortised top-plates were a contemporary introduction. It is quite likely that until this time rails were simply lapped to the heads of the posts by methods similar to those observed in an 11th-century Coppergate building. Alternatively, reversed assembly could have been used.

The introduction of mortised baseplates and top-plates would have made it necessary to ensure that all wall posts and studs were of equal height. With earthfast timbers this was a problem, and in practice the heads of posts may have had to be made level and any joints cut after erection: in stave structures, where a large number of identical timbers was required, there must have been a degree of prefabrication from the outset, and it may therefore be no accident that baseplates were first introduced in such structures. As Beresford (1982, 114) states, although 'various forms of mortise and tenon joint have been known from prehistoric times, they seem to have been generally avoided in the construction of larger timber buildings in the early middle ages, in favour of joints which were halved, slotted or dovetailed. The successful use of the mortise and tenon joint was frequently dependent upon some precise prefabrication, which would be difficult, although not impossible, to achieve in buildings where posts were set in the earth'. The introduction of baseplates allowed the necessary precision, as all the posts or staves were set at the same level. This would also have allowed the use of more complex joints in the roof structure of higher-status buildings, which was important for the future development of timber framing. Baseplates allowed a degree of rot-protection to both posts and cladding, although where tenons protruded into the soil, this is likely to have been of limited value. Although the appearance of mortised baseplates at Billingsgate in the early 11th century may represent a local innovation, it is worth stressing that baseplates had already been introduced for stave work by then. Elsewhere, their introduction was slow, even in high-status buildings, perhaps because carpenters used to the post construction tradition did not recognise their advantages. The introduction of early timber framing had little influence on smaller structures; post, post trench and baseplate construction were largely interchangeable, and often to be seen side by side.

In contrast to the material already discussed, the considerable technical complexity of the roof structures of large buildings thought to be of late Saxon date (Hewett 1980) has not been reflected in an archaeological context, largely because such structures leave no trace except when a collapsed building is left *in situ*. In addition, few individual roof elements have been recognised among surviving timbers from Billingsgate or elsewhere.

A pair of arcade posts from the aisled barn of Paul's Hall, Belchamp St Paul, Essex, one of which was dated by radiocarbon to 1026 +/- 95 (Hewett 1980, 23), shows the complex arrangement of braces and earthfast buttresses necessary in large aisled buildings of the period, but for which the only other evidence comes from 12th and 13th-century halls of the same type. Although the posts apparently rested on cement pads, they were originally supported by earthfast buttresses. If Hewett's dating is accepted, it may be inferred that technological advances, notably the use of squared timbers and accurately-cut pegged joints, occurred first in the development of roof structures for buildings where large spans were to be covered, or particular solutions were required. The Church may have been initially responsible for the spread of this technology, since it was the only institution with a continuous tradition of large-scale construction, which may have preserved late Roman solutions to such problems. As this technology became more widespread and was secularised, so it would have been employed in royal and aristocratic halls, although according to the evidence already discussed, such advances were not at this period extended to include non-structural, and therefore less important elements, such as wall frames. It has been noted that 'while it is not difficult to build a wall, adding a roof is a much more complex matter. For this reason, when attempts were made to prolong the lives of buildings, the main research effort was more often than not devoted to technological improvements in the roof structure' (Chapelot & Fossier 1985, 286).

Transitional and developed framing

Early framing, with its emphasis on earthfast principal posts and cleft-timber baseplates with unpegged mortises, survived to at least the mid 12th century in England, and to the end of the century

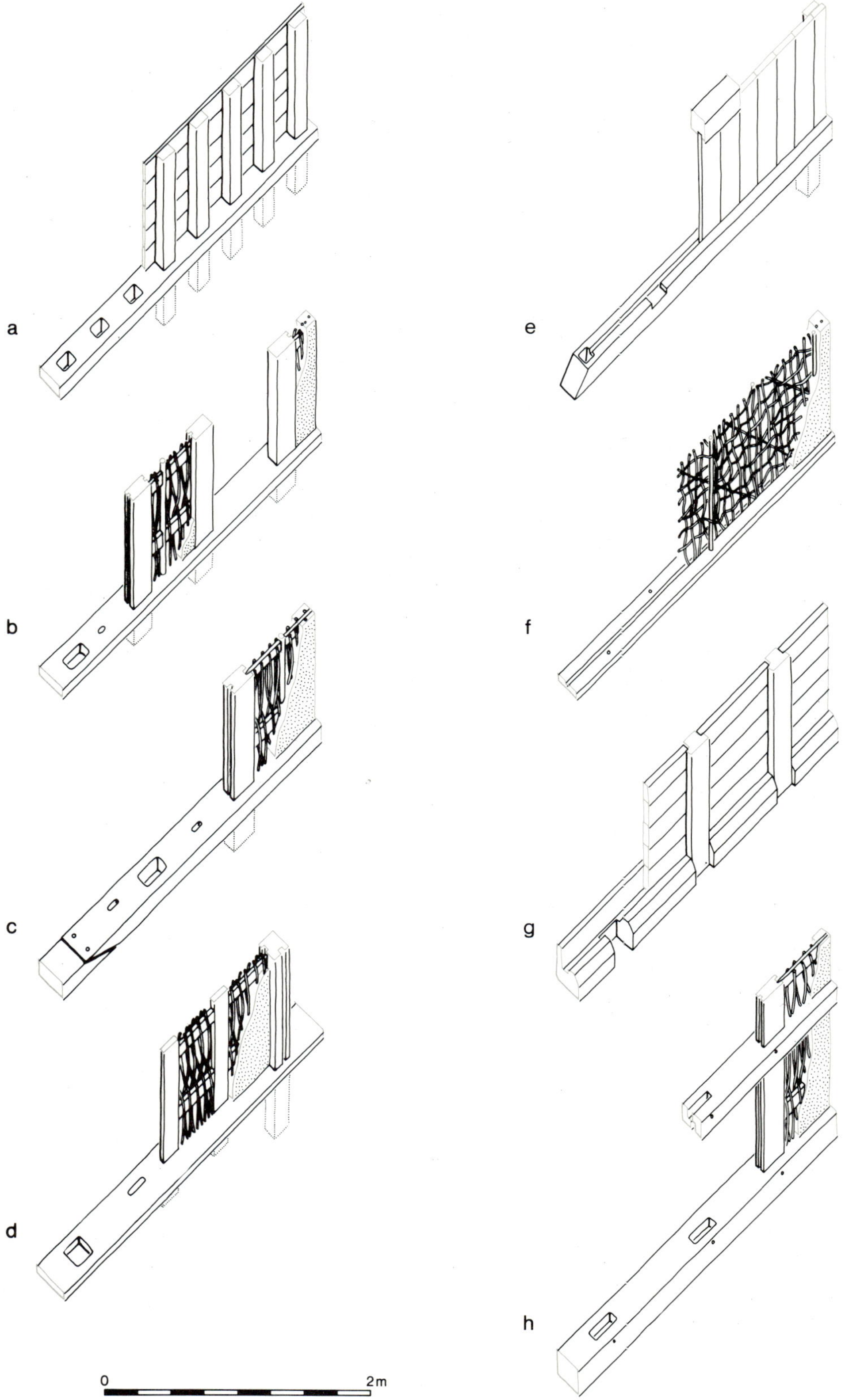
a
b
c
d
e
f
g
h
0
2m

in Ireland. Even then 'the (earthfast) tradition was to persist into the late 13th and early 14th centuries in buildings of relative importance like Fyfield Hall, Essex, but the 13th century saw the gradual abandonment of such buildings in favour of those set on sills or plinths' (Beresford 1982, 114).

Weoley Castle kitchen, however, demonstrates changes that were introduced towards the middle of the century, with the adoption of baseplates with pegged mortises, still 'interrupted' but now often tenoned into the wall posts to form a type of frame. Another innovation was the use of dwarf walls to support the baseplates, the principal posts being set within the walls or on padstones. In the south, this practice disappeared by the late 13th century (Smith 1965), having developed into full framing, but it was to survive for several more centuries in the north, for example at Horbury Hall, Yorkshire (*Med Archaeol*, **21**, 1987, 171-2), in the 15th-century Augustinian prebendal manor in Coffee Yard, York (*Med Archaeol*, **30,** 1986, 174-7, fig 60), and in a post-medieval house at South Holmes, Yorkshire.

Squared baseplates allowed tenoned posts to be held firmly in deep and precisely fitted mortises, whereas previously earthfast tusk tenons may have been used to give some stability. The depth of the baseplates also allowed pegs to be driven through the mortises to hold the posts without seriously weakening the timber, and this was repeated at top-plate level. The more accurate cutting of joints and the more confident use of timber was a great advance on the carpentry of the 11th and earlier 12th centuries, allowing prefabrication of all frames. This led to the extension of the baseplate to hold intermediate studs as well as the principal posts, thereby reversing the structural relationship of baseplate and post, and with the addition of the top-plate, creating a frame. Such frames thus became an integral part of the building but were initially used only in narrow structures with a roof span of less than 4.3m with wattle and daub or stave walls (Beresford 1982, 113).

96. Schematic reconstruction of Billingsgate Lorry Park baseplates drawn at 1:50 showing: a) close-studded wall; b) alternate large and small mortises and doorway; c) alternate large and small mortises and scarfing; d) large mortise for principal post, small mortise for studs/floor; e) stud-and-plank wall (NB scale 1:100); f) grooved baseplate and supporting rods; g) lipped baseplate in cellar; h) framed wall and mid rail.

Conclusions

This study of reused house timbers from the Billingsgate site therefore suggests that domestic timber framing developed from post construction, which was one of the three strands of vernacular building method present in Saxo-Norman England. Two separate building traditions which were largely in areas of Scandinavian influence, can be recognised. In one, earthfast stave construction was followed by the introduction of grooved baseplates to support stave and stave and plank walls; the other incorporated wattled walls, supported by light posts. Advances in post construction in the 11th century led to the appearance of full framing at the end of the 12th, and the slow decline of competing traditions of carpentry. These advances then percolated down to buildings of inferior function or status and in less developed regions; the appearance of full framing in 13th-century Dublin may be attributed to the Norman invasion in 1171.

During the course of its development, it is suggested that timber framing passed through the following phases: *Primitive:* roofs supported by earthfast, often unevenly spaced and aligned posts, sometimes in trenches. *Early*: mortised baseplates, usually of cleft timber, retaining wall studs. *Developed (Full):* squared baseplates and more advanced carpentry; fully self-supporting frames.

The introduction of squared timbers with accurately-cut joints required a corresponding change in structural philosophy, a change which may have occurred first in the construction of church roof frames, possibly during the expansion of Romanesque architecture before the Norman Conquest. The techniques learned would then have passed into the secular repertory by their application to the roofs and supporting frames of large high-status structures, including aisled halls. The final step extended this technology to the construction of the walls; as the new carpentry became more widespread, and therefore cheaper, improvements spread more rapidly, aided by the growth of the new urban and rural middle classes. It is suggested that the main elements of full timber framing were in existence by the Norman Conquest, although it took more than a century before they were successfully fused together by a gradual and logical series of developments. We must therefore disagree with the view that 'There is no intermediate phase between post-construction and timber-framing' (Charles 1982, 112).

6: WOODS AND WOODLAND: CARPENTERS AND CARPENTRY

Damian Goodburn

The assessments of revetment and house construction in Chapters 4 and 5 show that the techniques and traditions of timber building underwent a considerable change during the medieval period: that at least is the clear inference from the studies of the structural elements presented by Gustav Milne and Trevor Brigham. In this chapter, rather than consider the architecture of the revetments, the timber and roundwood from the London waterfront will be examined from a different viewpoint, as attempts are made to reconstruct the trees they were cut from and the woodland in which those trees once grew, as well as the methods used to convert logs into timber. As a consequence it is possible to suggest that major change can also be identified in medieval carpentry practice as well as in the contemporary woodlands.

Although the study of timber-framed buildings is well-developed, medieval woodworking practice has, with a few notable exceptions (*eg* Darrah 1982), received little attention in archaeological literature. Our new study must therefore be placed firmly in context, and to achieve this, practices evidenced in the Saxo-Norman and the later medieval periods will be contrasted. For further comparison, the post-medieval traditions represented by a riverfront revetment erected in *c.*1671 (BYI, p.76) will be considered, together with a summary of modern practice, based on the writer's experience as a waterfront carpenter in Shoreham dock, Sussex, in 1979. Links will then be drawn between carpentry and other woodworking practices, and some of the economic and social implications for medieval London highlighted. Some exploration is made of the nature of the woodland and tree resources used by Londoners with the emphasis on the human experience required to build the structures: on tools (Fig 97), techniques and logistical considerations. This approach has been supported by the results of systematic experimentation in early woodworking practice carried out by the writer and colleagues in ancient woodlands near London (*eg* Goodburn & Redknap 1988). However, if general assumptions concerning medieval woodworking practice are to be based on an examination of riverfront revetment structures, then the status of those structures must be taken into consideration, for this will be reflected both in the manner of construction and in the raw materials used.

From September 1988, the Museum of London's Department of Urban Archaeology operated a new systematic approach to timber recording (MOL 1990), and employed the author as the Archaeological Timber Specialist to coordinate the work. In spite of the very real constraints imposed on research conducted by rescue archaeologists (Milne 1990), new levels of information were being recorded, and site records can now be subjected to detailed reinterpretation (Goodburn 1990a; 1990b). Some of the first fruits of this work are presented here. Without considerable discussion with James Norman, Richard Darrah, Gustav Milne, and other Museum staff working on the Thames Exchange and Vintry projects, this chapter could not have been produced. Behind it all lies the toil, often in extraordinarily difficult circumstances, of the field excavation teams on all the recent waterfront sites.

97. Some basic tools used for timber conversion and carpentry: a) early medieval iron wedge. Scale 1:5; b) early medieval general purpose axe. Scale 1:5; c) T-shaped broad axe (partially reconstructed). Scale 1:10; d) narrow bladed adze of late Saxon date from Thetford. Scale 1:5; e) medieval spoon bit. Scale 1:5; f) late medieval cross-cut saw blade. Scale 1:5. g) Sawing timber on a single trestle (see-saw) from a 14th-century manuscript drawing. h) Post-medieval rip saws (pit saw) like this could be from 2m to 2.7m long. Similar saws were used in the London area from the mid 15th century onwards. i) Sketch showing pit saw used to cut timber laid horizontally over a pit or on two trestles.

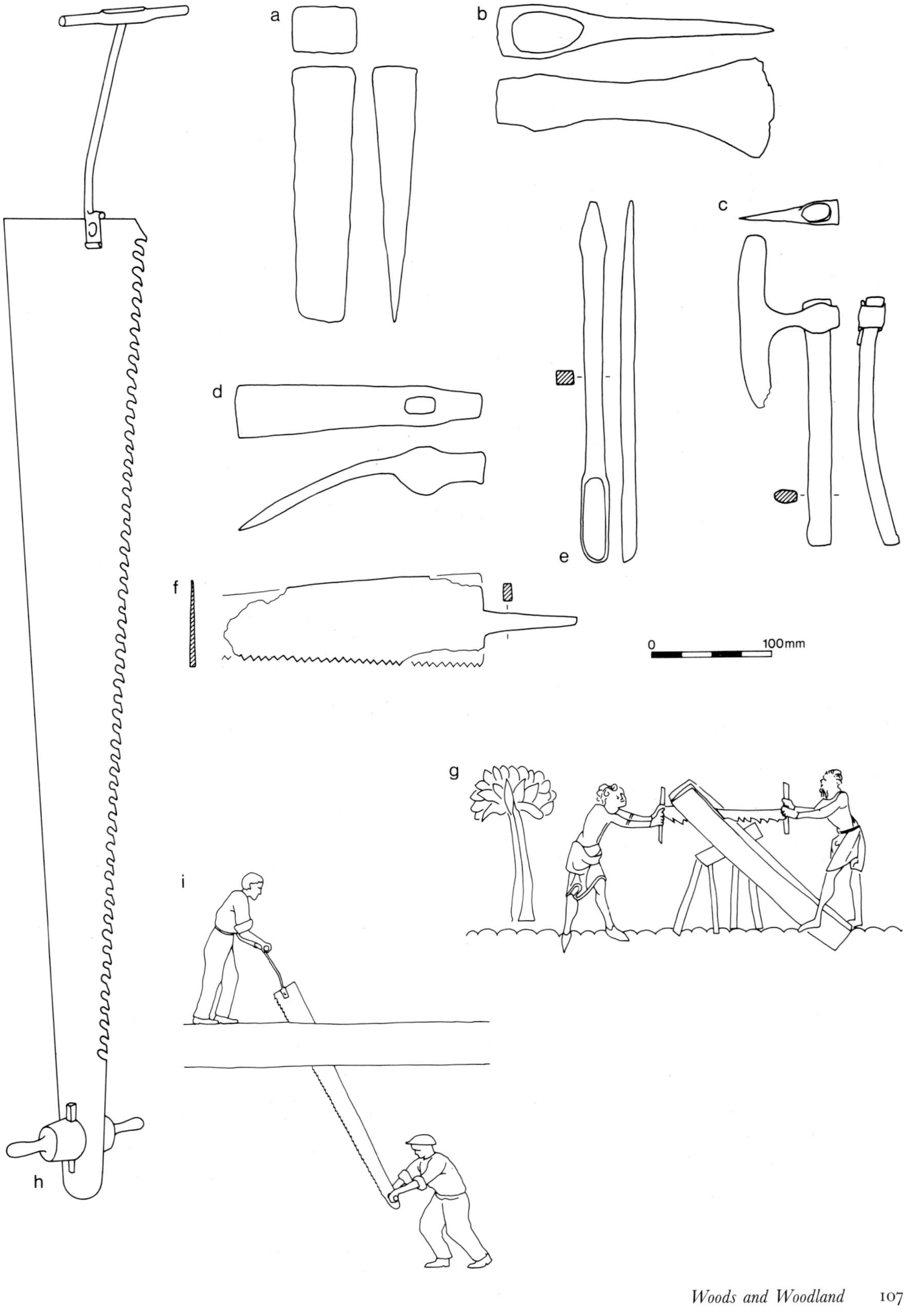
a
b
c
d
e
f
g
h
i
0
100mm

One fundamental factor in this study is the difference between WOOD, *Boscus*, and TIMBER, *Meremium*, two types of woodland resource often confused by archaeologists and some historians, although the legal distinctions and their relative importance in the medieval period were comprehensively defined by Rackham (Rackham 1976; 1980). Essentially wood is the small stuff, made up of poles cut from coppice stools, young trees or branches from older trees. Although there is no clearly-defined point at which a piece of wood becomes timber, as a rule of thumb any stem over 0.15m in diameter might be considered timber (Rackham 1980, 3): however, large oak branches could fall into either category and can be difficult to distinguish from crooked stem timber. Wood cut from trees or poles five to 20 years old was often used in light construction work and fencing, but mainly for fuel, either as wood or as charcoal. Without an abundant, carefully-managed supply of wood for fuel, virtually no continuous industrial, agricultural or domestic process could be conducted in the medieval period (*eg* McIntosh 1986, 143-4). In spite of the crucial importance of this basic commodity, it has yet to benefit from a substantial, dedicated study.

COMPARATIVE WOODWORKING PRACTICES

In the following section, summaries of woodworking practices in various periods are contrasted to stress the point that they underwent considerable development and change, particularly in the Saxon and later medieval periods. This point is not always appreciated when the subject is studied solely through the surviving documentation.

Species used

Saxo-Norman practice

The waterfront structures and the reused elements they incorporated were primarily oak (*Quercus robur; Quercus petraea*). However some plank fragments of ash (*Fraxinus excelsior*) were found on the Thames Exchange and Cannon Street (UTA88) sites. Where wood was used in wattle-work, hurdles or as timber make-up, a wider variety of species was used.

Later medieval practice

Most of the timber used and reused on the medieval waterfront was oak, although the planks from the BG13 revetment which were of a non-indigenous variety of pine are a noteworthy exception to this rule. However, some baseplates and piles used in the round were of elm (*Ulmus sp*) and beech (*Fagus sylvatica*) (Brett 1982). With the exception of piles, virtually no wood has been recorded on waterfront sites of this period.

Post-medieval practice

On the City of London Boys' School site (BOY86), a revetment dated to the 1670s was principally made of reused oak timbers with an imported softwood baseplate (Spence 1989, 28-9: see also site archive report). Elsewhere on the site large elm piles and planks were common in foundations dating to the 1690s.

Modern practice

Most present-day waterfront carpenters in south-east England use tropical hardwoods such as opepe (*Nauclea diderrichii*) and iroko (*Chlorophora excelsa*) from Africa; greenheart (*Ocotea rodiaei*) from South America; keruing (*Dipterocarpus sp*) from south-east Asia. A small amount of North American softwood such as British Columbian pine (*Pseudotsuga menziesii*) is also used, while an even smaller proportion of the timber is home grown elm (*Ulmus sp*) or larch (*Larix decidua*), a modern introduction (Edlin 1975, 168).

Felling

Saxo-Norman practice

There is no direct archaeological evidence from the City or documentary record to guide us. However, since no evidence for the use of any type of saw in this period has been recorded, woodmen must have used only axes for felling, as the ship-building scene on the Bayeux Tapestry suggests. Such axes would not have been the thin-bladed woodworking tools like the 'T' axe (cf. Fig 97c), but tools with a long helve and a heavy, narrow and compact bit (Wheeler 1927, 22; fig 6, Type I). Much wood was also harvested for structural purposes, but how and with what is uncertain. However, a similar type of felling axe to that just described would be suitable for cutting the larger poles. Detailed tree-ring studies on dated samples of ancient roundwood will ultimately provide important information concerning the coppice cycles utilised during the medieval period. In addition, it is often possible to estimate the time of year in which the wood was harvested, where the latest annual ring survives.

Later medieval practice

It is traditional practice in British woodlands to fell trees in winter, although medieval sources seem to suggest that felling timber could be carried out at any time of year (Harvey 1975, 115). The reasons for winter felling of both wood and timber are practical. It is easier to select trees for size and quality when they are not partly covered with foliage, and felling trees in winter causes less damage to young underwood growth. There is also less undergrowth in the woods to impede access and movement, while the trimming of branches is much easier once all the leaves have been shed in autumn.

Traces of a wide kerf or 'mouth' cut on one side of a tree during felling have been found on several recently excavated timbers (*eg* TEX88: 697). The wider, lower end of the timbers is facetted, suggesting that the cross-cutting was done with a felling axe. Although saws became more common during the later medieval period, it is possible that the practice of felling oak exclusively with axes may have continued, as was the case in parts of north-east England until recent times (Edlin 1949, 6).

Post-medieval practice

No archaeological evidence was recovered to show how the 17th-century timbers on the City of London Boys' School site were felled, although it is known that large two-man cross-cut saws were increasingly used for tree-felling in this period (Underhill 1986, 193), working towards a 'mouth' or 'drop' initially cut with a felling axe.

Modern practice

Chainsaws are used universally for felling trees to produce waterfront timbers today, although axes are still used to cut off buttresses from some large tropical trees. In general terms, the trend in British felling techniques has been towards producing the lowest possible stump with least waste of timber. Felling large trees with axes wastes up to 0.6m of the lower part of the best log the tree will provide: such waste is eliminated when chainsaws are used, although these rely on fossil fuels. Hand tools such as hatchets or billhooks are still used to fell underwood in parts of England, although light chainsaws are commonly used for even quite small soft or hardwood poles.

Barking

Where the bark of oak was harvested for tanning in recent times, felling was done in the spring, as the bark was more easily removed then (Edlin 1949, 87). Most medieval timbers excavated by the Museum of London have had no bark covering. This implies that bark was systematically removed, probably for tanning, an important medieval craft. The sale of bark is well documented in medieval records. No diagnostic marks left on oak timber from the bark-stripping process have yet been recorded in London, but they could survive, given the most favourable conditions.

Lopping (branch removal)

Most of the timber and wood excavated on the London waterfront had been lopped. However, since the branch chip debris characteristic of the lopping process has never been found on those sites, that work must have been undertaken elsewhere. Branches must have been removed before the timber was transported, since untrimmed logs are so awkward to move. Even where *top and lop* (the residue left after the main log has been cut from a tree) was used as make-up material in Saxon and early medieval embankments, it appears to have been brought in split and hewn to length. The working assumption must therefore be that lopping always took place very close to the felling spot.

Saxo-Norman practice

Documentary records throw no light on how lopping was done in the Saxon period. However, all the timber and wood excavated in the City has been neatly lopped with some form of edged tool, presumably axes and hatchets. Some of the more crooked cleft oak used as make-up in the Saxon embankments was made from large oak branch timber (*eg* TX2: Fig 108), while lighter rods may have been lopped with a billhook-type tool (*eg* Goodall 1981, 54; fig 6). Saws were clearly not used.

Later medieval practice

In terms of the tools and approach used by medieval carpenters or woodmen, the archaeological evidence is essentially the same as that for the preceding period. However, documentary references stress the importance of *top and lop* as a valuable fuel which could be sold by those who bought the tree or trees (Rackham 1980). However, Rackham also shows that shredding or shragging, the regular cropping of branches from standing trees, was practised in this period, although the use of terms such as the Shragged Oak (*eg* near Chatham, Kent) suggests that it was not a common landscape feature in some areas near London. No evidence of this practice in the form of healed cut branch scars has yet been recorded on London timbers.

Post-medieval practice

Seventeenth-century timbers used in the round recorded on the BOY86 site were neatly lopped with edged tools, not saws, as far as could be seen from surviving marks. Essentially the practice must have been similar to that used in the medieval period.

Modern practice

Lopping of timber trees and large softwood poles (*snedding*) is done with light chainsaws and felling axes. Smaller poles may be trimmed with billhooks, the hooked ends of which are specially adapted for that specific purpose. Most of the branches are then burnt on the spot, since only the largest of them are now used in Britain for fuel.

Bucking

Bucking is the cutting of the trimmed tree stem into logs of the required length: for example, *c.*3m for many of the revetment elements. On practical grounds, it is likely that the cross-cutting was done close to source, and no archaeological evidence for bucking on London waterfront sites has been recorded.

Saxo-Norman practice

No historical work illuminates this area of work. Timbers and roundwood from the TEX88 and VRY89 sites show slightly or roughly facetted ends without the long striations produced by large cross-cut saws, suggesting that bucking was done with axes.

Later medieval practice

Some 13th and 14th-century timbers recorded on the TEX88 site cut from trees over 0.3m in diameter had apparently square true ends. Close examination showed them to have been neatly cross-cut with axes, not saws. This may have been done at the bucking stage, but could represent later cross-cutting. The shape of two 13th-century revetment posts (TX4: 2028, 2081; Fig 111) suggests that the hewn lower ends were bucked before transport to the site with narrow-bladed axes with straight-ended blades between 100mm and 120mm wide. Cross-cutting of poles is still likely to have been done with axes but the unpointed ends of such timbers are rarely well preserved on the waterfront.

Tools which are probably bucking saws are listed in 15th-century inventories (Clark 1984) while bucking with two-man cross-cut saws is depicted on illustrations from the mid 16th century (*eg A Town in Winter* by Brueghel the Elder). Tools such as saw bucks must have been introduced when saws for bucking became common. The trend was to avoid the waste of timber created by using axes for cross-cutting, and as efficient two-man cross-cut saws became available, pressure to conserve timber and maximise profit encouraged their adoption.

17th-century practice

The ends of the thicker 17th-century timbers from the BOY86 site had been cut with saws, since no facets could be seen or felt, but this may represent bucking or subsequent cross-cutting. A reference to essential woodworking tools needed by settlers in the New World in 1622 implies that 'two-hand sawes' were considered the standard tools for bucking or heavy cross-cutting (Underhill 1986, 194).

Modern practice

Chainsaws are now used for all bucking work in England but since two-man cross-cut saws are

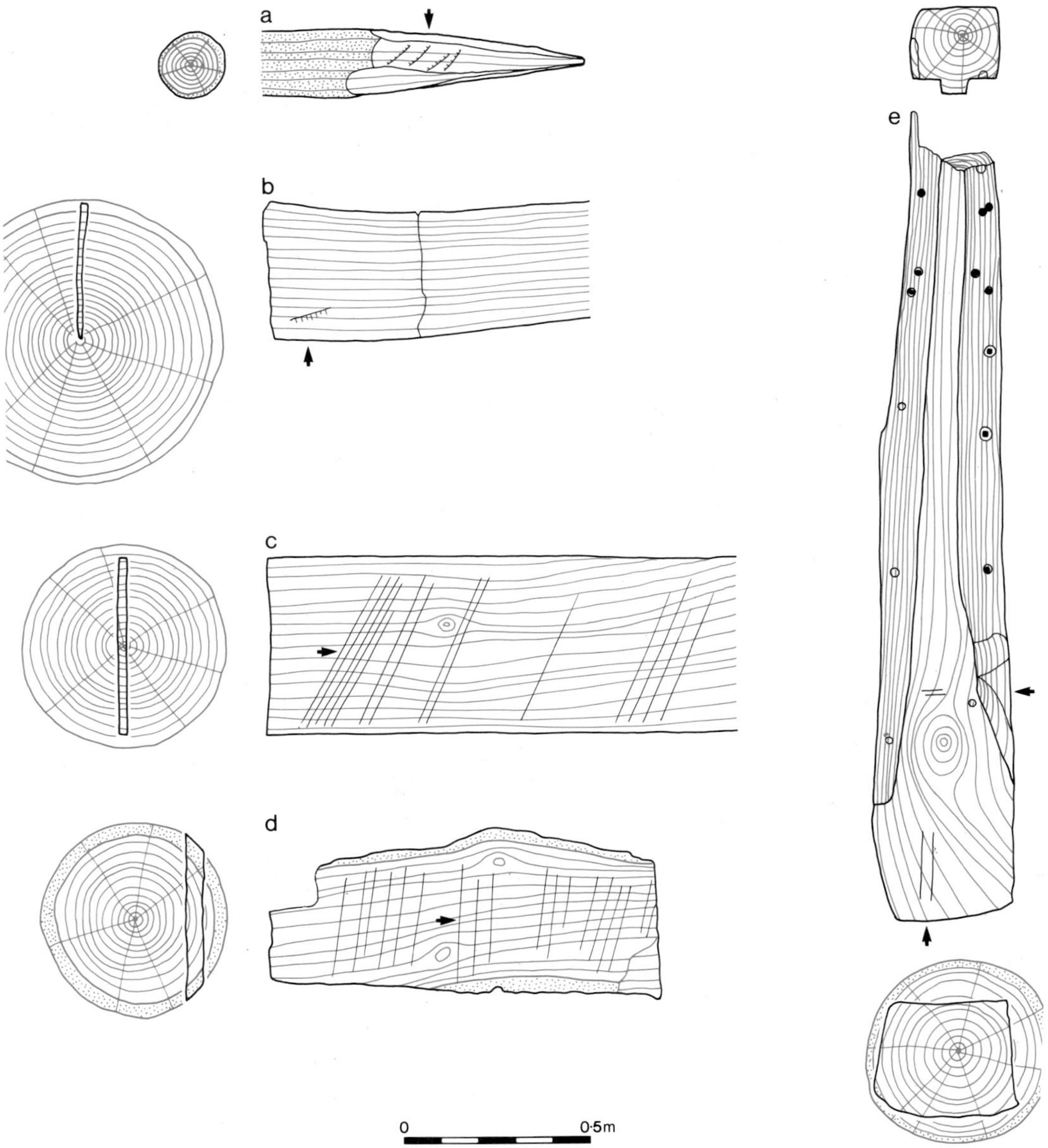

*98. Timber conversion: a) late Saxon pile used in the round sharpened to a point with an axe (*TEX*88, 2504); b) late Saxon radially-cleft plank, with broad-axe mark arrowed (*TEX*88, 2271); c) 13th-century trestle-sawn plank (*TEX*88, 3000); d) 17th-century pit-sawn plank (*TEX*88, 2167); e) late 12th-century boxed heart oak revetment post with marks of a broad axe and of a narrower bladed tool indicated with arrows (*TEX*88, 2028).*

exported to tropical countries where much of the timber for waterfront work is felled, two-man bucking must still be practised there.

Timber conversion

Having cut trimmed logs to the desired lengths, the woodworker is faced with the task of *converting* those logs into timbers, planks, boards or laths. As laths have not been used in waterfront carpentry, the following discussion concerns the other elements. Although space does not allow a full discussion of the infrastructure needed for some conversion processes, such as log handling, tools and equipment, some general comments will be made.

Regrettably, the *type of conversion* is often confused in the archaeological literature with the *method of conversion*. The *type of conversion* refers to the section of the log used: for example, whether the timber is a whole log, or the plank radially-faced. By contrast, the *method of conversion* concerns the way in which the plank, post or beam was cut out of the log, *ie* whether it was *hewn, sawn* or *cleft*. The wealth of detail relating to timber conversion methods recorded by the Department of Urban Archaeology will only be summarised here. For convenience, the reconstruction of parent logs is discussed separately from the examination of tool marks: both studies are, in practical terms, part of the same process.

Saxon practice

The wattle fences and revetments found at Thames Exchange (TEX88) and the Vintry site (VRY89) had uprights made of poles up to 120mm in diameter, while the portable wattle hurdles had smaller vertical 'sails' set in pairs or in threes, each *c*.35mm in diameter (*eg* Fig 102), with horizontal elements from 15 to 50mm in diameter. All the wood used was *uncleft* with the bark left on. No cleft roundwood has been recorded in wattle structures of this date.

Many small timbers between *c*.150 and 250mm in diameter were used *in the round* in simple plank and pile revetments (*eg* Fig 98a). Sometimes these timbers were roughly hewn square *(boxed heart)*, particularly when they appear to have been reused building timbers. Unfortunately, well-preserved tool marks have not been found on the surfaces of these squared timbers, although they generally 'ripple' in the manner of hewn timber. This hewing was probably accomplished with an axe or possibly two axes (perhaps one a narrow-bladed, the other a broad, thin-bladed tool) but the archaeological evidence is not clear on this point.

Another common type of conversion is *box-halving* (Fig 99), where half a log was used to make a plank between 70mm and 120mm thick and *c*.0.4m wide, often having sapwood and wane along its edges. Such planks from the London waterfront are usually described as *staves* (*eg* Fig 13). These were sometimes set vertically earthfast, and study of the joints cut on them shows that several had been reused from other revetments and buildings. The probable method of conversion will have included cleaving a log in half and hewing the halves to the shape of a plank with a sub-rectangular section. Unfortunately, the recorded surfaces were abraded, but although no clear wedge impressions or tool marks were observed, the irregularities and rippling surfaces imply cleaving and hewing.

99. Converting timber using Saxon methods: cleaving halved timbers from a medium-sized oak standard with hardwood wedges.

100. Cleaving boards using Saxon methods: this quartered oak log will be split into two, and then each section radially cleft in half again. This process produces c.30 boards from each tree.

The most common type of conversion for the thinner planks, often known as boards, was *radial cleaving* (Fig 100). This technique of converting a log relies on the availability of very straight-grained, relatively knot-free oak. The resultant boards, with a wedge-shaped cross-section and corrugated, slightly wavey surface, were normally trimmed and smoothed so as to assume a slightly lenticular cross-section.

The planking from the mid Saxon wells at Barking, Essex, incorporated radially-split timbers. Examination of these timbers by Richard Darrah showed that all subsequent shaping and cutting of joints was by axes, and not saws (McGowan 1987, 38). The well-preserved late Saxon board walk from TEX88 incorporated small, cleft oak planks, up to 200mm wide and between 35 and 50mm thick, with the sapwood and wane left on, the rough surface and wedge section being preserved (Fig 103). No wedge marks were observed, which could suggest that wooden wedges and large mauls were used rather than a large number of iron wedges.

Much of the board at Thames Exchange had been reused from clinker-built boats and smaller quantities from buildings. The boat planking was between 20 and 35mm thick and 150mm to 270mm wide in the case of boat planks from revetment 1743 at TEX88 (Fig 104). The planks had clearly been hewn to shape, probably with a thin-bladed 'T' axe rather than an adze, although no very clear facets survived (cf. Crumlin-Pedersen 1986). The radially-cleft boards reused in TEX88 revetment 1743 were up to 390mm wide with a maximum thickness of 28mm, tapering to a feather edge (cf. Fig 98b). They were punctured by small pegs and may once have been used as building clapboard. The edges had been trimmed and most of the sapwood removed but, despite their abraded surfaces, it seems that they were left largely undressed.

Later medieval practice

Small timber and underwood was still used in the round at least as late as the 14th century, but only as wattle fencing on the foreshore (*eg* BOY86), or more commonly, as small piles for retaining and supporting revetment baseplates. Some of the lighter front braces were also used with very minimal squaring by hewing, though most may have been mature coppice poles or possibly the top logs from small oak standards. Others, such as those in the 13th-century BG14 revetment (Fig 21), appear to have been branches from large oaks.

Contrary to the firm statement made by Harvey that 'it should be mentioned that there is no evidence whatever for the fatuous supposition that medieval boards were not sawn but hewn or split and then adzed to shape; sawing was universal' (Harvey 1975, 99), it can now be shown that *radially-cleft boards* of oak continued to be made in the medieval period. A survey of documentary sources suggests that *clove-board* was used throughout the country from at least the late 13th to the early 16th centuries (Carr-Laughton 1957). For example, documentary accounts mention *'Clouenbord'* used to cover the king's bath at Westminster in 1345 (Salzman 1952, 243). The radially-cleft board used as sheathing for medieval revetments in London was usually reused clinker boat planking or boards and muntins from buildings or large furniture (Tatton-Brown 1974, 128-32; Goodburn 1988).

There is much evidence for the hewing of beams and posts with a *boxed heart* in many medieval waterfront structures (*eg* TX4; Fig 51). Some timbers are marked by two different types of axe facet, one indicating the use of a fairly narrow blade, the other a wider, more curved blade (Fig 98e). This practice of hewing with a narrower-bladed tool to cross-cut and rough-out timber (*notch and chop*), followed by a thinner, wider-bladed axe (*broad axe*), is clearly illustrated in a mid 16th-century woodcut by Jost Amman.

A radically new method of timber conversion involving both hewing and *sawing* to produce two (or perhaps more) timbers from a large, hewn baulk, was used to make some of the timbers in medieval London revetments. This technique was used in the late 14th-century TL11 revetment at Trig Lane (Fig 78), for example. An example has been recorded of a baulk sawn three times to produce four *box-quartered* timbers (TEX88; 744). However, as is now fairly well documented for standing buildings, converting large logs into several beams and posts in medieval carpentry seems relatively uncommon (Rackham 1976). The most common type of conversion on the medieval London waterfront is *box heart*, and then *box halving*.

In medieval England, *plank* clearly meant wide, thick planks, while the thinner, narrower material was called *board* (Salzman 1952, 242). By the 13th century, the thicker planking used for sheathing framed waterfront revetments was usually sawn and not cleft. Fairly clear saw marks survive on the protected surfaces of the planking. In the TX4 revetment, the planking varied between *c*.0.3m and 0.4m in width, and from about 50 to 120mm in thickness, while the sawn oak planking in the slightly later revetment was up to 0.47m wide (Fig 98c). Large saws for *ripping* planks were therefore in common use during this period. Although the marks are rarely sufficiently well preserved to clarify the actual *method of sawing*, clear examples of the crossing saw-marks identical to those observed

101. Billingsgate Lorry Park: a sawn plank from the 13th-century BG14 *revetment. The diagonal saw marks preserved on the reverse face diverge either side of the 2 x 100mm scale, leaving the triangular signature characteristic of timber sawn on a single trestle, by the 'see-saw' method.*

in some standing medieval buildings have been recorded on the Vintry, Thames Exchange and Billingsgate sites (Fig 101). These show that these 13th-century timbers were sawn on a trestle (the *see-saw* method: Fig 97g), a technique also used by the Romans (Goodburn 1990b). By the later 15th century, sawing over a pit seems to have become common, when references to *'putte saws'* appear in London documents (Clark 1984).

Post-medieval practice

Documentary accounts of this aspect of woodworking craft (Edlin 1949) and extensive studies of timbers in standing contemporary buildings provide more information on this topic than the evidence from archaeological sites of this period in London. Nevertheless, it is worth noting that the use of timber (principally elm) *in the round* for the foundation piles of waterfront buildings was still common (*eg* BOY86). Although roundwood of small size was not apparently used in London structures in this period, it may have been in more rural contexts.

Cleaving as a conversion technique was rarely used for planks or boards used or reused in revetments, although a section of radially-cleft clinker boat planking of possible 17th-century date was excavated on the Blackfriars Road site (Goodburn 1988, 427).

Plain sawing was the common method used to produce the thick elm and oak carvel ship's planking found reused on the BOY86 site (Goodburn 1988, 427-8). Several fragments of timberyard waste from the TEX88 site included very waney planks of oak with clear saw marks on them and a distinctive triangular area of split surface where the pit-sawn plank had finally separated from the rest of the sawn log (Fig 98d). This pattern of marks shows that the planks were from a log that had been plain-sawn over a pit or level trestles.

The sawing of most or all the faces of timber was also becoming widespread, as is shown by the sawn faces of the *boxed heart* oak post from the BY1 revetment (Fig 79). This structure also shows how imported *softwoods* were starting to be used to provide beams and planks. Softwood coming into 17th-century London appears to have been imported in the form of hewn baulks which were then sawn as required. It is likely that some of the timber converted in London at this time was actually converted by water-powered reciprocating mechanical saws (Edlin 1949, 16). The extensive use of such sawmills in the New England colonies suggests that some American softwood may have been imported as sawn plank ready for use (Perlin 1989). No clear evidence of the use of powered mills has been recorded in London, but some of the many 17th and 18th-century oak piles on the BOY86 site had such regular saw marks that they might have been sawn with a reciprocating mill.

Hewing as a technique of timber conversion was rarely used except in the manner described above, but was used as a method of dressing sawn timber and planks. For example, ship's planking reused in the BY1 revetment and adjacent structures was extensively dressed with adzes after being sawn out.

Modern practice

With the proliferation of modern softwood plantations, home-grown conifer, particularly larch poles, is still used *in the round* for waterfront carpentry in rural areas. As the technical literature on modern timber conversion is large (see *eg* Bramwell 1976), all that need be said here is that myriad forms of powered saws dominate the scene, powered by fossil fuels, grid electricity, or waste from the milling process. However, timber was still being imported as hewn boxed heart baulks from some tropical countries for waterfront work in England as late as 1979. Rather than discuss the developments in conversion technology and practice, briefly summarised above, it is more useful to consider this area together with the next section which deals with the types of trees used.

THE MEDIEVAL WOODSCAPE

Reconstructing the trees from which the London waterfront structures were cut

This type of study was pioneered by Oliver Rackham in his systematic work on the medieval timber-framed Grundle House (Rackham 1972), and developed in works such as the analysis of the 13th-century timber roof of Gloucester friary (Rackham *et al* 1978). Though attempts at reconstructing the parent trees used in a structure is now an accepted part of some vernacular building studies, the approach has not been adopted by many archaeologists in Britain working in urban historic contexts. This is unfortunate, since much of the history of the countryside lies buried in the towns. Such a study allows ancient landscapes to be reconstructed in surprisingly subtle ways, especially when combined with dendrochronological, palynological and historical research. It can also tell us about types of woodland management, economy and the status and 'cost' of the structure itself. If this study of *timber* could then be combined with a systematic study of *wood* then a broader picture of the use of trees and wood in early London could be drawn. That these studies should become part of current archaeological practice was stressed in the recently published guidelines for the processing and recording of waterlogged wood (Milne 1990).

Some nautical archaeologists have already attempted to reconstruct the parent trees used to build ancient boats. One of the most useful and exciting fruits of the increasingly systematic programmes of experimental medieval boat building being carried out in Denmark and latterly in England has been the new understanding it has given us about the nature of timber conversion technology and its relationship with the availability and growth of different types of timber trees (Crumlin-Pedersen 1986; Goodburn 1988; 1991).

To carry out this process successfully with timbers recovered from archaeological sites, certain stages have to be worked through systematically with people who have practical experience of the technologies relevant to the period, and of the growth patterns of the tree species concerned. In the DUA this approach has only become possible with the revision and upgrading of the timber recording system (MOL 1990). Listed below are the essential elements that the drawn record of each timber must incorporate:

1 size and shape of the timber;
2 grain and the disposition and shape of the larger knots;
3 cross-sections indicating the type of timber conversion used;
4 presence and disposition of sapwood or wane;
5 original edges, distinguished from those damaged by later cuts;
6 notes on the width of growth rings and the regularity of growth if available;
7 cross-checking of this information with the results of tree-ring study to confirm the identification of timber conversion, or the survival of sapwood. However, it should be stressed that a tree-ring specialist will not always be able to identify correctly the type of timber conversion from a single dendrochronological sample.

Given the reliable recording of Points 1 to 6 in good light when the sample is fairly clean (not always possible in rescue archaeology), the next stages can be attempted.

8 Hypothetical *parent logs* can be sketched to scale, provided that the timber being assessed survives to its full length, or has other significant features which suggest the size of the tree.
9 Using the information recorded about grain patterns, tapering, position of knots *etc*, a reconstruction of the *parent tree* can now be attempted. A working assumption here is that the heart of a large oak is normally found in the middle which, it is accepted, is not always the case.
10 Bearing in mind the shapes in which oak trees are now known to grow given particular conditions, tentative reconstructions can be made of the *growth environment,* the type of woodland, field or hedgerows that those specific trees represent.

There is as yet no generally accepted way of representing analyses of this type. However, Figs 102 to 112 attempt to show the results of a pilot study of timbers and wood from a selection of structures mainly from the Thames Exchange site, by way of an example.

*102a. Above: 10th-century wattle-work woven around collapsed earthfast posts on the foreshore on the Thames Exchange site, looking south (*TEX88, *1512). The structures were traced for 17m.*

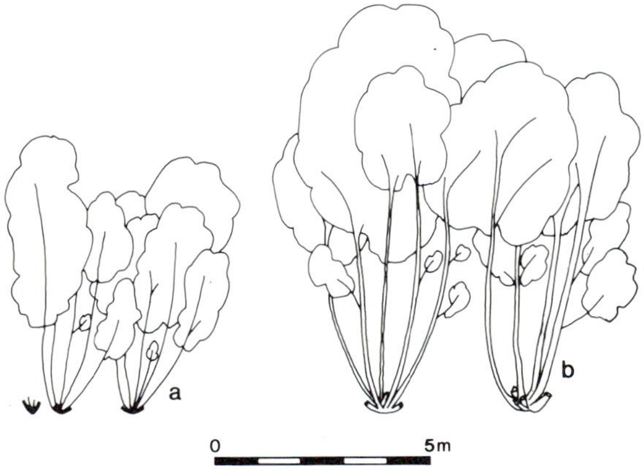

102b. Diagram showing types of trees from which wood used in the construction of the wattle-work shown in Fig 102a was derived. The horizontal rods (a) between 15 and 50mm in diameter and the straight regular stakes (b) up to 120mm in diameter must have been harvested from a form of coppice, perhaps the Silva minuta *mentioned in the Domesday Book (Rackham 1976, 59).*

103. Above: late Saxon board walk excavated on the Thames Exchange site (TEX88, 3171), looking north. The 5 x 100mm scale rests in a machine cut trench which sliced through the feature, exposing the two joists onto which the cleft boards were pegged. Remains of a later structure can be seen in the section above the board walk to the north.

104. Diagram showing type of trees from which were derived the timbers used in the construction of the board walk shown in plan and side elevation (right). The waney planking (a) was radially-cleft from an oak with a diameter of up to 0.45m, probably between 80 and 110 years old. The oak rails were minimally trimmed. The east rail (b) was smaller and knottier, perhaps the top log from a small standard. The west rail (c) was a lower log c.230mm in diameter, c.25 to 40 years old. Their combined length suggests that the parent tree was straight for its usable length of 5.5 to 6m.

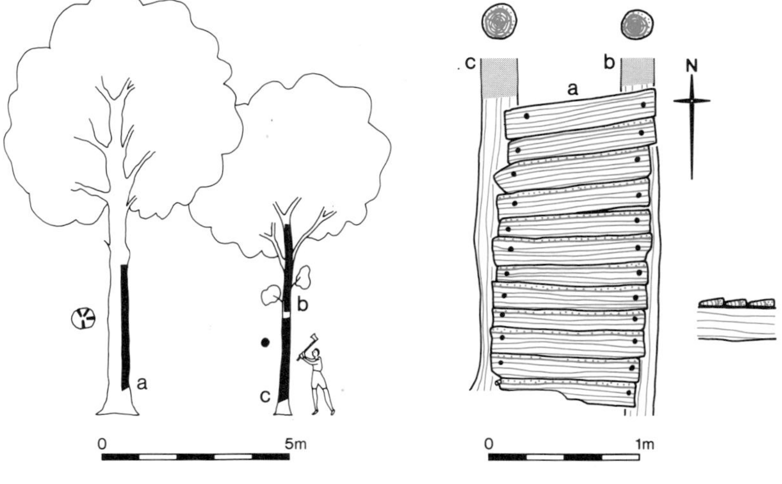

105. Diagram showing types of trees (left) from which were derived the timbers used in the construction of the revetment shown in north facing (landward) and side elevation on the right. A 19m length of this late Saxon structure was recorded on the Thames Exchange site (TEX88; 1743). Most of the sheathing (a) comprised articulated sections of radially-cleft clinker boat planking between 150mm and 270mm wide and 25 to 30mm thick, with no sapwood. This was cleft from straight-grained knot-free logs. By analogy with the contemporary Graveney boat (Fenwick 1978), the logs may have varied between 1.5 and about 7m long, suggesting that large oaks c.0.8-0.9m in diameter were used. These must have grown in dense groves of oaks 150+ years old, either in what had once been Roman managed woodland or more likely in parts of remaining 'wildwood'.

Reconstructing the late Saxon woodscape

Little has been written about Saxon woodlands because, to date, little is known beyond Rackham's summary based on a critical assessment of historical and place name evidence (Rackham 1976; 1990 & forthcoming). The archaeological pilot study presented here is therefore seen as a preliminary reconnaissance exercise, with the emphasis placed on the depiction of late Saxon structures and associated parent trees.

Our evidence shows that a variety of types of tree-producing land must have existed in late Saxon south-eastern England. There must have been large areas of woodland managed as coppice for the harvesting of raw material for wattlework. This probably took the standard later medieval form, in which coppice stools were interspersed with standard timber trees. Small timber oaks must have grown in woodland, possibly on old coppice stools. Medium to fairly large-sized timber oaks, up to 0.6m in diameter, could have grown in woodland, hedges or wood pasture (*Silva Pastilis*). Since Saxon conversion technology was limited to cleaving and hewing, knotty (heavily branching) trees with very curved grain were apparently little used for building.

The straight-grained timber trees used for cleaving thin board were often very large with diameters over 1m being common. The straightness of the grain shows that they grew in high woodland, perhaps in remnants of the *wildwood* or in former Roman managed woodland which had subsequently overgrown. These large oaks were clearly relatively common near late Saxon London as there is little evidence for large-scale timber import at this date. Indeed, the recent dendro-provenancing of the wide, radially-cleft late Saxon boat planking from New Fresh Wharf and other sites shows that the

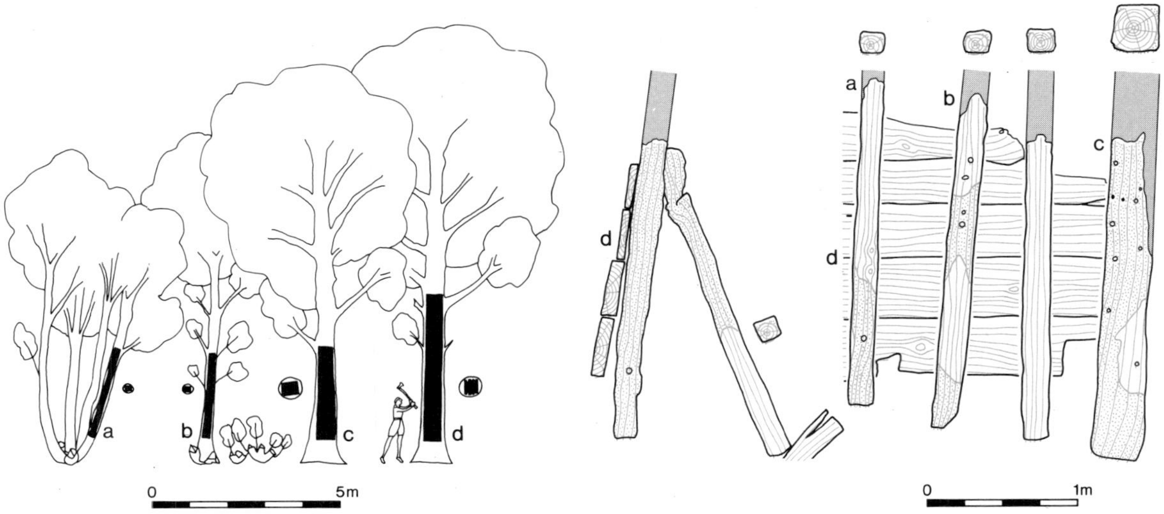

parent trees grew in south-east England (I Tyers, pers comm). The presence of such trees shows that significant areas of high, dense woodland of semi-natural appearance must have been a feature of the late Saxon landscape in south-east England. Trees with a large girth and low branches are also likely to have grown in wood pasture, although Saxon woodworkers could not, or did not commonly, convert them.

106. Diagram showing types of trees (left) from which were derived the timbers used in the construction of the revetment shown in south facing (riverward) and side elevation on the right (TEX88; *1734). This late Saxon pile and plank revetment used varied types of reused timbers in its construction. The radially-cleft, feather-edged oak boards (a) may originally have been used as building clapboard. They were c.0.39m wide with some sapwood along their edges. These boards were cleft from straight-grained knot-free logs over 0.85m in diameter. The parent trees could either have been wildwood oaks or from a grove of old oaks in dense woodland. The piles were also apparently reused from buildings. Some (b) were tangentially-cleft from logs c.0.3m in diameter and one (c) used in the round was 0.2m in diameter. They could have been cut from small standards or even coppice stems 30 to 70 years old.*

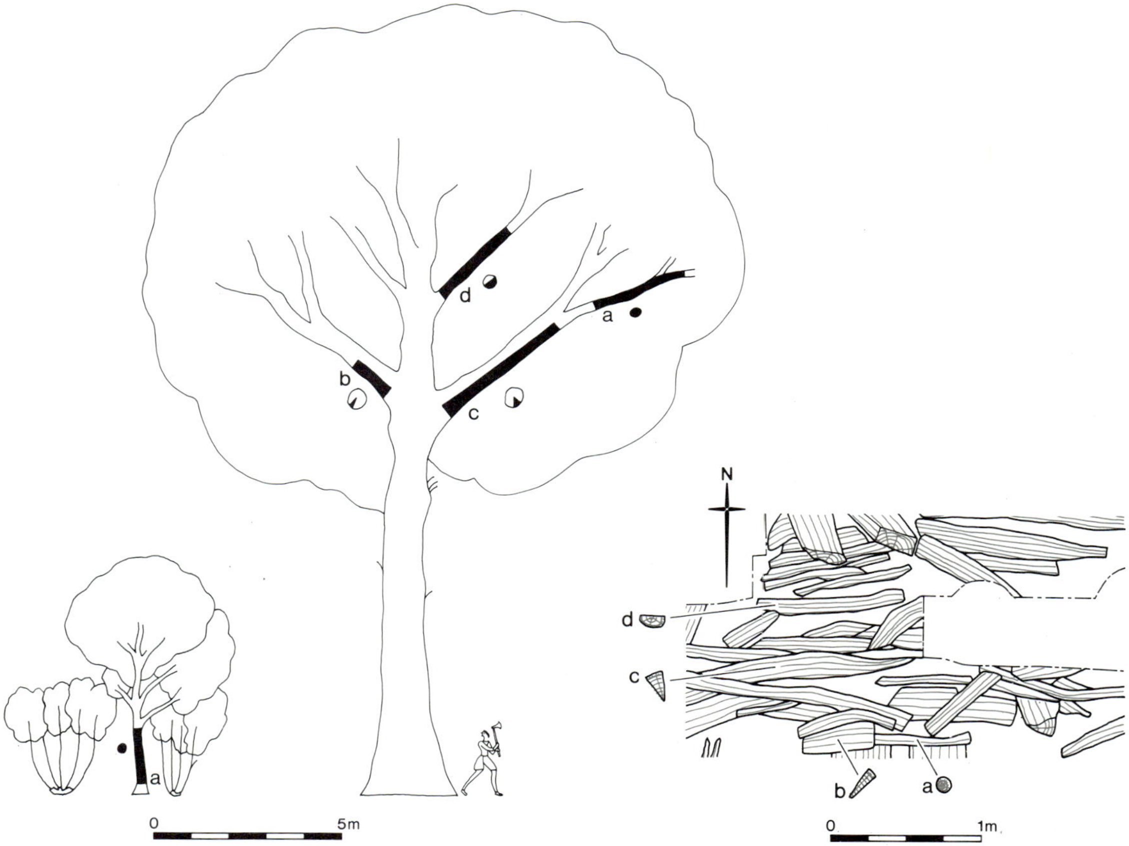

*107. Above: diagram showing types of trees (left) from which were derived the timbers used in the construction of the embankment shown in plan (right): see Fig 102 (*TEX88; TX2*). This late Saxon timber, wood and earth embankment incorporated cleft oak timbers (b, c, d) from stems and branches 0.2 to 0.4m in diameter, and a few pieces of large roundwood (a) of oak and other species used as 'make up' material. Much of the oak may be top and lop from large oaks over 40 years old, the rest perhaps local tree clearance.*

108. Thames Exchange: 11th-century TX2 *stave structure, set into the foreshore next to 5 x 100mm scale, looking north. Behind the staves (beneath the steel girder), is part of a dump of cleft timber and branches.*

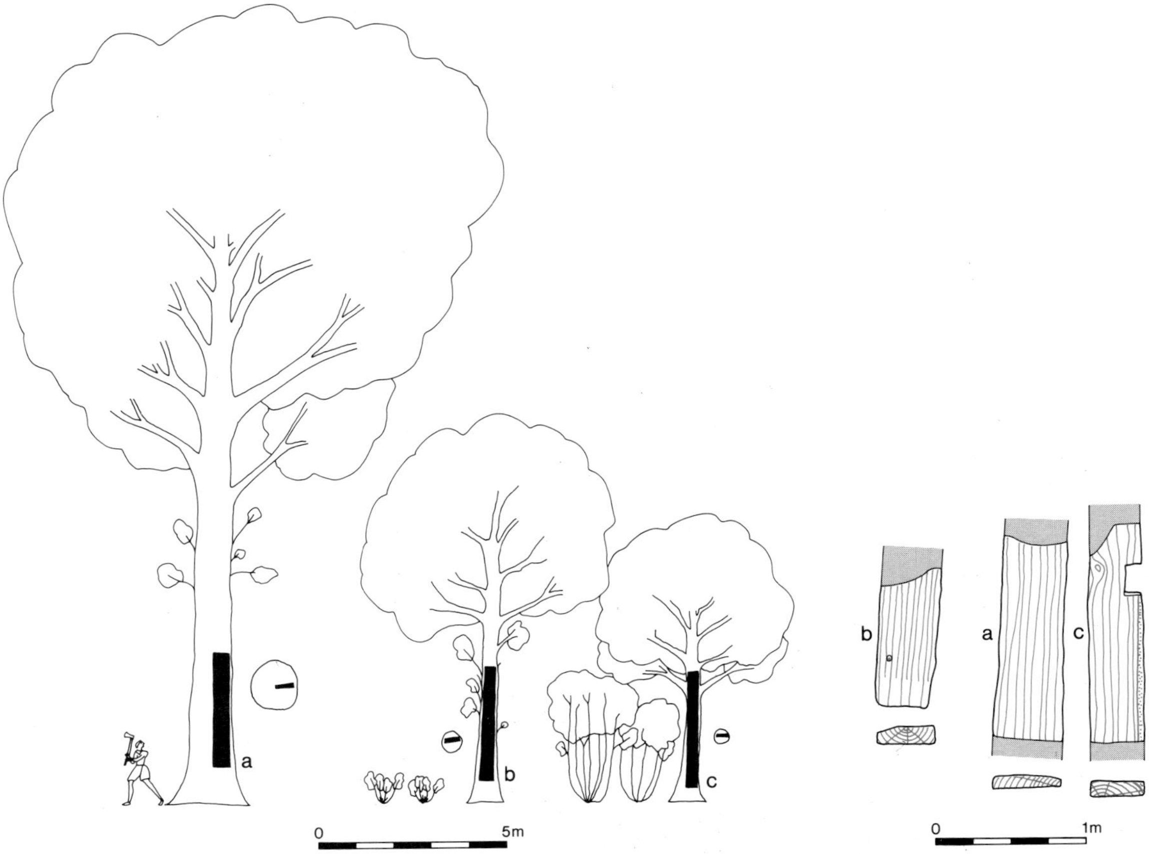

109. Diagram showing types of trees (left) from which were derived the timbers used in the construction of a stave-built revetment, some members of which (a, b, c) are drawn in elevation on the right (TEX88; TX2). A section of this late Saxon revetment was recorded for over 10m and lay immediately south of the embankment described above (see Figs 101–2). The tangentially cleft and hewn staves had some wane and sapwood surviving. They appear to have derived from moderately straight logs between 0.3 and 0.45m in diameter and perhaps 2.5 and 3m long. The parent trees probably grew as 60 to 90 year-old standards in coppice woodland.

*110. Diagram showing types of trees (left) from which were derived the timbers used in the construction of the revetment shown in side elevation and in south facing (riverward) elevation on the right. The 12th-century earthfast structure (*TEX88; TX7*) was hurriedly recorded during the watching brief, but the conversion of some of the timbers was noted. The main posts were boxed-heart or box-quartered. Although the conversion method was not recorded, the cross-section may imply cleaving. The quartered example shown (a) was originally c.3.5m long by 0.31m wide and 280mm thick, with no apparent wane. It was cut from a moderately straight oak log c.0.95m diameter, which may have been cut from a parent tree c.180 to 250 years old in a wood or possibly relic wildwood.*

The radially cleft oak planking (b) was between 0.3m and 0.41m wide and 60 to 80mm thick including a little sapwood, but only 1.2m long. It had been cross-cut with an axe, but was probably cleft in lengths of at least 2.5m to avoid excessive waste or labour. The logs must have been up to 1.3m in diameter, moderately straight grained but need not have been long, as the planks were not very thin or regular. Perhaps the parent tree was a large oak c.200 years old, grown in a wood pasture environment, the Silva Pastilis *mentioned in Domesday Book (Rackham 1976, 59). The intermediate posts (c) were 150mm square, moderately straight hewn boxed-heart waney oak, probably cut from old oak coppice or very small standards perhaps about 25-40 years old.*

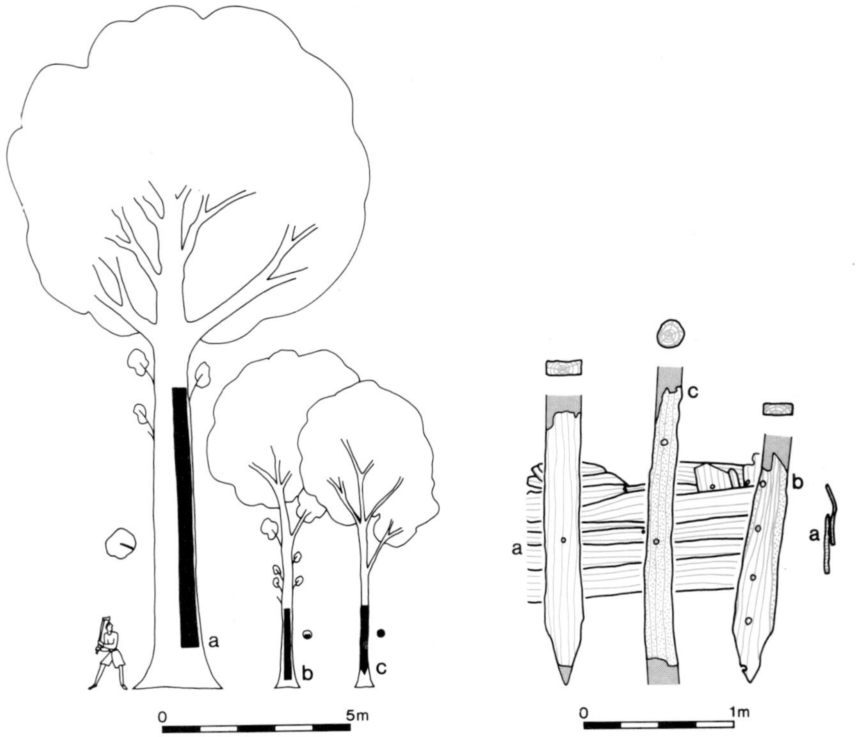

111. Diagram showing types of trees (left) from which were derived timbers used in the construction of the revetment shown in side elevation and south facing (riverward) elevation on the right. This was an early 13th-century earthfast front-braced structure (TEX88; TX4). The minor posts (a, b) were waney, hewn boxed-heart oak: typical examples were 2.5m long, 170mm wide and 140mm thick. The major posts were waney and somewhat crooked, boxed-heart hewn oak over 2.2m long: an example (c) was 0.37m wide and 0.33m thick. It was cut from a parent tree perhaps 80 to 100 years old, which had grown in a coppice- with-standards wood or even possibly as a hedgerow or wood pasture tree.

The plain-sawn planking (d) was 0.30m to 0.42m wide, 50 to 120mm thick and 3.35m long with little sapwood on the edges. These planks exhibited wavey grain and some large knots suggesting an origin either in top logs from a large woodland tree or more likely, the bole of a hedgerow or pasture tree. A typical log was at least 0.55m in diameter, cut from a tree 80 to 120 years old.

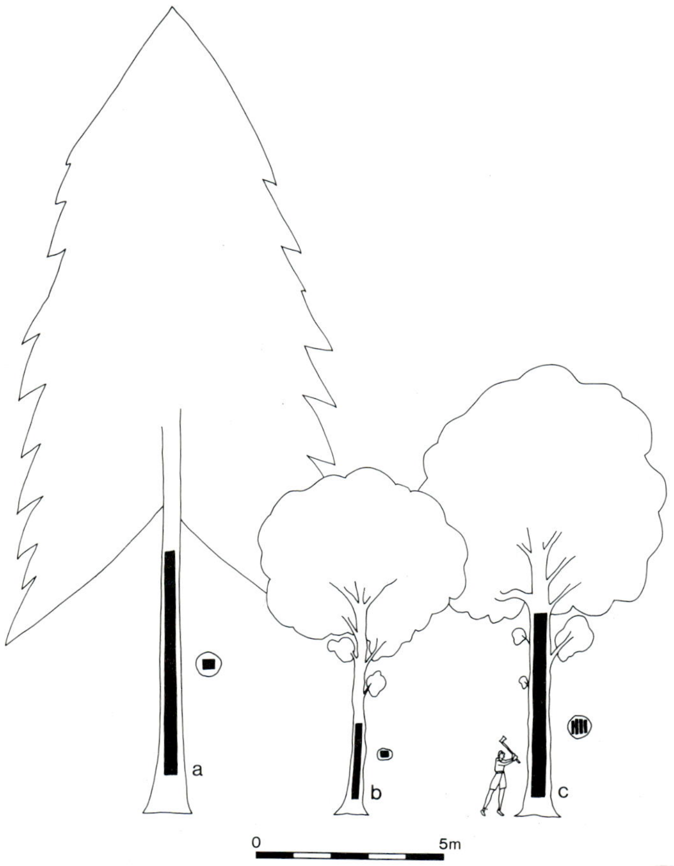

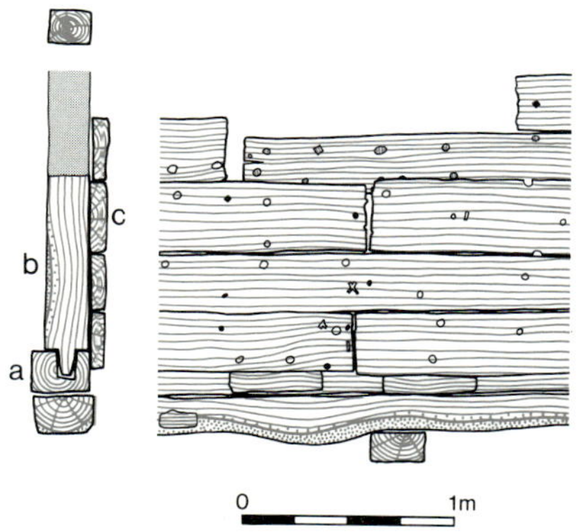

*112. Above: diagram showing types of trees (left) from which were derived timbers used in the construction of the 17th-century revetment shown in side elevation and in north facing (landward) elevation on the right. This structure was part of a revetment built in c.1670 and the elevations combine information from the controlled excavation and the watching brief on the Boys' School site (*BOY86; BYI*). The softwood (pine sp) baseplate (a) was sawn and hewn from a straight pine log at least 2.5m long probably imported from either Scandinavia or the New World colonies. Dendro-provenancing might identify the most likely origin.*

The boxed-heart, slightly waney oak post (b) was 0.22m wide and about 155mm thick, apparently sawn out from an oak log at least 2m long. This was probably a small standard oak 40 to 60 years old. The plain-sawn oak planking (c) was reused from a large carvel-built ship. It varied from 0.26m to 0.36m wide and 60 to 70mm thick, and was reused in lengths over 2m long. They were cut from moderately straight logs about 0.45m in diameter derived from a variety of types of trees from 70 to 100 years old.

The sawyer's revolution and the later medieval woodscape

Converting the timber represented in the waterfront material by cleaving and hewing required little infrastructure: one or two people could fell, hew and cleave the largest of trees on the spot. Several people, a cart or a wagon could then carry the converted timber to the nearest watercourse for longer-distance transport. By contrast, when large saws were adopted for producing plank, in or by the late 12th century, more infrastructural support must have been developed. Large heavy logs had to be moved to a place convenient for sawing. Initially this would probably have involved the lifting of each log onto a trestle to provide the space for the sawyers to work, sawing vertically. There is no evidence from this country of conversion saws being used horizontally, as is the case in Asia, although the largest logs may have been 'broken' into lighter sections by this method. Medieval timber conversion using saws also therefore involved the use of lifting tackle, larger wagons, and larger work teams than would have been necessary during the late Saxon period.

The use of saws also revolutionised tree selection for timber building. Smaller, younger and knottier trees could now be used to provide wide planks and occasionally beams and posts. As discussed previously, Rackham's description of a typical medieval woodland comprises stands of coppice producing mainly wood, interspersed with small timber, with a few larger trees up to perhaps 0.6m in diameter for sawn plank. The presence of short lengths of very knotty sawn planks with crooked grain in later medieval waterfront structures suggests that trees which had been grown in open pasture were now being used.

However, the straight-grained radially-cleft oak planking reused in many contemporary London waterfront structures represents another class of tree, which may be termed a *board tree*. Although much cleft oak board was imported from Baltic countries and Germany during the medieval period (Salzman 1952, 206), it is very unlikely that all of it was imported. This particularly applies to the long curved boards required to make the clinker boat planking found reused in medieval revetments, as these would have been very difficult to order and transport. Though London may have imported much of its short standardised cleft oak board together with some softwood mast and scaffold spar timber, most of its needs for wood and timber were met from renewable local managed woodlands or, to a lesser extent, from parks, forests and trees growing in pasture land and orchards.

113. Left: converting timber using later medieval methods in 1990. Timber planks are being sawn on a single trestle (see-saw), replicating the methods used to prepare many of the sawn planks and boxed-halved oak timbers found in the London riverfront revetments. Knotty timber of modest size can be sawn into wider planks and beams than could have been obtained by cleaving.

Destruction of woodlands in the post-medieval period

In the post-medieval period the timber grown close to London was increasingly supplemented by large quantities of imported timber, mainly softwood. Whether this is an indication of a reduction in supply or more simply that home-grown and converted plank or beam simply cost the buyer more than an imported equivalent is not clear. It could be suggested, however, that with the rapid economic development of south-east England in the 16th and 17th centuries, the extant stands of working woodland were insufficient to supply the expanding market.

Though the use of constructional timber of non-oak species is documented for the medieval period, there is very little evidence for the use of non-oak timber (as opposed to roundwood piles) on the contemporary London waterfront. However, the amount of sawn elm plank and beam-section timber found on a 17th-century site (BOY 86) indicates that medium and large-sized elms must have been fairly common in the London hinterland, as we have no evidence that this timber was imported. Most elms grow reasonably straight even when in hedgerows or small areas of woodland. However, the study of the growth and character of elms is a complex field and it is not possible to establish the growth environment of the elms used for the 17th-century planks found in London (but see Rackham 1980).

The development of world markets during the first phases of the economic domination by European expansionism is given material expression in the archaeology of timber structures of the post-medieval period, both above and below ground. The adoption of an approach to harvesting timber which destroys foreign forests rather than develops a system of sustainable supply, can be seen to have occurred at this time in northern Europe and especially in Britain.

This uncontrolled harvesting for short-term gain moved gradually from the temperate and northern coniferous forests to the tropics, but only became an issue of popular concern in the 1980s. In the late 1970s when this writer worked as a waterfront carpenter, there was little consideration given to the environmental consequences of using cheap, imported timber from distant sources, such as West Africa. Indeed this is still sadly the case in most waterfront and municipal carpentry, and also in boat-building in south-east England. The archaeological record world-wide could be used to inform this crucial debate with profit, since most work taking a long view of this subject has been dominated by interpretations of historical sources which, for Britain at least, are often misleading. For example, one recent study (Perlin 1989) only uses selected historical sources in the section on Britain, taking no account of archaeological evidence. It is also unfortunate that archaeological and historical data is ignored by present-day scientific researchers studying intensive tree-growing systems and the problems currently being experienced in mono-cultural coppicing.

JOINTS AND FASTENINGS

Cutting out joints

This section considers developments in medieval carpentry observed from changes in the way joints were cut in structural timbers. Discussion is restricted to changes in the practice of cutting mortises and tenons, though reference is made to other types of joint to illustrate particular points.

Saxon practice

(Fig 114a-c)

Thick, tangentially cleft and hewn oak planks have often been found in late Saxon contexts on City waterfront sites, and these are often interpreted as plate timbers derived from buildings (Chapter 5). Unfortunately there is as yet no evidence as to how the wall posts articulated with them, since no recognisable shouldered tenons on posts or studs have been found (but cf. bare-faced tenons used in the Saxon Tamworth mill; Rahtz & Sheridan 1972). We are immediately confronted by a problem of terminology for it is not possible to discuss mortise and tenon development if *no* tenons have been recorded: a mortise is only a mortise if it articulates with a tenon. This lack of evidence remains a significant blank area in our knowledge of Saxon carpentry: the implications for our understanding of English carpentry development are considerable.

We can however describe how the Saxons made 'mortises', which were little more than rectangular holes. The joints vary in form from roughly-cut square holes chopped out from both sides (which closely resemble prehistoric 'mortises') to more neatly-made rectangular 'mortises' (Fig 114a). Whilst the rougher type of square hole could have been cut out with a narrow-bladed axe relatively easily, the orientation of the facet in the end of the rectangular 'mortise' in timber 2305 (TEX88) suggests the use of a narrow-bladed adze-like tool. Strap adzes of this form have been excavated from late Saxon or Anglo-Scandinavian contexts (*eg* at Thetford). A clear example of the augering-out of the corners of large square 'mortises' was found in an oak plank in London (Fig 114b).

Joints such as grooves, rebates and laps have often been found in reused timbers and it is clear that many of these joints were cut out with hewing tools, and that saws were not used. Fig 114c shows a typical reused late Saxon cleft and hewn plank with a hewn lap joint cut into its edge near one end. No marks such as those left from the marking out of joints have yet been found, and at this stage it would seem fair to generalise that Saxon carpentry was not characterised by the cutting and laying out of accurate joints and integrated frames.

*114. Cutting joints. a) Late Saxon tangentially cleft oak plate broken across a mortise, showing axe or narrow adze marks in end grain, with facet 55mm wide (*TEX88*; 2305). b) Late Saxon tangentially cleft oak plank with square 'mortises' showing auger holes in corners, bored to prevent over cutting with the axe (*TEX88*; 2741). c) Late Saxon tangentially cleft oak planks with lap joints cut in their edges: axe marks visible on the lower joint (*TEX88*; 2401). d) 13th-century chase mortise in an oak revetment post, showing concave auger marks left by the tip of a spoon bit (*TEX88*; 730). e) late 12th to 13th-century notched lap joint cut in an oak back brace showing a probable twybill mark 60mm wide in the end grain (*TEX88*; 2044). f) Tenon on foot of 13th-century oak revetment post with roughly hewn shoulders (*TEX88*; 2123). g) 13th-century oak jetty brace with squinted lap joint, showing scribed marking-out line (*TX5*). h) Tenon on foot of 17th-century oak revetment post showing saw and chisel trimming marks (*BY1*). i) 17th-century mortises in a reused oak timber, showing flat-based impressions left by the concave tip of a post-medieval auger (*TEX88*; 2170).*

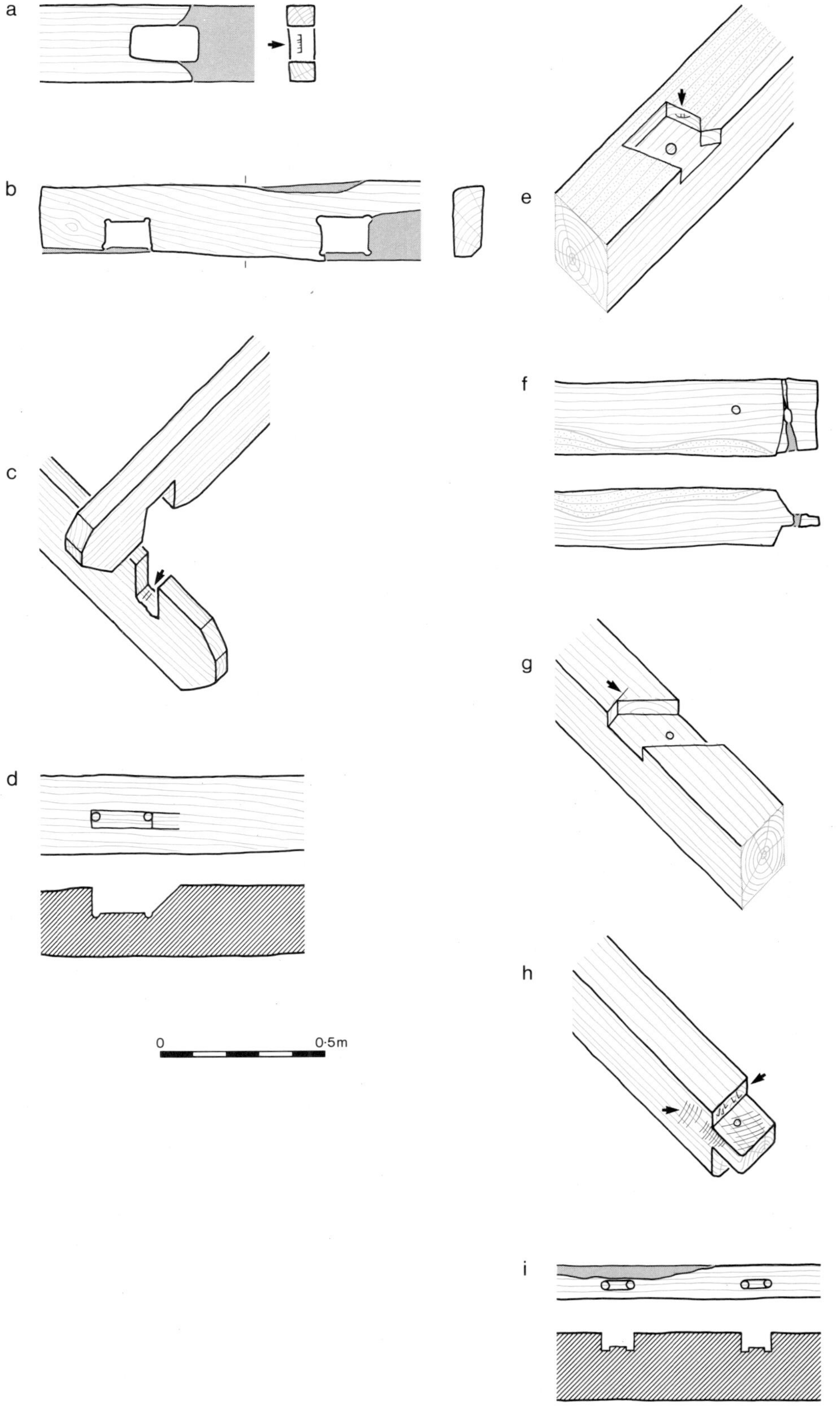
a
b
c
d
e
f
g
h
i
0
0·5m

Later medieval practice

(Fig 114d-g)

Taking the whole of the medieval period together is obviously difficult, when the types and complexity of joints used by carpenters is known to have undergone major changes. However, some general observations on the actual practice of cutting joints can be made on the basis of the waterfront evidence. This is of particular significance, since descriptions of how joints were cut by medieval carpenters have previously been based on recent practice, rather than on study of the material remains. For example, it has been suggested that the tool called a 'mortise wimball' was 'a large auger for drilling a series of holes to start the sinking of a mortise which could then be easily trimmed out and squared with a chisel' (Harvey 1975, 153). It is clear from the marks left by the protruding convex tips of spoon bits in the bottoms of mortises that they were only augered across their ends (Fig 114d). The rest of the waste appears to have been chopped or levered out, not with chisels, but with hewing tools such as the *twybill* which could be used to chop and pare when cutting joints. In a protected part of a notched lap joint in a back brace from TX4 (p. 53), a clear facet over 60mm wide was recorded which was probably cut with a twybill-type tool (Fig 114e).

The shape of medieval mortises also differs from Saxon examples, becoming more elongated and rectangular. Most later examples are not through-mortises and are more carefully made, designed to clasp the tenon inserted into them tightly. The tenon was prevented from withdrawing by a cleft and tapered oak peg.

Tenons tend to be poorly preserved on archaeological timbers, frequently being damaged in reuse or during the dismantling of a structure. However, the shape and surviving tool marks on some 13th-century tenoned timbers show that they were carefully hewn out rather than sawn (Fig 114f), as they presumably were by the later medieval period.

Although marking-out lines are often observed in surviving medieval buildings, they rarely survive on excavated timbers. However, on one of the oblique lap joints used in the construction of a 13th-century jetty, a faint scribed line survived, possibly cut with the tip of a knife (Fig 114g).

Post-medieval practice

(Fig 114h-i)

It is clear from the shape of the auger holes found in reused timbers from both the TEX88 and BOY86 sites that a new type of auger was introduced which had a flat non-convex end. These were used, possibly alongside the older spoon type, for the drilling out of the ends of mortises (Fig 114i). The tenons on posts used in waterfront structures appear to have been sawn out and then trimmed with chisels as in recent practice (Fig 114h). In general terms, the cutting of most joints appears to have been carried out in much the same way as in the 9th century. Another general feature demonstrated in structures excavated at the BOY86 site is that the form of joints, particularly scarf joints, became much simpler to cut: this could be seen as appropriate in an age when economics and costs were increasingly becoming a feature of daily life.

Modern practice

Modern waterfront carpentry does not involve much joinery, the joining of timbers usually being effected with galvanised steel brackets and other fastenings. Mortises are drilled out with numerous holes and finished with a narrow but thick-bladed iron-bound mortising chisel or mortising machine. Simple edge-halved scarves and lap joints are also used which are cut out with power saws, though trimming such joints may be done with broad-bladed 'shipwright's adzes'. Regular scantlings, tight joints, metal fastenings and measurements typify modern 'scientific carpentry': there are some echoes of Roman practice here.

Fastenings

Saxon practice

Late Saxon waterfront builders rarely seem to have used fastenings at all. They relied on the weight of dumped deposits to hold their structures together, or used driven stakes or piles, or occasionally used twisted withy rope to bind timbers or wood in place. However, in the TEX88 board walk (Fig 103) and in reused building timbers from revetments, pegs made from cleft billets or small whole stems of soft deciduous wood such as willow were used (Fig 115a, b).

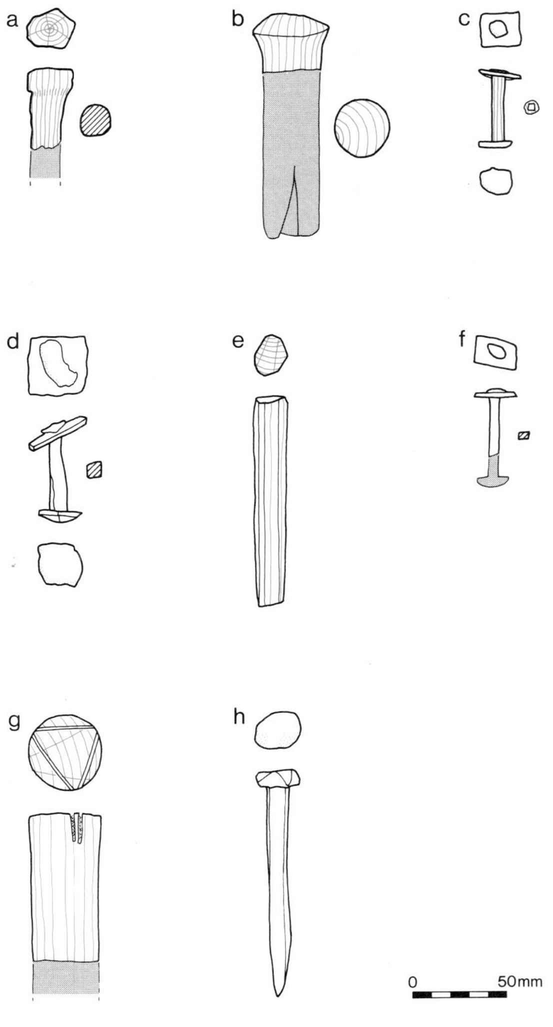

*115. Fastenings: a) late Saxon treenail, in the round (*TEX88*; 3171); b) late Saxon-style non-oak wedged treenail; c) late Saxon boat rivet driven through wooden plug (*TEX88*; 1743); d) later medieval boat rivet (*HOR86*, Kingston); e) later medieval cleft timber peg; f) 17th-century boat rivet (245 Blackfriars Bridge Road,* SE1*); g) 17th-century wooden treenail with expanded head (*BY1*); h) 17th-century wrought iron spike (*BY1*).*

Later medieval practice

In later medieval carpentry, pegs could be used in two ways: to lock joints or to pin timbers together. The most common size was roughly an inch in diameter. They were usually made from cleft oak billets and roughly trimmed with an axe (Fig 114e). Iron nails with square shanks were also occasionally used to fasten planks to timbers on revetments dating from the mid to late 13th century. Such iron nails are easily distinguished from the iron rivets used in contemporary ship construction and frequently found in boat planking reused as riverfront revetment cladding in Saxon (Fig 115c), later medieval (Fig 115d) and post-medieval structures (Fig 115f).

Post-medieval practice

By the 17th century, pegs of cleft softwood as well as oak were used mainly for securing joints, while large square-section tapering wrought iron spikes were used to fasten planks to timbers (Fig 115h): the plank sheathing of the BOY86 revetment was spiked to the posts of the revetment in such a way (Fig 79). In addition, these reused planks had been pierced by many distinctive ship's treenails (Fig 115g) in which the heads were expanded by caulking.

PRELIMINARY CONCLUSIONS

Although the preceding sections have dealt only briefly with aspects of changing carpentry practice, some specific trends are apparent. It seems clear that the builders ('carpenters' seems too specialised a term here) of the Saxon waterfront structures invested a minimum of labour and skill in the building of what are now considered to be low-status structures. In marked contrast, the later medieval structures demonstrate a considerably greater investment of labour, logistical organisation, and skills, shown in the use of elaborate joinery and particularly in the use of sawn planks and timber.

However, it also becomes clear that during this same period there was a decline in timber quality, as defined in modern terms (*ie* long, knot-free lengths of large girth). This may be related to the greater contemporary importance placed on underwood, which was needed for the provision of fuel and fencing. This in turn led to the intensification of the classic *coppice-with-standards* woodland management system which became so common in lowland England after the Norman Conquest. It is possible that the short coppice rotations (3 to 12 years) apparently so typical of medieval managed woods would have encouraged even lower heavy branching in standard oaks than would be seen if longer coppice rotations (12+ years) were used. The large trees that were tall, straight-grained and suitable for cleaving into thin board (*board trees*) seem to have become less common, resulting in a market for imported cleft oak board or wainscot. However, the medieval working woods and other types of tree lands supplied London's need for most other types of wood and timber from an essentially renewable resource. Much of the timber used in London came downriver, having been gathered at Kingston, or upriver from Essex. However, there is documentary evidence for the carriage of timber, on royal request, from as far away as the Forest of Dean (Salzman 1952, 238).

All woodland belonged to somebody in the medieval period. Although there were customary *botes* or rights for tenants to take timber or wood, most of it was bought and sold as any other commodity (Rackham 1976, 83): as a consequence, the timber or wood on excavations must not be taken too readily as a sample of the *nearest* woodland, as its presence on site will have been as much governed by economic factors as is the occurrence of pottery or stone.

By the 17th century, with the development of European colonisation of the New World and expanding world markets, greater quantities and new species of timber began to be imported. This new supply came from the highly mechanised, New England merchants and from the regions of Scandinavia and the eastern Baltic where labour was cheap and timber plentiful. The sudden, enormous demand for timber for rebuilding London after the Great Fire of 1666 added impetus to the sea-borne supply of London with foreign timber. This is manifested in the use of softwood in waterfront carpentry of the post-medieval period. The destructive habit of laying waste the forest lands of foreign countries was begun by Britain in this period and now the focus of destructive exploitation for short-term gain has moved to the tropical forests of Africa and South America.

In England today, the majority of carpenters consider that timber comes from timber yards rather than grows on trees, since they no longer select trees in the wood: the link between the management of renewable local resources and woodworking has been lost. They require timber that is, firstly, foreign and, secondly, sawn down to size from large trees. Cost is all-important, and work is done with fast machine tools that depend on a huge industrial infrastructure to operate. Even 'traditional' heavy carpentry is rarely 'traditional' and it mirrors its age as accurately as mechanical engineering. Thus in 1990, substantial quantities of English oak growing on the edge of London cannot be sold for buildings, boats, or even fences, but only to make coarse paper or cardboard.

To conclude, some key areas for future work should be outlined. Many of the themes discussed in this pilot study would benefit from a consideration of a wider range of material from City and Greater London excavations. Many qualifications and greater precision may also become possible when the dendrochronological work has been completed on material from recent projects in London: it must be stressed that tree-ring studies have far more to offer the archaeologist than merely estimated felling dates, indispensible as they undoubtedly are. Local historical, paleo-environmental and field study of ancient woodland in the area could amplify some of the suggestions made about reconstructing local woodlands. Considerations of logistics and the transportation of timber and wood could usefully be expanded, as could the social and economic implications. Parallel studies of developments in other types of woodworking such as shipbuilding or cooperage and woodland crafts like hoop or hurdle-making will also broaden the view, as would a study of wood as fuel for medieval London.

7: LESSONS FROM THE LONDON WATERFRONT

Gustav Milne

This study has examined the development of medieval timber building techniques from three different angles, by considering the structure of the riverfront revetments, reused timbers incorporated in waterfront features, and evidence of changing carpentry and woodland management practice identifiable in timbers from both sources. The three authors of these separate studies did not reach complete agreement on all matters of interpretation, as the conclusions in each section show. Nevertheless, consensus was achieved in some major areas, and these, together with the principal disagreements, are summarised in advance of the concluding discussion.

1 Both the *stave* and the *earthfast* building techniques were not static traditions: both underwent major developments during the early medieval period.

2 A rich and varied selection of earthfast structures has been identified, representing a tradition which had all but disappeared by the 14th century.

3 Neither the saw nor the standard mortise and tenon joint were known before the Norman Conquest; nor were they in common use until over a century later. As such, they do not therefore represent features directly introduced by the Normans in the late 11th century.

4 Timber-framed buildings were not introduced suddenly into medieval London in a fully-formed state, but evolved in the 12th to early 13th centuries, and continued to develop thereafter. However, there is a measure of disagreement on the manner of that evolution. In Chapter 5 it is suggested that framing developed from the earthfast tradition, although in Chapter 4 a fusion of elements from both the earthfast and the stave techniques had been advocated. Brigham and Goodburn support the proposition that the impetus for the development of the new framing techniques should be sought in work on high-status structures, while Milne sees such a development as part of a more widely-based medieval ethic to improve the life and effectiveness of timber structures. Thus Brigham assumes that structural developments recorded in the riverfront revetments were pioneered elsewhere and subsequently relegated to the waterfront, whereas Milne suggests that such developments reflect contemporary, rather than archaic, practice. However, all agree that the techniques recorded on the waterfront reflect more general timber-building practice: the only point of contention is whether an 11th-century revetment incorporates 10th- or 11th-century building techniques. Either way, the wider relevance of the study of the riverside installations is clear.

5 The full implications of this work for the English woodscape are still under consideration: much more research needs to be done on establishing the changing coppice cycles and tree forms in the early, middle and late medieval period. What is clear is that profound change did take place, and that the woodscape in AD800 was not the same as that in 1100 or in 1400: the countryside changed as much as the townscape in this formative period.

Medieval vernacular buildings in London

It has already been argued that the London carpenters who erected the medieval revetments were familiar with whatever techniques of earthfast post, framed or stave building were currently used for dry-land buildings (Fig 116). As a consequence, examples of all three techniques are represented on the City waterfront. Of these three, the presence of forms of stave work in later medieval London is probably the least expected, although the accomplished examples found on the waterfront unequivocally demonstrate that the tradition was maintained. It has already been pointed out that stave work should not be considered simply as a Saxon technique, but had a wider chronological application (Milne & Milne 1978, 102; Meeson 1983, 29-30). Buildings with earthfast posts were common in London before the 13th century, and the techniques are represented both in the group of reused timbers from the Billingsgate Lorry Park

*116. Sunlight Wharf: late 13th-century riverfront revetment (*SUN86*; 886). Arrangement of vertical posts and diagonal braces reflects contemporary house-building techniques; scale 5 x 100mm.*

site and in the revetments themselves. Structures such as TX6 and TX7 provide a graphic impression of how elaborate this general class of building could be, and are of especial importance, since no comparable medieval buildings with earthfast posts survive above ground.

However, these three techniques did not exist in isolation. Just as on the waterfront stave work was incorporated into the milieu of frame building, front braces were used on both earthfast and framed revetments, and back braces on both framed and stave revetments, so, it is argued, a number of hybrid building designs would have developed on dry land. In other words, not only was there development *of* a technique, there would also have been development *between* the techniques. The result would have been the erection of buildings with elements of earthfast post construction combined with timber-framing (cf. TX4), such as the East Hall II at Cheddar (Rahtz 1979, 178-83, figs 63-4), or the strange admixture of stave-type timbers in a framed building as at Baguley Hall (Smith & Stell 1960). The development of stave work, initially set earthfast (*eg* TX2), then in baseplates but with earthfast posts at the corners (*eg* TL1) is well known (Herrnbrodt 1958, fig 78), and perfectly illustrates the process of transition between techniques. Other hybrid building forms have been identified by archaeologists, for example, the *primitive framed buildings* described by Guy Beresford (Beresford 1977, 227-8), while the *interrupted sill-beam technique* (Smith 1965, 153-6; fig 11) is another hybrid of the post-with-frame building.

To sum up, it is not always possible or even desirable 'to draw the clearest possible distinction between the three systems (post building, framing and stave-building)' as some have suggested (*eg* Charles 1982, 101): indeed, Cedar Park, an early 18th-century prefabricated framed building on earthfast posts, shows how artificial such otherwise convenient classifications can be (Hobley 1982, fig 24). It is argued here that there was a fusion of elements from the stave-building and earthfast-post building traditions in the 12th century, which led to the evolution of timber-framed building in the 13th century.

A direct result of this continuing development and hybridisation was the variety of forms observed on the waterfront. In the early 14th century, for example, front-braced, back-braced, stave and framed revetments all existed alongside masonry river walls. By comparison, the Pilgrim's Hall at Winchester, built in 1308, incorporated elements of timber-framing, crucks and a variety of roof trusses including hammer-beams (Crook 1991), while in the same period at Wintringham, Huntingtonshire, a small manorial site enclosed a base cruck Hall, a timber-framed kitchen, a building with its walls built on the ground surface, and one with earthfast foundations (Beresford 1977, 226). A similar range of 14th-century foundation forms have been recorded in York, for example (Addyman 1979). The pattern is repeated on rural sites, for a considerable number of medieval house types were noted in Worcestershire (Field 1965), Derbyshire and Lincolnshire (Beresford 1975). Such a blend of youth and experience must surely have been the hallmark of medieval London, with examples of many techniques existing side by side.

Study of the house timbers and revetments from the London waterfront has therefore shown that a rich variety of timber buildings were present in 11th, 12th and 13th-century London, and some of the techniques employed are illustrated in Fig 117. This clearly shows how earthfast buildings were succeeded by framed ones, how regular studding replaced the irregular, how the scantling of timbers

117. Timber buildings in medieval London: a-e) reconstructions of construction techniques based on study of 11th to 13th-century house timbers described in Chapter 5 (cf. Fig 94). Reconstructions of timber-framing based on study of changing building techniques represented by riverfront revetment construction: f) early 13th century: note overlapping baseplates and lapped braces; g) 14th century: note tenoned braces and jowled timbers at corner.

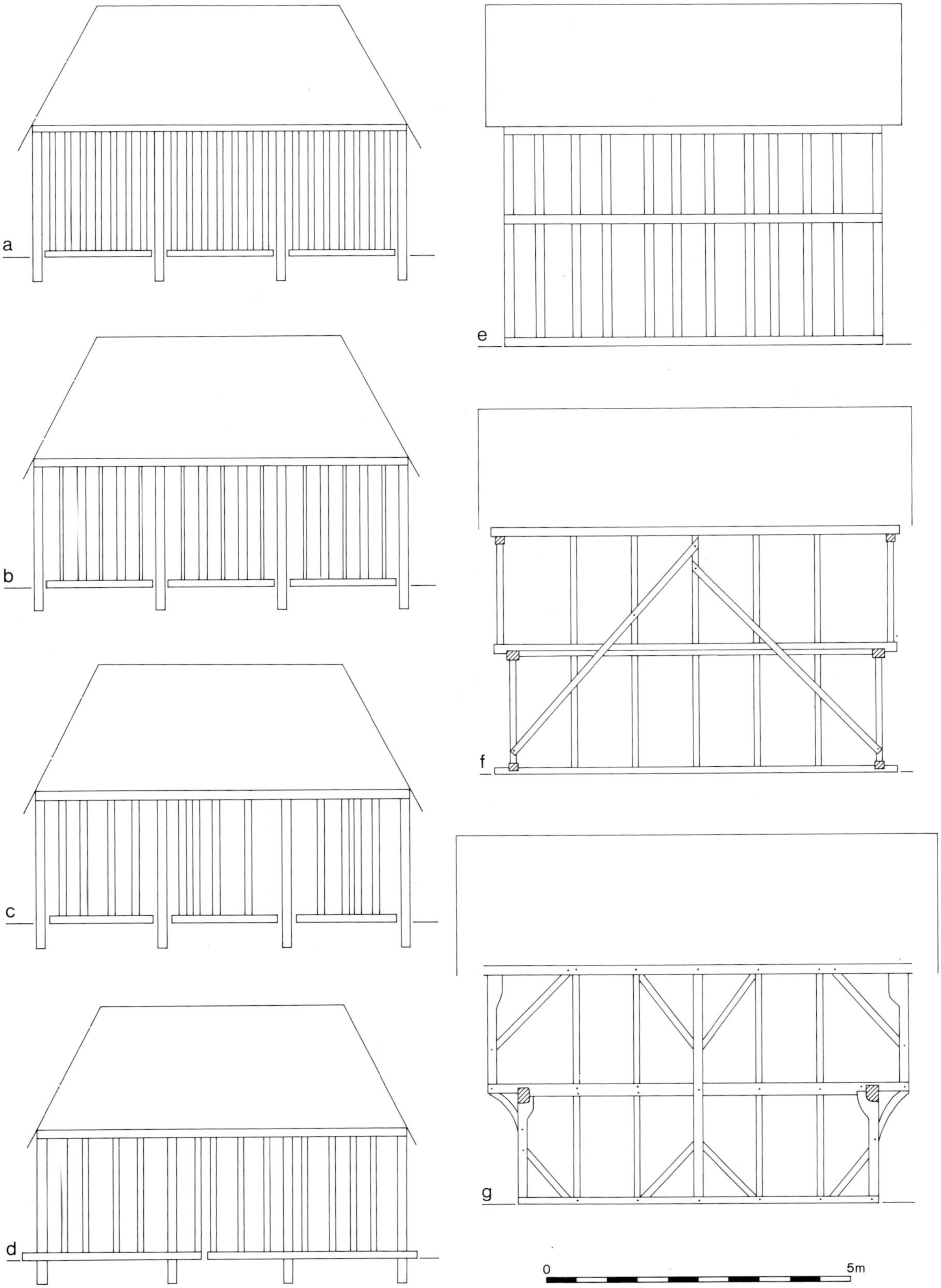

a
b
c
d
e
f
g
0
5m

became more uniform, how the use and shape of baseplates developed, how diagonal braces were initially applied, and subsequently became integral, to framed structures. It is even possible to show that several of the main posts in 12th-century structures tapered from bottom to top, since they were used the same way up as the trees from which they were cut had stood: by contrast, jowled corner posts such as that in the 14th-century TX11 revetment were used inverted, a feature of later medieval structures (cf. Fig 50 with Fig 78).

The possible incentives for such widespread innovations deserve some consideration. It has been suggested that a principal stimulation for the development of techniques in vernacular building came from the solving of problems in a different class of structure, such as the roofs of parish churches. In Chapter 5, Trevor Brigham presents detailed arguments to support the case that such innovations then percolated down to more mundane structures such as riverfront revetments. This type of 'trickle-down' theory is widely held: for example, Hewett argued that 'the technological development of carpentry, like that of other crafts, resulted from royal patronage of the finest craftsmen, and all that is debatable is the period of time necessary for their developments to become available to the majority of craftsmen' (Hewett 1980, 320). While it is clear that the king did employ the best craftsmen, there is little evidence that he trained them as well: perhaps it would be more accurate to suggest that once carpenters had demonstrated the order of their skill, then royal patronage might ensue. The earliest example of an edge-halved scarf with bridled abutments does not appear in the hammerbeam roof at Westminster, but on a revetment on the London waterfront (TL11). Nevertheless, it must be said that many of London's carpenters would have had the opportunity (not necessarily voluntarily) to work on major royal and ecclesiastical projects in the area, little of which now remain.

118. The early 13th-century transition from earthfast building to timber-framed structures on the Thames Exchange site, looking north-east. The 5 x 100mm scale rests against the earthfast TX4 *revetment, to the south of which part of a baseplate and braced trestle of the* TX5 *jetty can be seen. Although erected shortly after the revetment, it ultimately functioned with it.*

While it is clear that the lower orders did not have access to the same level of resources as the Church or the king, it does not necessarily follow that they lacked all innovatory skills as well: on the contrary, necessity, rather than lavish funding, is the mother of invention. Although a medieval manor-house must be sufficiently elegant to accommodate a lord, the contemporary long-house must be robust enough to house restless cows, a more testing structural propostion. Again, while little thought was expended on the aesthetics of the riverfront revetments, our study has demonstrated that constant consideration was given to their improvement, in the battle to withstand the daily scourging by the River Thames. Innovations were adopted and adapted wherever and however circumstances demanded: it was only the manner of the adoption which was dictated by the available resources. For example, the gradual changeover from earthfast to framed building was precisely the same on the waterfront (Fig 118) as it was on dry-land: no fully framed structure, regardless of 'status', has yet been found which can be shown to be significantly earlier than the first decades of the 13th century, the date for the earliest group of baseplated structures from the London waterfront (BG14, TX5, TX8, TL2, SH3), be they ever so humble.

It is suggested that the desire to improve the efficiency (*ie* the longevity) of the revetments, that led to the continual innovation on the London waterfront, was a manifestation of the same drive by medieval carpenters 'to elaborate to the limit of practicability structural principles of long-established reliability' (Hewett 1977, 295). London's buildings would have reflected this evolutionary situation.

Another form of stimulation would be the necessity of working with whatever timber was available: of especial interest in this respect is the common practice of reusing timber derived from dismantled buildings. The series of contracts published by Salzman (Salzman 1952, Appendix B) shows that the carpenters were often responsible for pulling down the old building and reusing as much of the old timber as possible either in the new building or in future work: 'He (the carpenter) is to have as much of the timber on the site as is not fit for reuse' (Salzman 1952, 418). It was therefore in the carpenter's best interest to dismantle old buildings carefully, which would have provided an opportunity to observe which joints and techniques had or had not failed, and how the trusses and frames had been put together. In this way, the work of an earlier generation of carpenters could have been scrutinised by a later one. This could have facilitated the development of successful attributes, and the avoidance of less desirable elements. This much is speculation: all that can be demonstrated is that the design of the London revetments grew from a desire to improve upon the structure being replaced, given the constraints of the site and available timber.

Timber-framing and the townscape

The study of the development of fully framed timber buildings in London is important for several reasons, quite apart from the intrinsic interest of the technological details. Such structures became a common and enduring feature of the medieval townscape after *c.*1200 and their widespread adoption changed the character of the City in many ways. Earthfast buildings needed to be replaced every generation or so, or at least substantially repaired and underpinned. Indeed, a recent study of some fifty Saxo-Norman timber buildings in London demonstrated that few had a life of longer than 15 to 25 years (Horsman *et al* 1988, 109). By contrast, the new timber frames, raised as they were on stone sills, lasted much longer, as the survival to this day of timber-framed buildings of 13th and 14th-century date in many parts of the country testifies.

This simple fact has a number of important implications, particularly with regard to property ownership and the development of the burgage plot. At the most basic level, before 1200 a timber building could not be seen as a long-term investment or as an item that could be inherited: after 1200, it could be. From that period onwards, the urban property was not just the plot itself, but also the timber building upon it. Such 'permanent' buildings might reflect this longevity further in the manner of their construction and in more ornate designs. If desired, resources could be lavished upon the structure, the real estate, in a way which might have seemed inappropriate previously. The movement away from earthfast construction also led to the introduction of durable vernacular housing in the countryside during the 13th century, and some of the varied implications of that crucial development have been considered in recent articles (*eg* Wrathmell 1984; Dyer 1986).

Another significant difference between framed and earthfast buildings is that the former could readily support two or three stories, and it seems that such structures were built in London shortly after the adoption of timber-framing. The second storey may well have been jettied beyond the wall line of the ground floor from the start: jetties were clearly common by 1244 when an order was made to amend all those which were considered a nuisance (Chew & Weinbaum 1970, 152). A jettied building uses a separate wall plate and baseplate for each storey, which overcomes the potential problem of weakening a wall plate by cutting joints for studs and joists in three of its four faces.

With multi-storey buildings, the number of people occupying a particular burgage plot could, if required, be doubled or trebled. The owner of a 'permanent' multi-storey building could therefore generate income by renting out rooms more conveniently than in the earthfast era. Quite apart from such financial considerations, this factor also directly affects estimates of the changing population of medieval London as a whole. To take a hypothetical example: the *area* of the town occupied in, say, 1150 and in 1250 may appear to be the same: it may even have contracted. Nevertheless, it need not be assumed the the population remained static or fell, for it could now be argued that, with the new-found facility to build upwards, the population could have expanded two- or even three-fold without encroaching upon new land within or without the City walls.

Timber-framing and the woodscape

As Damian Goodburn has shown, the change to timber-framed buildings would have been affected by, and would have continued to have an affect upon, the woodscape or the areas surrounding the town. A simple wattlework structure need only survive some ten years before the coppice cut to provide the wattles has regrown: such buildings, often disparagingly labelled as 'flimsy' by archaeologists (Beresford & Hurst 1971, 95-6), therefore represent an efficient use of a renewable resource. By contrast, a structure like the 1st-century Roman timber quay in London, which functioned for a mere 30 years, incorporated timbers up to 200 to 300 years old: although a spectacular example of civil engineering, it was therefore positively profligate in its inefficient use of timber (Milne 1985, 65-6). The dilemma facing a steadily increasing population of Saxon England was that, wattle-based structures and reused timbers aside, there was a limit to the number of earthfast buildings which could be built using substantial timbers (*c.*80 years old) if they had to be replaced before standards of a suitable size had grown up to replace them: the supply of timber would soon be limited to whatever remnants of the dwindling *wildwood* survived.

The development of mortar and stone sills in the pre-Conquest period represents serious attempts at prolonging the life of timber buildings in London, and therefore of making more effective use of the woodland resource. The development of the bipartite revetments on the Thames waterfront is another example, whereby the serviceable life of the structure was increased and the drain of the woodlands therefore decreased (cf. TL3 & TL11).

The introduction of 'permanent' timber-framed buildings is argued to be a natural extension of the same tradition, since these structures were designed to last longer than the oldest tree felled to build them: in other words, the native woodlands could be managed in cycles appropriate for the supply of the standards needed for framed buildings, but could not cope indefinitely with the greater demands imposed on them by the earthfast regime.

In any era in which timber is not imported on a significant scale, the nature of the timber buildings will directly reflect the contemporary woodscape. As a consequence, it has been possible to show that the native woodlands which supplied the material for London's Saxo-Norman buildings were different from those which provided for the timber-framed town. The precise details of the layout and spacing of standards in these woodlands need further research, and a number of important questions await answers.

It is known that provincial carpenters worked in medieval London, as is shown by such names as Reginald de Swaffham, Richard de Shropshire and John de Chelmsford. The different traditions and ideas they brought with them would have stimulated the development of timber-framed building in the City. However, cruck building never became a feature of medieval London's townscape (Alcock 1981). This cannot have been because the technique was unknown but may reflect the fact that the local woodlands were not managed to provide the appropriate raw material.

Taking a wider view, it seems that the dramatic development of timber building from *c.*1050 to 1250 reflects the major feature of the period, the rising population, which may well have doubled from the time of the Domesday survey to the early 14th century (Bolton 1980, 65). This is graphically demonstrated in three closely related ways by the material from London. To begin with, there is the disappearance of the *wildwood* trees towards the end of the period, representing the extent of *assarting* (the deliberate clearance of waste or woodland for new settlements, fields or pasture) at this time. More rigorous woodland management systems had then to be developed and extended, given that a much smaller woodland resource had to supply the fuel and building needs of a much larger population in 1250 than had existed just two centuries earlier. Evidence for such changes has been identified in the London material, with the use of younger trees for building timber and with the development of longer-lasting timber-framed buildings, for example.

Thirdly, the development of multi-storied buildings to house the rising population is evident from 1200 onwards. It is also worth mentioning that the majority of land won from the Thames during the medieval period had been reclaimed between 1000 and 1300, and is seen, in part at least, as another response to the land hunger of the expanding town (cf. Milne 1981), first expanding outwards, and then upwards.

A lost townscape rediscovered

In conclusion, it may be said that although London's timber buildings have long since been destroyed, their shadow lingers on the waterfront. The innovations and techniques evident in the riverfront revetments bear a pale but welcome witness to the wealth of timber building that once existed within the City.

Study of this evidence is argued to relate directly to the study of the lost medieval townscape, as Fig 117 tries to show. Here a sequence of timber buildings is presented, working from the superficially unpromising waterfront data to portray a selection of the types of structure which, our evidence implies, would have stood within the medieval town. That the London house developed dramatically throughout this period seems clear: for the first time, the variety and suggested form of those substantial modifications can now be presented for discussion and comment.

As a result of the work in London, significant changes in techniques, such as the change from earthfast to framed building, have been identified, recorded and dated. Since 1980, the Vernacular Architecture Group have published an annual list of dendro-dated buildings sampled from all parts of the country (*Vernac Architect*, 1980-90). To this work, the London waterfront catalogue can now be added, providing as it does, dendro-dated examples of sawn timbers, particular joints and early timber-framed structures. In addition, it provides a dated series of earthfast structures of comparable age to the Bishop's Palace, Hereford, which is one of the oldest standing medieval timber buildings in England dated by dendrochronology (Blair 1987; Haddon-Rees *et al* 1990, 46-7).

Had one of the 11th or 12th-century timber structures in London been discovered above ground, encased within the carcass of a Victorian office block, it would have been hailed as a unique survival, lovingly listed and carefully restored for future generations to admire. Unfortunately, the remarkable sequence of medieval timber structures described in this volume was all uncovered below ground where different laws apply: none were listed, and only a pitiful proportion of timbers were saved (at considerable cost): these are now on display in the Tower Hill Pageant museum, London. Since 1988, a representative selection of joints from recently-excavated timbers has been freeze-dried to form the nucleus of a timber reference library.

These exceptions aside, the majority of the London timberwork was and is ignominiously discarded, since the cost of conserving it for posterity far exceeds the not inconsiderable cost of its excavation. It is now represented solely by record sheets and photographs. This fact highlights the importance of a comprehensive and comprehensible recording system, for the further study of London's medieval building techniques must be based, not on an examination of the timbers themselves, but on the perusal of paperwork.

APPENDIX: MEDIEVAL WATERFRONT SITES ON THE THAMES

THAMES NORTH BANK (west to east)

All sites recorded by the Department of Urban Archaeology (DUA) unless indicated otherwise.

18-20 York Buildings 1988 (DGLA) TQ30368054
Supervisor: B Cowie

Part of a mid Saxon embankment, the earliest medieval waterfront structure recorded in London, was located in a small trench and observed elsewhere on this site. The brushwood and rubble embankment lay over the sandy foreshore, and incorporated oak and alder stakes, traces of wattlework and some vertically-set oak planks. The trees from which the planks were cut were probably felled *c*.AD 670 to 690, according to provisional dendrochronological analysis (Cowie & Whytehead 1989).

Old City of London Boys' School 1986-7 (BOY86) TQ31548092
Supervisor: C Spence

(See p. 76) The controlled excavations located a mid 14th-century masonry river wall built out onto the Thames foreshore, over 50m south of the previous frontage. Shortly after the Great Fire of 1666, a timber revetment (BY1) was erected to the south, marking a further advance of the waterfront, and incorporating some reused ships' timbers (Spence 1989, 28-9).

Bridewell/Tudor Street 1978 (BRI78 & TUD78) TQ315809
Supervisors: D Gadd; A Thompson

Following extensive excavation of the early 16th-century Bridewell Palace, a series of more limited observations were made of underlying and adjacent deposits to establish how and when the land at the confluence of the Fleet and the Thames was reclaimed. A 15th-century piled revetment incorporating boat planking was recorded to the west of the Fleet, as well as traces of a possible 14th-century piled revetment and later medieval masonry river walls.

Queen Victoria Street 1985 (QVS85) TQ31688091
Supervisor: K Steedman

Limited controlled excavation of a site on the east bank of the Fleet, at the confluence with the Thames exposed a section of late 13th or 14th-century medieval masonry river wall. This survived until the Great Fire of 1666, after which further reclamation took place.

Mermaid Theatre 1979 (THE79) TQ31828090
Supervisor: P Herbert

Baseplates of a mid 13th-century front and back-braced revetment were recorded (see Figs 85-7) representing the earliest reclamation on the riverfront in this area (Hillam & Herbert 1980).

Baynard's Castle 1972-81 (BC72; BC75; BYD81) TQ319808
Supervisors: P Marsden (Guildhall Museum); C Hill; J Burke-Easton

The main excavation priorities on this 200m x 100m site were the Roman riverside wall (Hill *et al* 1980) and the 15th-century masonry building known as Baynard's Castle (*Med Archaeol*, 1973, **17**, 162-4; Marsden 1981), which were examined over several years. In addition, observations were made of a series of medieval waterfront structures marking phases of riverside reclamation after the collapse of the Roman wall, but before the construction of Baynard's Castle (*Med Archaeol*, 1982, **26,** 192). There was no evidence for any major medieval waterfront development before the 13th century, and the structures incorporated examples of squared baseplates (Hill *et al* 1980, 46-7), stave work and scarf joints (see Figs 4e; 8b).

Sunlight Wharf 1986-7 (SUN86) TQ32138082
Supervisor: R Bluer

(See p. 64). An extensive watching brief investigated an area gradually reclaimed from the late 12th to the 15th century: a number of timber revetments were observed, together with waterfront buildings and other features (Hunting 1988; Spence 1989, 24-5).

Trig Lane 1974-6 (TL74) TQ32088086
Supervisors: G & C Milne

(See p. 64). Extensive controlled excavation of this 450 sq m site recorded a well-preserved series of timber and masonry structures erected during the piecemeal reclamation of the area from the mid 13th to the 15th century (Milne & Milne 1978; 1981; 1982).

Bull Wharf 1979; 1990 (BLL79; UPT90) TQ32408075
Supervisors: C Milne; J Ayre

Limited watching brief observations in 1979 demonstrated that the south part of the site was not reclaimed until the 13th century. Fragments of a front-braced revetment were recovered and a masonry river wall seen.

Major excavations to the north-east in 1991 exposed the substantially robbed 3rd-century Roman quay, the most westerly sighting of this feature in London. It was sealed by waterlaid deposits, over which were laid pre-Conquest embankments revetted with earthfast posts and piles incorporating reused ships' planking. There was evidence of subsequent inundations, and of further reclamation in the medieval period.

Vintry House 1988 (VRY88) TQ32398080
Supervisor: R Malt

A series of controlled sample excavations combined with an extensive watching brief revealed a complex pattern of reclamation dating from the Roman period to the 16th century.

Overlying the remains of the Roman quay were waterlaid deposits, suggesting a rapid rise in river level. Saxon wattle and clay embankments were replaced by a sequence of timber-revetted reclamation deposits which advanced the waterfront on either side of a major inlet. The reused material incorporated within the revetment structures (see Fig 119) included many boat and ship timbers as well as a post from a pre-Conquest aisled hall.

119. Revetments, boats and buildings exposed on the London waterfront on the Vintry site in 1991. Part of the southern face of an 11th-century revetment (VRY89 786) comprising earthfast posts driven deep into the foreshore with a cladding of reused boat timbers to the left, and a reused house timber, the top of a late 10th-century aisle post, to the right. The 5 x 100mm scale rests on an arbitary excavated level beneath the contemporary foreshore.

Thames Exchange 1988-90 (TEX88) TQ32458075
Supervisors: M Colquhoun, C & G Milne & J Stevenson

(See p. 42). Controlled excavation of a sample area 90m x 11m (less than a third of the whole site) combined with an extensive watching brief recorded a series of waterfront structures and buildings overlying the remains of the Roman quay. The earliest medieval reclamation was associated with Saxon piled revetments and embankments, after which a long series of structures including earthfast post and framed revetments was examined, of which the latest was probably 14th-century.

Dowgate 1959 (PCD59)
Supervisor: P Marsden (Guildhall Museum)

During the construction of the Public Cleansing Depot a waterfront embankment was observed. It comprised tree trunks and branches in grey silt or clay over a brushwood raft and was sealed by dumps containing 13th-century pottery revetted by a front-braced horizontally-planked revetment (Guildhall Museum Excavation Register, 6, 30-1; 51; Steedman *et al* forthcoming).

Cannon Street Station 1988 (UTA88) TQ32588075
Supervisor: R Bluer

Limited excavation of reclamation deposits and structures sealed beneath, and to the south of, foundations of the late 12th-century Hanseatic Guildhall (later the Steelyard) exposed Saxon embankments of clay, brushwood and rubble; a stave wall of possible 12th-century date; and also a late medieval masonry river wall 10m north of the present-day frontage (Spence & Grew 1990, 22-3).

Swan Lane 1981 (SWA81) TQ32738070
Supervisor: G Egan

A fragmented but extensive watching brief following controlled excavation of a sample area revealed a series of medieval timber revetments and masonry river walls. Reclamation had extended the line of the waterfront southwards from the robbed remains of the Roman quay in the 10th or 11th century and throughout the medieval period (Egan & Pritchard 1991, 9-10).

Seal House 1974 (SH74) TQ32778067
Supervisor: J Schofield

(See p. 37). Controlled excavation of a 40m-long trench was followed by a limited watching brief. The pattern of medieval reclamation from the 11th to the 15th century was plotted (Schofield 1975; Hobley & Schofield 1977).

New Fresh Wharf 1973-8 (NFW74; SM75; FRE78) TQ32958066
Supervisors: G Clewley; J Schofield; L Miller

A series of controlled excavations in 1973-4 and 1975-6 recorded remains of a 3rd-century Roman quay, sealed by waterlaid deposits. The earliest medieval waterfront embankment was of late 10th or early 11th-century date. The remains of a contemporary boat were found on the foreshore. The watching brief in 1978 recorded successive advances of the waterfront from the 12th century onwards (Miller 1977; Steedman *et al* forthcoming).

Billingsgate Lorry Park 1982-3 (BIG82) TQ33008065
Supervisor: S Roskams

(See p. 24). The 24 x 18m area examined under controlled conditions revealed a sequence of Saxon embankments overlying the remains of the Roman quay. Subsequent reclamation saw the waterfront advanced with the erection of timber revetments in the 12th and 13th centuries: reused ship and house timbers were also recovered. A series of well-preserved waterfront buildings including part of the church of St Botolph was recorded overlying the reclaimed land.

Observations made during the subsequent watching brief were of later medieval reclamation (Brigham 1990; Steedman *et al* forthcoming).

Custom House 1813-17 TQ33208062

During construction of the Custom House in the early 19th century, three distinct lines of wooden embankment and a river wall faced with Purbeck stone were observed (Laing 1818, 5-6).

Old Custom House site 1973 (CUS73) TQ33308055
Supervisor: T Tatton-Brown

On this 50m x 20m controlled excavation, the 2nd-century Roman quay was sealed by waterlaid deposits, over which no trace of Saxon embankments was found. The earliest reclamation deposits in this part of the waterfront were of 13th to 14th-century date. They were initially retained by an earthfast post revetment (Fig 82) which incorporated a substantial section of ship's timbers, and subsequently by a framed front-braced structure (Fig 83). Part of a jetty was also found, as were the foundations of the medieval and later Custom House. This work was published with exemplary speed (Tatton-Brown 1974; Tatton-Brown 1975).

THAMES SOUTH BANK (west to east)

All sites excavated by Department of Greater London Archaeology (DGLA) unless indicated otherwise.

Kingston Horsefair 1986-7 TQ178694
Supervisor: G Potter

Extensive excavations of an abutment and three piers of Kingston Bridge, constructed in the 1180s, also revealed a series of 14th to 15th-century piled revetments incorporating articulated slabs of ship and boat planking erected during reclamation of land adjacent to the Bridge (Goodburn 1988; Potter 1991).

245 Blackfriars Bridge Road 1987 TQ31688042
Supervisor: N Shepherd

A late 16th-century channel was recorded flowing north into the Thames. The west side was revetted with parts of a 16th or 17th-century boat, and the baseplates of a contemporary bridge survived in the base of the channel.

5-15 Bankside 1987 TQ32408040
Supervisor: J Bowsher

Flooded and reclaimed marshland with medieval drainage channels were recorded. A 14th-century riverfront revetment incorporating clinker-built planking from a boat was found beneath the chalk rubble which formed the base of the later 14th-century masonry river wall.

37-46 Bankside 1987 TQ32188051
Supervisor: P Thompson

A series of timber revetments was found, one of which incorporated parts of a 16th-century wheelbarrow.

Winchester Palace (Pickfords B Wharf) 1983-4 TQ32608041
Supervisor: D Seeley

As part of a major excavation programme designed to examine the Bishop of Winchester's mid 13th-century palace, areas of the associated Thames frontage were excavated. Three waterfront structures were found, of which the earliest had been extensively robbed, leaving the beech baseplates. The next phase was better preserved, incorporating substantial triangular back braces, dated by dendrochronology to *c*.1354 (cf. TL10; TL11: Figs 75; 77). This was superseded by a 15th to 16th-century masonry river wall (Yule 1989, 37-9).

Fennings Wharf 1984 TQ32818037
Supervisor: G Dennis

The landward abutment of the medieval London Bridge (1176-1209) was recorded during contractors' building works, surviving largely intact up to the level of the base of the arch vaulting, and was observed to a depth of *c*.8m. Dendrochronological samples taken from the foundations were derived from trees felled in 1185-7. Sealed beneath the foundations was a substantial oak box-work structure, which had been rebuilt three times. On its upstream side an inlet and ramp gave access to the river. The structure may represent part of the first medieval London Bridge (*Med Archaeol*, 1985, **29**, 178).

Toppings Wharf 1970-2 TQ32858035
Supervisor: H Sheldon (Southwark & Lambeth Archaeological Excavation Committee)

Controlled excavations and observations demonstrated that the bank of the Thames had been damaged by a major flood, presumably that recorded in October 1294. Subsequent development included an inlet with 14th and 15th-century timber features, with the remains of a possible jetty to the west (Sheldon 1974).

London Bridge City 1986-92 TQ332802
Supervisors: H Jones; J Hunter; A Thompson; R Bluer

Controlled excavations and observations in the Morgans Lane, Abbots Lane and Vine Street area examined parts of two moated enclosures on the south bank of the Thames. Substantial sections of the moat enclosing the house built for Sir John Fastolf in *c*.1443 were recorded. The earliest phase of revetting utilised wattle-work, while the later phases incorporated much reused timber, including parts of a clinker-built boat and a fragment of a late 13th-century 'Flanders chest'.

Parts of the Rosary, a moated house built for Edward II in *c*.1325, were also recorded, together with the remains of two timber-revetted inlets facing the Thames. These showed evidence of alterations and repair, and the earliest phase of one inlet was associated with pottery dated *c*.1280-1350. The most recent phase of excavations on this site revealed timber structures thought to represent part of a late medieval watermill.

Platform Wharf, Rotherhithe 1986-7 TQ 34807972
Supervisor: E Norton

Excavations between Rotherhithe Street and Cathay Street located the remains of a moated enclosure on the south bank of the Thames, thought to represent a mid 14th-century residence built for Edward III (Norton 1988).

BIBLIOGRAPHY

Addyman, P, 1979 Vernacular buildings below ground, *Archaeol J*, **136**, 69-75

Alcock, N, 1981 Cruck construction, CBA Res Rep, **42**

——, Barley, M, Dixon, P, & Meeson, R, 1989 *Recording timber-framed buildings: an illustrated glossary*, CBA Practical Handbook, **5**

Aldsworth, F, & Harris, R, 1988 The tower and Rhenish helm spire of St Mary's church, Sompting, *Sussex Archaeol Coll*, **126**, 105-44

Alford, B, & Baker, T, 1968 *The history of the carpenters company*

Baillie, M, 1982 *Tree-ring dating and archaeology*, London

Bans, J, & Gaillard-Bans, P, 1984 Continental roofs 1, *Vernac Architect*, **15**, 56-64

Beresford, G, 1975 *The medieval clayland village: excavations at Goltho and Barton Blount*, Soc Medieval Archaeol Monogr Ser, **6**

——, 1977 The excavation of a moated house at Wintringham, Hunts, *Archaeol J*, **134**, 194-286

——, 1982 The reconstruction of some Saxon buildings at Goltho, Lincs, in Drury 1982, 113-23

——, 1987 *Goltho: the development of an early medieval manor 850-1150*, English Heritage Archaeol Rep, **4**

Beresford, M, & Hurst, J, 1971 *Deserted medieval villages*, London

Biddle, M, Hudson, D, & Heighway, C, 1973 *The future of London's past*, Worcester

Blair, W J, 1987 The 12th-century Bishop's Palace at Hereford, *Med Archaeol*, **31**, 59-72

Bolton, J, 1980 *The medieval English economy 1150-1500*, London

Bramwell, M, 1976 *International book of wood*, London

Brett, D, 1978 Dendrochronological analysis, in Milne & Milne 1978, 98-101

——, 1982 Dendrochronology and carbon 14 dating, in Milne & Milne 1982, 74-83

Brigham, T, 1990 The late Roman waterfront in London *Britannia*, **21**, 99-183

Brown, F, 1976 Aisled timber barns in east Kent, *Vernac Architect*, **7**, 36-40

Brunskill, R, 1971 *Illustrated handbook of vernacular architecture*, London

Carr-Laughton, L, 1957 Clove-board, *Mariners Mirror*, **43**, 247-9

Carver, M, 1979 Three Saxo-Norman tenements in Durham City, *Med Archaeol*, **23**, 1-80

Chapelot, J, & Fossier, R, 1985 *The village and house in the middle ages*

Charles, F, 1974 Scotches, levers, sockets and rafter holes, *Vernac Architect*, **5**, 21-4

——, 1982 The construction of buildings with irregularly spaced posts, in Drury 1982, 101-12

Chew, H, & Weinbaum, M, 1970 *The London Eyre of 1244*, London Record Society, **6**

Christie, H, Olsen, O, & Taylor, H, 1979 The wooden church of St Andrews at Greensted, Essex, *Antiq J*, **59**, 92-112

Clark, J, 1984 Richard Crips the wheeler: a medieval craftsman and his tools, *Tools & Trades J*, **2**, 13-29

Coles, J, Coles, B, & Dobson, M, (eds) 1990 *Waterlogged wood*, WARP Occ Pap, **3**

——, & Goodburn, D, (eds) 1991 *Wet site excavation and survey*, WARP Occ Pap, **5**

Cowgill, J, de Neergaard, M, & Griffiths, N, 1987 *Medieval finds from excavations in London: 1 knives and scabbards*

Cowie, R, & Whytehead, R, 1989 Lundenwic: the archaeological evidence for middle Saxon London, *Antiquity*, **63**, 706-18

Cowie, R, 1989 *An archaeological excavation at 18-20 York Buildings* (YKB88), unpublished archive report for the Dept Greater London Archaeology

Crook, J, 1991 Pilgrims Hall, Winchester, *Archaeologia*, **109**, 129-59

Crumlin-Pedersen, O, 1970 The Viking ships of Roskilde, in *Aspects of wooden shipbuilding*, National Maritime Museum Monogr Ser, **1**, 7-23

——, 1986 Aspects of Viking-age shipbuilding, *J Danish Archaeol*, **5**, 209-28

Currie, C, 1972 Scarf joints in north Berkshire and Oxfordshire area, *Oxoniensia*, **37**, 177-86

——, 1990, Gazetter of archaic roofs in Herefordshire & Worcestershire churches, *Vernac Architecture*, **21**, 18-23

Darrah, R, 1982 Working unseasoned oak, in McGrail 1982, 219-29

Drury, P, (ed), 1982 *Structural reconstruction: approaches to the interpretation of the excavated remains of buildings*, BAR, **111**

Dyer, C, 1986 English peasant buildings in the later middle ages, *Med Archaeol* **30**, 19-45

Dyson, T, 1981 The terms quay and wharf, and the early medieval London waterfront, in Milne & Hobley 1981, 37-8
——, 1987 Early harbour regulations in London, in Herteig (ed) 1987, 19-24
——, 1989 *Documents and archaeology: the London waterfront,* MOL

Edlin, H, 1949 *Woodland crafts in Britain*
——, 1975 *The Observer book of trees*
Egan, G, & Pritchard, F, 1991 *Medieval finds from excavations in London: 3, dress accessories* c.*1150*-c.*1450*

Fenwick, V, 1978 *The Graveney boat,* BAR, **53**
Field, R, 1965 Worcestershire peasant buildings, household goods and farming equipment in the later middle ages, *Med Archaeol,* **9**, 105-45
Fletcher, J (ed), 1978 *Dendrochronology in Europe,* BAR Int Ser, **51**

Garmonsway, G (ed), 1972 *Anglo-Saxon chronicle,* revised edn, London
Good, G, Jones, R, & Ponsford, M, (eds) 1991 *Waterfront archaeology: proceedings of the third international conference, Bristol, 1988,* CBA Res Rep, **74**
Goodall, I, 1981 The medieval blacksmith and his products, in D Crossley (ed) 1981, *Medieval Industry,* CBA Res Rep, **40**, 51-62
Goodburn, D, 1988 Recent finds of ancient boats from London, *London Archaeol,* **5**.16, 423-8
——, 1990a Recording and processing ancient timbers in the DUA, Museum of London, in Hoffman 1990, 67-77
——, 1990b Some unfamiliar aspects of early woodworking revealed by recent excavations, in Hoffman 1990, 143-58
——, 1991 Waterlogged wood and timber as archives of ancient landscapes, in Coles & Goodburn 1991, 51-3
——, & Redknap, M, 1988 Replicas and wrecks from the Thames area, *London Archaeol,* **6**.1, 7-10; 19-22
Green, M, 1976 Excavations of the Palace defences and Abbey precinct at Abingdon Street, Westminster 1963, *J Brit Archaeol Ass,* **129**, 59-76
Grew, F, & de Neergaard, M, 1988 *Medieval finds from excavations in London: 2, shoes and pattens*
Grimes, W, 1968 *The excavation of Roman and medieval London,* London

Haddon-Reece, D, Miles, D H & Munby, J, 1989, List 32: tree-ring dates from the AM Lab, HBMC, *Vernac Architect,* **20**, 46-9
Hall, R, 1982 10th-century woodworking in Coppergate, York, in McGrail 1982, 231-44
——, 1984 A late pre-Conquest urban building tradititon, in P Addyman & V Black (eds), *Archaeological papers from York presented to M W Barley,* 71-7
Harris, E, 1973 Bergen, Bryggen 1972: The evolution of a harbour front, *World Archaeology,* **5**.1, 61-73
Harris, R, 1978 *Discovering timber-framed buildings,* Aylesbury
Harrison, M, 1975 Trig Lane, *Current Archaeol,* **49**, 57-9
Harvey, J, 1975 *Medieval craftsmen*
——, 1987 *English medieval architects: a biographical dictionary down to 1550*
Haslam, J, 1972 Medieval streets in London, *London Archaeol,* **2**.1, 3-7
Hauglid, R, 1976 *Norske Stravkirker: Bygningshistorick Bakgrunn og Utvikling,* Oslo
Heighway, C, Garrod, A, & Vince, A, 1979 Excavations at 1 Westgate Street, Gloucester, *Med Archaeol,* **23**, 159-213
Herrnbrodt, A, 1958 *Der Husterknupp, eine Niederheinische Burlange des Frühen Mittelalters,* Köln
Herteig, A, 1975 The excavation of Bryggen, Bergen, Norway, in R Bruce-Mitford (ed) 1975, *Recent exacavtions in Europe,* 65-89
——, 1981 The medieval harbour of Bergen, in Milne & Hobley 1981, 80-7
——, (ed), 1987, *Proceedings of the 2nd international conference on waterfront archaeology in north European towns,* Bergen
Hewett, C, 1973 The notched lap-joint in England, *Vernac Architect,* **4**, 18-21
——, 1977 Scarf jointing during the later 13th and 14th centuries, *Archaeol J,* **134**, 287-96
——, 1980 *English historic carpentry,* London & Chichester
Hill, C, Millett, M & Blagg, T, 1980 *The Roman riverside wall and monumental arch in London,* London Middlesex Archaeol Soc Special Paper, **3**
Hillam, J, 1987 Problems of dating and interpreting results from archaeological timbers, in R Ward (ed), *Applications of tree-ring studies,* BAR Int Ser, **333**, 141-55
——, forthcoming in Steedman *et al* forthcoming
——, & Herbert, P, 1980 Tree-ring dating: the Mermaid Theatre, London, *London Archaeol,* **3**.16, 439-44
Hobley, B, 1982 Roman military structures at the Lunt Roman fort, in Drury 1982, 223-74
——, & Schofield, J, 1977 Excavations in the City of London, first interim report, 1974-5, *Antiq J,* **57**, 31-66
Hoffman, P (ed), 1990 *Proceedings of the 4th* ICOM *group on wet organic archaeological materials conference,* Bremerhaven
Holdsworth, P, 1980 *Excavations at Melbourne St, Southampton, 1971-6,* CBA Res Rep, **33**
Horsman, V, Milne, C, & Milne, G, 1988 *Aspects of Saxo-Norman London 1: building and street development,* London Middlesex Archaeol Soc Special Paper, **11**
Huggins, P, 1976 The excavation of an 11th-century Viking hall and 14th-century rooms at Waltham Abbey, Essex, 1969-71, *Med Archaeol,* **20**, 75-133
Hunting, P, 1988 *St Pauls Vista,* London
Hutton, B, 1981 Some Yorkshire scarf-joints, *Vernac Architect,* **12**, 30-7

James, S, Marshall, A, & Millett, M, 1984 An early medieval building tradition, *Archaeol J,* **141**, 182-215

Laing, D, 1818 *The New Custom House,* London

Long, C, 1975 Excavations in the medieval city of Trondheim, *Med Archaeol*, **19**, 1-32

Marsden, P, 1979 The medieval ships of London, in McGrail 1979, 83-91
——, 1981 Shipping and the waterfronts of London, in Milne & Hobley 1981, 10-16
McGowan, K, 1987 Saxon timber structures from the Barking Abbey excavations 1985-6, *Essex Archaeology*, **22**.2, 35-8
McGrail, S (ed), 1979 *Medieval ships and harbours in northern Europe*, BAR int ser, **66**
——, (ed), 1982 *Woodworking techniques before* AD *1500*, BAR int ser, **129**
——, (ed), 1990 *Maritime Celts, Frisians and Saxons*, CBA Res Rep, **71**
McIntosh, M K, 1986 *Automomy and community: the royal manor of Havering 1200-1500*
Meeson, B, 1983 Plank-walled building technique and the church of St Lawrence, Rushton Spencer, *Vernacular Architect*, **14**, 29-35
Miller, L, 1977 New Fresh Wharf: 2, the Saxon and early medieval waterfronts, *London Archaeol*, **3**.2, 47-53
Millett, M, 1983 Excavations at Cowdreys Down, Basingstoke, Hants 1978-81, *Archaeol J*, **140**, 151-279
Milne, G, 1979 Medieval riverfront revetment construction in London, in McGrail 1979, 145-53
——, 1981 Medieval riverfront reclamation in London, in Milne & Hobley 1981, 32-6
——, 1985 *The Port of Roman London*, London
——, 1990 Recording, sampling and conservation of structural wood: an urban archaeologist's view, in Coles *et al*, 1990, 6-8
——, Battarbee, R, Straker, V, & Yule, B, 1983 The London Thames in the mid-1st century, *Trans London Middlesex Archaeol Soc*, **34**, 19-23
——, & Goodburn, D, 1990 The early medieval port of London, AD700-1200, *Antiquity*, **64**, 629-36
——, & Hobley, B (eds), 1981 *Waterfront archaeology in Britain and northern Europe*, CBA Res Rep, **41**
——, & Milne, C, 1978 Excavations on the Thames waterfront at Trig Lane, London, *Med Archaeol*, **22**, 84-104
——, & ——, 1979 The making of the London waterfront, *Current Archaeol*, **66**, 198-204
——, & ——, 1981 Medieval buildings at Trig Lane, *London Archaeol*, **4**.2, 31-7
——, & ——, 1982 *Medieval waterfront development at Trig Lane, London*, London Middlesex Archaeol Soc Special Paper **5**
MOL 1980 *Archaeological Site Manual*, Museum of London
MOL 1990 *Archaeological Site Manual*, Museum of London
Morgan, R, & Schofield, J, 1978 Tree rings and the archaeology of the Thames waterfront in the City of London, in Fletcher 1978, 223-38
Morris, C, 1979 Wooden objects, in Heighway *et al* 1979, 197-200
Munby, J, 1988 Wood, in J Blair & N Ramsay (eds), *English medieval industries*, London, 379-405
Murray, H, 1981 Houses and other structures from the Dublin excavations 1962-76: a summary, *Proc Eighth Viking Congress*, Odense University Press, 57-68
——, 1983 *Viking buildings in Dublin*, BAR, **119**
Murray, J, 1982 *Excavations in the medieval burgh of Aberdeen, 1973-84*, Waverley

Oswald, O, 1962-3 Excavation of a 13th-century wooden building at Weoley Castle, Birmingham, *Med Archaeol*, **6-7**, 109-34

Perlin, J, 1989 *A forest journey: the role of wood in the development of civilisation*, New York
Platt, C, & Coleman-Smith, R, 1975 *Excavations in medieval Southampton*, Leicester
Potter, G, 1991 The medieval bridge and waterfront at Kingston-upon-Thames, in Good *et al* 1991, 137-49

Rackham, O , 1972 Grundle House: the question of timber in certain East Anglian buildings in relation to local supplies, *Vernac Architect*, **3**, 3-8
——, 1976 *Trees and woodland in the British landscape*, London
——, 1980 *Ancient woodlands*, London
——, forthcoming, Trees and woodland in the Saxon period: the documentary sources, in *Anglo-Saxon Environment and Economy*, CBA Res Rep
——, Blair, W, & Munby, J, 1978 The 13th-century roofs and floor of the Blackfriars Priory at Gloucester, *Med Archaeol*, **22**, 105-22
Rahtz, P, 1979 *The Saxon and medieval palaces at Cheddar*, BAR, **65**
——, & Sheridan, K, 1972 Fifth report of excavations at Tamworth, Staffs, 1971. A Saxon watermill in Bolebridge Street, *Trans South Staffordshire Archaeol Soc*, **13**, 9-16
Reimers, E, 1982 *Einige Mittelalterliche Hauskonstruckionen in Bergen*, Bryggens Museum
Rhodes, M, 1982 The finds, in Milne & Milne 1982, 84-92
Rigold, S, 1975 Structural aspects of medieval timber bridges, *Med Archaeol*, **19**, 48-91

Salzman, L, 1952 *Building in England down to 1540*, Oxford
Schweingrüber, F, 1988 *Tree rings*, Dordrecht
Schofield, J, 1975 Seal House, *Current Archaeol*, **49**, 53-7
——, 1981 Medieval waterfront buildings in the City of London, in Milne & Hobley 1981, 24-31
——, 1984 *The building of London from the Conquest to the Great Fire*, London
——, 1987 *The London surveys of Ralph Treswell*, London Topographical Soc, **135**
——, 1991 Construction of medieval and Tudor houses in London, *Construction History*, **7**, 3-28

Sheldon, H, 1974 Excavations at Toppings and Sun Wharves, Southwark, *Trans London Middlesex Archaeol Soc,* **25**, 1-116
Smith, J T, 1965 Timber-framed building in England, *Archaeol J,* **122**, 133-58
——, 1970 The evolution of the English peasant house to the late 17th century: the evidence of buildings, *J Brit Archaeol Ass,* **33**, 122-47
——, & Stell, C, 1960 Baguley Hall: the survival of pre-conquest building traditions in the 14th century, *Antiq J,* **40**, 131-51
Spence, C, (ed) 1989 *Digging in the City: the annual review 1988,* Museum of London
——, & Grew, F, (eds) 1990 *The annual review 1989,* Museum of London
Spencer, B, 1982 Pilgrim souvenirs and kindred objects, in Milne & Milne 1982, 106-8
Steedman, K, Dyson, T, & Schofield, J, forthcoming, *Aspects of Saxo-Norman London, 3: waterfront development around the bridgehead and Billingsgate to 1200,* London Middlesex Archaeol Soc Special Paper, **14**
Sturdy, D, & Munby, J, 1985 Domestic sites in Oxford: excavations in Cornmarket and Queen Street, Oxford, 1959-62, *Oxoniensia,* **50**, 47-94

Tatton-Brown, T, 1974 Excavations at the Custom House, London, 1973, *Trans London Middlesex Archaeol Soc,* **25**, 117-219
——, 1975 Excavations at the Custom House Site, London, 1973; Part 2, *Trans London Middlesex Archaeol Soc,* **26**, 103-70
Thompson, F (ed), 1980 *Archaeology and coastal change,* Soc Antiq Occ Pap, **1**
Tooley, M, 1990 Sea-level and coastal changes during the last 5,000 years, in McGrail, 1990, 1-16
Tyers, I, 1985 Tree-ring dating by x-ray scanner, *London Archaeol,* 5.4, 87-9
——, 1990 List 37: tree-ring dates from the Museum of London, *Vernac Architect,* **21**, 45-6

Underhill, R, 1986 *Woodwrights workbook,* Chapel Hill, USA

Vince, A, 1985 The Saxon and medieval pottery of London: a review, *Med Archaeol,* **29**, 25-93
——, 1990 *Saxon London: an archaeological investigation*

Wacher, J, 1975 Bargate Street, in Platt & Coleman-Smith (eds) 1975, 149-161
Wallace, P, 1981 Dublin's waterfront at Wood Quay, 900-1317, in Milne & Hobley 1981, 109-18
——, 1982 Carpentry in Ireland, AD 900-1300: the Wood Quay evidence, in McGrail 1982, 263-99
Welch, C, 1912 *The boke of the ordinances of the Brotherhood of Carpenters of London,* London
Wheeler, R, 1927 *London and the Vikings,* London Museum Catalogue, **1**
Woodward-Smith, N, & Schofield, J, 1977 A late 15th-century account for a wharf at Vauxhall, London, *Trans London Middlesex Archaeol Soc,* **28**, 278-91
Wrathmell, S, 1984 The vernacular threshold of northern peasant houses, *Vernac Architect,* **15**, 29-33

Yule, B, 1989 Excavations at Winchester Palace, Southwark, *London Archaeol,* **6**.2, 31-9

Unpublished Archive Reports

(these may be consulted in the Museum of London by written request)

BOY86: *Old City of London Boys' School site, Whitefriars*
Site report by C Spence
Timber report by D Goodburn (1990)

BIG82: *Billingsgate Market Lorry Park*
Periods IV *to* XII by T Brigham with S Roskams
Dendrochronology reports by J Hillam & C Groves (1985) and by J Hillam (1988a; 1988b; 1990)

SH74: *Seal House*
Site report by J Schofield
Dendrochronology report by R Morgan revised by J Hillam

SUN86: *Sunlight Wharf*
Site report by R Bluer
Provisional dendrochronology report by I Tyers

TEX88: *Thames Exchange*
Site report by M Colquhoun & J Stevenson
Provisional dendrochronology report by N Nayling (1991)

TL74: *Trig Lane*
Site report by G & C Milne
Dendrochronology report by D Brett & C Harding (1977)
Revised dendrochronology report by I Tyers (1991)

ACKNOWLEDGEMENTS

This report, building as it does on the results of a series of excavations conducted over almost two decades as well as on the work of Trevor Brigham, Damian Goodburn and Chrissie Milne, incorporates the field work, research and advice of too many individuals to mention all by name. However, the study could not have begun without the hard work of the field teams who excavated and recorded the waterfront structures considered here, in conditions that were always damp, usually difficult, and often dangerous. It is to them that this report is dedicated, especially those who were regrettably made redundant during the reorganisation required by the recession and the needs of the new Museum of London Archaeological Service.

The work of the professional archaeological teams was greatly assisted on several of the projects by volunteer support, especially from the enthusiastic City of London Archaeological Society.

The catalogue on which much of the study was based was prepared from the field records and archive material from sites supervised by, among others, Richard Bluer, Morag Colquhoun, Steve Roskams, John Schofield, Craig Spence, Jo Stevenson and Kieron Tyler. Additional assistance was given by many colleagues, including Bob Cowie, Geoff Egan, Dick Malt and Gary Richards.

Francis Grew and Tony Dyson made many useful suggestions as to the improvement of this report, as did Dr Julian Munby to whom especial acknowledgement is made for his wise and detailed comments. Our studies were additionally informed and inspired by the work of Cecil Hewett, Oliver Rackham and many more whose own research is cited in the bibliography. However, the responsibility for errors and misinterpretations in this report remains that of the authors.

The majority of the drawings were prepared for publication by Tracy Wellman from material supplied by the authors, and most of the photographs were taken by the Department of Urban Archaeology's photographic team, of whom Jon Bailey, Maggie Cox, Trevor Hurst and Jan Scrivener deserve special mention. Other photos were by Valerie Fenwick (Figs 98, 99), David Harrison (Fig 73) and Chrissie Milne (Figs 42, 113). The dendrochronological report was compiled by Nigel Nayling and Ian Tyers, who also prepared Figs 9, 11, 28, 39, 63, 66. The translations of the summary into French and German were kindly undertaken by Agnes Shepherd and Frederike Hammer.

The excavations summarised in the catalogue were funded by several organisations. These include, in alphabetical order, the City of London Archaeological Trust, Corporation of the City of London, Department of Environment (now English Heritage), Kumagai Gumi UK Ltd, Manpower Services Commission, Morgan Guaranty Trust Co and LEP Group Plc. However, this study could not have been completed without the financial support of the English Heritage publication programme overseen by Gill Andrews and Roger Thomas.

SUMMARIES IN FRENCH AND GERMAN

Résumé

L'endiguement de la Tamise pendant l'époque saxonne tardive et l'édification de digues se succédant, l'une devant l'autre jusqu'à l'époque médiévale, produisirent une succession de poutres de revêtement, parmi lesquels vingt-cinq exemples minutieusement datés sont décrits dans ce rapport. Ceux ci s'échelonnent entre le dixième et le quatorzième siècle et furent sélectionnés parmi les digues fouillées sur quatre sites: Billingsgate Lorry Park (1982-3), Seal House (1974), Trig Lane/Sunlight Wharf (1974-6/1986/7) and Thames Exchange (1988-9). Un revêtement datant de la fin du dix-septième siècle provenant du site à 'City of London Boys' School' (1986/7) fut aussi inclu. Cette étude examine ces édifices tout d'abord en temps qu'exemples de pratique de construction en bois plutôt qu'en temps que digues. Bien que toutes ces constructions furent conçues pour arriver aux même fins: c'est à dire revêtir et protéger la berge, on remarquera des différences importantes entre les techniques de construction des échantillons les plus anciens et les techniques utilisées avec les tardifs. On peut noter alors, que ces différences reflètent en général, les changements à tous les niveaux des coutumes de menuiserie du pays; comme par exemple le passage de bâtiments construient à partir de pieux enfoncés en terre aux bâtiments construient à partir de charpentes de bois et de poutres de soubassement.

Les deux premiers chapitres donnent des renseignements d'introduction sur les sites mentionnés, les recherches précédentes, les conventions utilisées et comprend un glossaire illustré ainsi qu'une discussion de l'étude dendrochronologique sur laquelle la datation utilisée dans le rapport fut principalement basée. Le catalogue illustré des vingt-cinq constructions en bois formant les digues représentent le chapitre 3, et la discussion est dans le chapitre 4: ces parties de l'étude sont principalement le travail de Gustav Milne.

Ces conclusions peuvent être comparées dans le chapitre 5, avec les recherches faites par Trevor Brigham, sur les poutres en bois provenant à l'origine de bâtiments médiévaux édifiés dans la Cité de Londres. Un grand nombre de ces poutres furent identifiées comme étant réutilisées dans la construction des digues trouvées sur la fouille de 'Billingsgate Lorry Park'. Une fois de plus, l'attention est portée sur le développement des bâtiments à charpente de bois pendant l'époque médiévale, mais cette fois à travers l'examination des poutres de soubassement subsistantes et en particulier le changement de type de mortaises.

Dans le chapitre 6, Damian Goodburn approche l'étude des changements de bâtiments médiévaux en bois différemment, en observant les changements de pratique de menuiserie, d'outils, et d'exploitation de terrain boisé. Ces changements furent démontrés à partir de l'étude de poutre en bois récemment trouvés sur des fouilles archéologiques des bords de la Tamise. Une tentative fut faite de reconstituer le changement d'exploitation de pays boisés médiévaux, avec l'appui d'illustrations représentant les types d'arbres et les morceaux de bois d'oeuvre qu'ils contiennent en utilisant les morceaux de bois trouvés sur les sites situés au bord de la Tamise.

En conclusion, les idées avancées dans les chapitres précédents sont réunies et une estimation des traditions de construction et des types de bâtiments en bois qui, d'après nos recherches, auraient été présents dans la cité médiévale de Londres.

Zusammenfassung

Die Uferbefestigungen der Themse in später Sachsenzeit und deren Ausbau während des gesamten Mittelalters brachte eine Reihe von Holzkonstruktionen mit sich. In diesem Bericht werden 25 eng datierte Beispiele beschrieben. Sie reichen vom 10. bis ins 14. Jahrhundert und stammen von vier Ausgrabungsstätten (Billingsgate Lorry

Park 1982-3, Seal House 1974, Trig Lane/ Sunlight Wharf 1974-6 & 1986-7 und Thames Exchange 1988-9). Zusätzlich wurde noch ein fünftes Beispiel aus dem späten 17. Jahrhundert herangezogen (City of London Boys' School 1986-7). Dieser Bericht konzentriert sich in erster Linie auf die handwerkliche Praxis und nicht so sehr auf die Aspekte einer Uferbefestigung. Obgleich alle Baumaßnahmen demselben Ziel dienten, nämlich das Ufer auszubauen und zu schützen, unterschieden sich die in früherer Zeit verwendeten Techniken deutlich von den späteren. Dieser Bericht vertritt die Auffaßung, daß die Unterschiede die weitreichenden Veränderungen in Praxis und Technik der heimischen Zimmerleute widerspiegeln. Das gilt besonders für den Wandel von der Erdbefestigungs- zur Holzrahmen-Bauweise.

Die ersten beiden Kapitel beschreiben den Hintergrund des Projektes, liefern ein illustriertes Spezialwörterbuch und eine Erleutergung der dendrochronologischen Untersuchungen, auf denen ein gut Teil der Datierung basiert. Kapitel 3 enthält einen illustrierten Katalog der 25 Uferbefestigungen, die dann in Kapitel 4 diskutiert werden. Diese Kapitel beruhen im wesentlichen auf der Arbeit von Gustav Milne.

Kapitel 5 gibt Gelegenheit, die in Kapitel 4 gezogenen Schlüsse mit der Untersuchung von Trevor Brigham zu vergleichen, der sich mit mittelalterlichen Holzgebäuden in der City befasst. Ein grosser Teil solcher Hölzer wurde in der Uferbefestigung wiederverwendet, die unter dem Billingsgate Parkplatz ausgegraben wurde. Auch in dieser Studie liegt das Hauptaugenmerk auf der Entwicklung handwerklicher Praxis bei der Errichtung mittelalterlicher Fachwerkbauten, nur daß hier zur Untersuchung Fundamentbohlen und die sich ändernden Formen von Nut and Zapfen im Vordergrund stehen.

In Kapitel 6 verwendet Damian Goodburn einen anderen Ansatz bei der Untersuchung mittelalterliche Holzgebäude, indem er Veränderungen in der Holzbearbeitung, der Werkzeuge und der Holzbewirtschaftung mit in Betracht zieht. Die Ergebnisse beruhen auf der Untersuchung einer Auswahl von Hölzern, die jüngst bei den Ausgrabungen von Uferbefestigungen zu Tagen kamen. Mit Hilfe von Zeichnungen der verwendeten Baumarten des Bauholzes wird hier versucht, den Wandel der mittelalterlichen Waldlandschaft aufzuzeigen.

Dem Material der vorherigen Kapitel folgt eine Zusammenfassung aus heutiger Sicht, welche Bautraditionen und Holzbautypen wohl im mittelalterlichen London vorhanden waren.

INDEX

In this index, page numbers are shown in arabic numerals, while references to illustrations are in italics. The index may be used in conjunction with the table in Fig 120, which shows which structural attributes were present in each of the structures described in the catalogue in Chapter 3.

	C10th	C11th		C12th			late C12th					
POSTS	TX1	BG3	TX2	BG10	SH1	TX3	BG12	BG13	SH2	TX4	TX7	TL1
set earthfast *	*	.	.	.	.	.	?	?	*	*	*	.
set in baseplate ■	.	.	.	.	.	.	.	.	.	.	.	.
roundwood *	*	.	.	.	.	.	.	.	.	.	.	.
squared x	.	.	.	.	.	.	.	.	x	x	x	.
same scantling ■	.	.	.	.	.	.	.	.	.	.	.	.
FRONT BRACES												
roundwood *	.	.	.	.	.	.	.	.	.	*	*	*
squared ■	.	.	.	.	.	.	.	.	.	.	.	
BACK BRACES												
roundwood *	.	.	.	.	.	*	.	.	.	.	.	.
squared x	x	.	x	x	.	x	.	.	.	x	x	.
PLANKS												
cleft *	*	.	.	.	.	.	.	.	*	.	*	.
sawn ■	.	.	.	.	.	.	.	■	.	■	.	.
FASTENINGS												
pegged *	.	.	.	.	.	.	.	.	.	*	.	.
nailed x	.	.	.	.	.	.	.	.	.	.	.	.
spiked ■	.	.	.	.	.	.	.	.	.	.	.	.
STAVES												
cleft *	.	*	*	*	.	.	.	.	.	.	.	*
sawn ■	.	.	.	.	.	.	.	.	.	.	.	.
set earthfast *	.	*	*	.	.	.	.	.	.	.	.	.
e-fast & baseplate x	.	.	.	.	.	.	?	.	.	.	.	x
set in baseplate ■	.	.	.	■	■	?	.	.	.	.	.	.
STAVE BASEPLATES												
grooved *	.	.	.	*	*	.	.	.	.	.	.	*
mortised ■	.	.	.	.	.	.	.	.	.	.	.	.
SPECIES												
native *	*	*	*	*	*	*	*	.	*	*	*	*
imported ■	.	.	.	.	.	.	.	■	.	.	.	.
JOINTS												
edge-trench *	.	.	*	*	.	.	.	.	.	.	.	.
squint lap x	.	.	.	.	.	.	.	.	.	.	.	.
notched lap ■	.	.	.	.	.	.	.	.	.	■	.	.
splayed recess *	.	.	.	.	.	.	.	.	.	.	.	.
chase mortise x	.	.	.	.	.	.	.	.	.	.	.	.
square mortise *	*	.	*	*	.	.	.	.	.	.	.	.
central mortise ■	.	.	.	.	.	.	.	.	.	.	.	.
scarf *	.	.	.	.	.	.	*	.	.	.	.	.
	TX1	BG3	TX2	BG10	SH1	TX3	BG12	BG13	SH2	TX4	TX7	TL1

120. Structural attribute table showing structures described in Chapter 3 grouped chronologically. The various symbols show which of the features listed in the left hand column were recorded in each revetment.

Index of structures: Billingsgate Lorry Park site, BG3 *p.26,* BG10 *p.28,* BG12 *p.30,* BG13 *p.30,* BG14 *p.32,* BG16 *p.35.* *Seal House,* SH1 *p.37,* SH2 *p.39,* SH3 *p.40.* *Thames Exchange,* TX1 *p.45,* TX2 *p.47,* TX3 *p.50,* TX4 *p.53,* TX5 *p.56,* TX6 *p.59,* TX7 *p.60,* TX8 *p.62,* TX9 *p.63.* *Trig Lane/Sunlight Wharf,* TL1 *p.66,* TL2 *p.68,* TL3 *p.68,* TL7 *p.70,* TL10 *p.72,* TL11 *p.74.* *City of London Boys' School,* BY1 *p.76.*

C13th									C14th			C17th
BG14	BG16	SH3	TX5	TX6	TX8	TX9	TL2	TL3	TL7	TL10	TL11	BY1
.	.	.	.	.	.	.	.	.	.	.	.	.
■	■	■	■	■	■	■	■	■	■	.	.	■
.	.	.	.	.	.	.	.	.	.	.	.	.
x	x	.	.	.	.	.	.	.	.	.	.	.
.	.	■	■	■	■	.	.	■	■	.	.	■
*	.	.	.	.	.	.	*	.	.	.	.	.
.	■	■	■	■	■	■	.	■	.	.	.	.
.	.	.	.	.	.	.	.	.	.	.	.	.
.	.	.	.	x	x	x	.	x	x	x	x	.
.	.	.	.	.	.	.	.	.	.	.	.	.
■	■	?	.	?	■	?	.	.	.	.	.	■
*	*	*	.	*	*	*	.	.	.	.	.	.
.	x	.	.	x	.	.	x	x	.	.	.	.
.	.	.	.	.	.	.	.	.	.	.	.	■
.	.	.	.	.	.	.	.	.	.	*	.	.
.	.	.	.	.	.	.	.	.	.	.	■	.
.	.	.	.	.	.	.	.	.	.	.	.	.
.	.	.	.	.	.	.	.	.	.	.	.	.
.	.	.	.	.	.	.	.	.	.	■	■	.
.	.	.	.	.	.	.	.	.	.	*	.	.
.	.	.	.	.	.	.	.	.	.	.	■	.
*	*	*	*	*	*	*	*	*	*	*	*	*
.	.	.	.	.	.	.	.	.	.	.	.	■
.	.	.	.	.	.	.	.	.	*	*	*	.
.	.	.	x	.	x	x	.	.	.	.	.	.
.	.	.	.	.	.	.	.	.	.	.	.	.
*	.	*	.	.	*	*	.	.	.	.	.	.
x	.	x	.	x	x	.	x	x	.	x	x	.
.	.	.	.	.	.	.	.	.	.	.	.	.
■	.	■	■	■	■	■	■	■	■	■	■	■
.	*	*	.	.	.	*	.	*	*	*	*	.
BG14	BG16	SH3	TX5	TX6	TX8	TX9	TL2	TL3	TL7	TL10	TL11	BY1

Do you remember?

Copy these sentences, and think of a sensible word to fill each gap.

1. When fish sleep their _______ slow down.
2. The slippery sides of a bath make it _______ for a spider to climb out.
3. Bats have special _______ to help them hang upside down.
4. Budgies' feet are naturally _______ when they sleep.
5. An _______ has large ears to help to keep it cool.
6. Fish swim in shoals to _______ themselves from attack.

More to think about

Write a sentence to answer each question.

1. Do spiders get into baths by coming up the plug hole?
2. Why might it be unsafe for bats to roost on the ground?
3. How can we tell that birds naturally clench their feet?
4. Give three reasons why fish often swim in shoals.
5. What happens to a fish's brain pattern when it sleeps?

Now try these

1. Find a word or phrase in one of the passages that means the same as:
   a) the place where fish live
   b) to hang upside down
   c) gripping firmly
   d) very large
   e) creatures likely to attack other creatures
2. Think of a sensible ending for each of these sentences.
   Write the complete sentences in your book.
   A reference book may be useful to check your answers.
   a) Giraffes evolved with long necks so that ...
   b) Some people think wolves howl at the moon because ...
   c) We know what dinosaurs looked like by ...
   d) Tigers have stripes to ...
   e) Cactuses have thorns to prevent ...

UNIT 2 The Big Match

Danebridge Primary School's team are leading 3–2 against Shenby School when disaster strikes!

The cup match became an exciting end-to-end battle as the teams threw everything they had left at each other and both goals survived narrow squeaks. Time was rapidly running out, though, for Shenby when they forced Chris to tip the ball round the post for yet another corner and Tim signalled everyone back into the penalty area to protect their slender lead.

The winger played a neat short-corner before whipping the ball across into the box through a great ruck of bodies. It suddenly loomed up in front of Duggan who reacted by blocking it with his hand in panic before a Shenby player could get at it.

As he booted it away, the Shenby team and their supporters were already loudly demanding a penalty for hand-ball and he slumped to the ground in distress.

"It was an accident, I didn't mean to," he pleaded, shaking his head and failing to find any excuse for his stunned team-mates. "I don't know why I did it – it just happened..."

The referee had no choice but to award a penalty and all their hard work seemed to be wasted. Duggan's eyes were not the only ones to be fixed on the goalkeeper Chris in the desperate hope that he could yet somehow rescue the situation.

The spectators grew hushed in anticipation of the duel, the final shoot-out, and some of the players grouped around the edge of the area hardly dared to watch as the Shenby captain prepared to run in to take the penalty.

Duggan stood, head bowed, hoping for a miracle.

Grandad removed the pipe from his mouth, moistened his lips with his tongue and said a little silent prayer.

Mr Jones wiped his hand nervously down his face as the suspense and tension mounted.

But they could do nothing more to help. It was simply all up to Chris.

Rob Childs

Do you remember?

Write a sentence in your book to answer each question.

1. Which two teams were playing the match?
2. Who was Danebridge's goal-keeper?
3. Who was Danebridge's captain?
4. Why was it a bad day for Duggan?
5. Who took the penalty?

More to think about

1. Find these phrases in the passage, and write them in your own words.
   a) when disaster strikes
   b) a great ruck of bodies
   c) both goals survived narrow squeaks
   d) rescue the situation
   e) Time was rapidly running out
   f) hushed in anticipation
   g) their slender lead
   h) hoping for a miracle
2. Write a sentence in your book to answer each question.
   a) Why was it an important match?
   b) Why did Duggan touch the ball?
   c) How do we know Duggan was deeply upset?
   d) Why did some of the players hardly dare to watch when the penalty was being taken?
3. Write a few sentences describing how you imagine the story finishes.

Now try these

1. How would you have felt, and what thoughts would have been going through your mind, if you were:
   a) Duggan b) Chris c) Grandad d) The Shenby team captain?
2. Duggan and Chris loved football. It was their favourite game. Do you have a favourite sport? Give your reasons. If you don't like any sports or games say why.

UNIT 3 A Clever Way to Catch a Thief

There's an old West Indian tale about a rich man who found that he was constantly losing things from his house. He suspects that one of his servants may be stealing, but which servant, and how could he possibly be sure? Then he thought of a plan.

One evening, when it was getting dark and the servants had finished their day's work, he brought them all together.
"Sadly," he said, "we seem to have a thief amongst us, but with your help I think we can rid ourselves of him or her." The servants looked at each other, sorry to think that one of their number was untrustworthy, but uncertain how the rich man could possibly detect the culprit.
"I have placed a table in the centre of the room next door, and on the table is a box. I have put into the box an old cockerel that possesses magic powers. In turn I want each of you to go into the room. It is dark in there, but don't put on any light. Feel your way to the table and gently rest your left hand on the box."
"But what will that show?" asked one of the servants, quite perplexed.
"If you are not the guilty one, nothing will happen – but if you are the thief, the magic cockerel will immediately detect this and will crow so loudly we shall all immediately hear, and know who is to blame."
The servants glanced at each other, some thinking the rich man might be going mad! Other servants were anxious, not sure whether the cockerel really did possess magic powers. What might happen to them, they thought, if left alone in the dark room with the strange creature?
"If you are innocent you have nothing to fear," reassured the rich man.
So, one by one, the servants went into the room, but not a sound was heard. Not once did the magic cockerel crow.

"Excellent!" exclaimed the rich man as the last servant emerged from the dark room. "Now we know for sure who is the guilty person."
The servants were totally puzzled. "There is a very good reason why the cockerel made no sound. There was no cockerel in the box to make a sound! Each of you now show me your left hand. There was no cockerel, but there was soot on top of the box," said the man. "You," he exclaimed, thrusting his finger towards the only servant with a clean hand, "must be the guilty person. You were the only person frightened to place your hand on top of the box!"

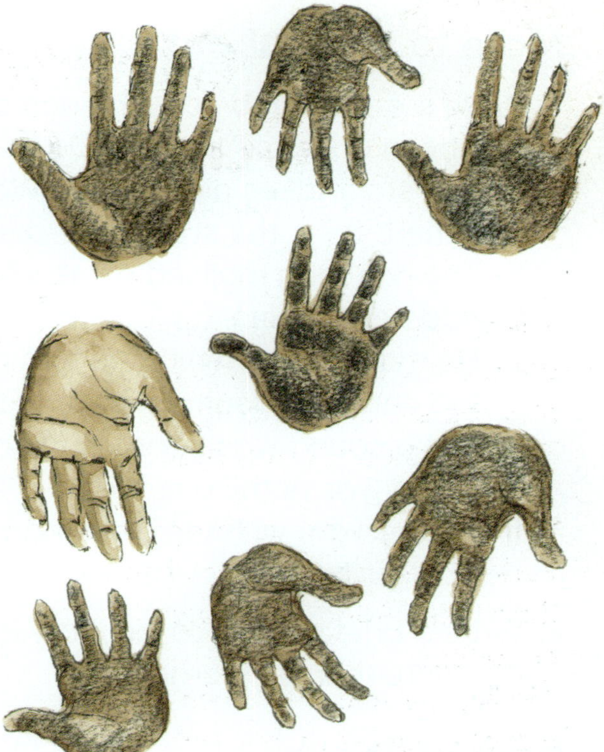

Do you remember?

Copy these sentences into your book, choosing the best ending.

1. The rich man thought his things were being stolen by
   a) a burglar who had broken in.
   b) one of his servants.
   c) the gardener.
2. The servants were
   a) sorry to think one of them was untrustworthy.
   b) cross that the rich man suspected them.
   c) sure they knew who had stolen the goods.
3. The rich man told his servants to
   a) go together into the darkened room.
   b) go one at a time into the darkened room.
   c) not to go into the darkened room.
4. Inside the room there was
   a) an empty box on the table.
   b) a box on the table with a cockerel inside.
   c) a policeman.
5. The box was
   a) painted black.
   b) covered in black soot.
   c) covered with a black cloth.

More to think about

1. Write a question to go with each of these answers. The first one has been done to help you. Don't forget your question marks.
   a) The story takes place in the West Indies.
      Where does the story take place?
   b) The rich man realised some of his things had been stolen.
   c) He made each servant in turn go into the darkened room and touch the box.
   d) Not a sound was heard in the room.
   e) There was nothing in the box.
   f) The servant with the clean hand was guilty.

2. Write a brief version of the story in not more than 40 words.

Now try these

1. Write some sentences to answer these questions.
   a) This story took place many years ago. Do you think this method of detection would work now? Say why.
   b) If this story were to happen now, and you were a police officer, how would you set about solving the crime?

2. Copy these lists next to each other in your book. Draw a line between the words or phrases that have similar meanings. The first one has been done to help you.

detect	cried out
culprit	guilty person
perplexed	find out
guilty	straight away
immediately	uneasy
anxious	not guilty
innocent	pushing
thrusting	puzzled
exclaimed	committed an offence

3. Did you enjoy reading this short story?
   Write a few sentences describing to a friend who hasn't read the story what you think they would like most about it, or what they might not like about it.

UNIT 4 The Invisible Dog

Rupert, the great Dane, died when Janie was only two, but many years later, when she was looking around in the garage, Janie found his collar and lead.

The collar was a very big, broad, brass-studded one with a round metal disc attached to the buckle. She rubbed the disc clear of dust and there, scratched on the face, was the name RUPERT and, underneath, their telephone number.

Janie put the collar to her nose. It smelt of leather and dog, and just for a moment it made her feel sad to think that this faint smell was all that was left of the creature whose great neck the collar had encircled. How many hundreds of times in his eight years of life would he have gone for a walk wearing it, with Mum or Dad holding the end of the thick plaited lead?

Janie went out of the garden gate and wandered up the lane, the loop of the lead in her left hand, the empty collar dangling. She looked down at the thick leather circlet and imagined the shape and sweep of the great neck, the Great Dane neck, within it. She saw the dog clearly in her mind's eye as it walked beside her.

Lost in a daydream, she almost bumped into Mrs Garrow, an elderly widow who lived alone in one of the cottages at the top end of the village.

"Hullo, Janie! Where are you off to then?" said the old lady with a loud laugh. Mrs Garrow's laugh sounded like nothing so much as a duck quacking.
"I'm taking my dog for a walk," said Janie.
"I can see that," said Mrs Garrow, and she put out a hand and patted the air behind the dog's collar, just where the dog's back would have been.
"Who's a good boy then?" said Mrs Garrow. "He's looking ever so well, Janie; you must be proud of him," ... and she went on her way quacking loudly.
Some people never grow too old for games of make-believe, thought Janie. That's nice. And two can play at that.
"Heel!" she said, and she walked on, the invisible dog pacing at her side.

Dick King-Smith

Do you remember?

Write the correct answer to each question in your book.

1. Who was Rupert?
   a) Rupert was a pet dog. b) Rupert was Janie's brother.
2. What type of dog was Rupert.
   a) He was a Great Dane. b) He was a Labrador.
3. How old was Janie when Rupert died?
   a) Janie was eight when Rupert died.
   b) Janie was two when Rupert died.
4. How old was Rupert when he died?
   a) Rupert died when he was eight. b) Rupert died when he was two.

4. Ask one of your audience to feel the matchstick inside the handkerchief, and to break it.

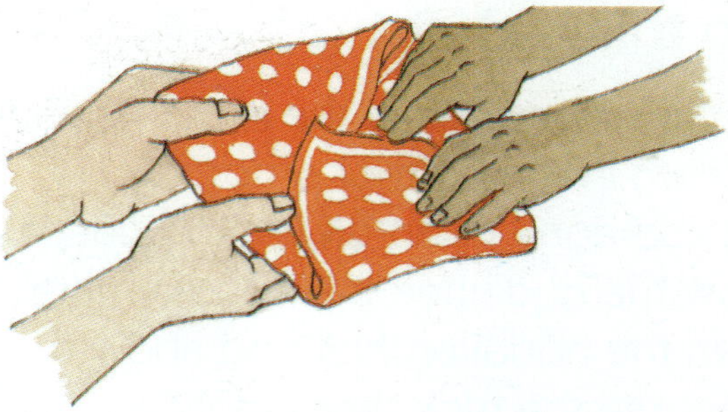

5. Shake the handkerchief, allowing the unbroken matchstick to fall onto the floor!

The secret:

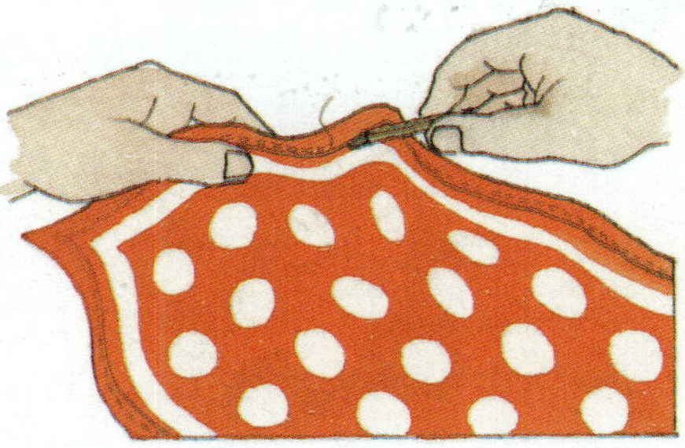

Before you begin the performance, slip a matchstick into the hem of the handkerchief. When you ask someone to break the wrapped-up matchstick make sure that they break the one hidden in the hem (when they feel it they will think it is the one which they saw you wrap into the handkerchief).
It's a good idea to have two or three handkerchiefs with matchsticks already secreted in the hems, as your audience is bound to be flabbergasted and ask you to do the trick again. But don't let them realise that you are changing handkerchiefs, or they may become suspicious!

Do you remember?

What words are missing? Choose a word from the box to fill each gap. Write the missing words in your book.

practise	tricks	women	audience	magician
thoroughly	embarrassed	hats	rabbits	work

Magicians often seem to perform impossible __1__. The most famous tricks are getting white __2__ from __3__ and cutting __4__ in half! If you want to be a __5__ the most important secret is to __6__ your tricks __7__. If you don't practise, your tricks will not __8__ and your __9__ will laugh and you will feel __10__!

More to think about

1. These sentences about the matchstick trick have been muddled up. Write them in the correct order.
   Ask someone to break the matchstick in the handkerchief.
   Show the audience the handkerchief.
   Open the handkerchief and show the unbroken matchstick.
   Rehearse the trick thoroughly.
   Collect together a handkerchief and some matchsticks.
   Wrap the matchstick in the handkerchief.
   Show the audience a matchstick.

2. Do you know a magic trick? If you do, write the instructions step by step like those for the matchstick trick. If you don't, write instructions to teach a young child how to cross a busy road.

Now try these

1. Which word in the passage means:
   a) fascinated (in the first paragraph)
   b) not possible (in the first paragraph)
   c) practising (in the first paragraph)
   d) hidden (in the last paragraph)
   e) amazed (in the last paragraph)
   f) doubtful (in the last paragraph)

2. Imagine that you really do have a magic wand. You can use it to change three things, but three things only!
   Write in your book what you will change, and say why.

UNIT 7

The Shark

A treacherous monster is the Shark
He never makes the least remark.

And when he sees you on the sand,
He doesn't seem to want to land.

He watches you take off your clothes,
And not the least excitement shows.

His eyes do not grow bright or roll,
He has astounding self-control.

He waits till you are quite undrest,
And seems to take no interest.

And when towards the sea you leap,
He looks as if he were asleep.

But when you once get in his range,
His whole demeanour seems to change.

He throws his body right about,
And his true character comes out.

It's no use crying or appealing,
He seems to lose all decent feeling.

After this warning you will wish
To keep clear of this treacherous fish.

His back is black, his stomach white,
He has a very dangerous bite.

Lord Alfred Douglas

Do you remember?

Copy these sentences into your book.
Find words from the poem to fill the gaps.

1. The poem is about a _______ .
2. He watches as the boy takes off his _______ .
3. He pretends to take no _______ .
4. The shark even pretends that he's _______ .
5. Then suddenly he throws his _______ about.
6. You can then see he has a black _______ .
7. He has a white _______ .
8. He has a very dangerous _______ .

More to think about

1. Write a sentence to answer each question.
   a) Why are sharks said to be treacherous?
   b) Explain why the poet says the shark has 'astounding self-control'.
   c) Why does the shark pretend to be asleep as the boy runs down to the sea?
   d) What is the 'true character' of the shark?
   e) Is this poem fair to all sharks? Give your reasons.
2. Rewrite the poem as if it were an article for a newspaper. The poem doesn't tell us what happened in the end, but your article should.

Now try these

1. Write these phrases in another way. Use a dictionary to help you.
   a) a treacherous monster (line 1)
   b) never makes the least remark (line 2)
   c) not the least excitement shows (line 6)
   d) astounding self-control (line 8)
   e) his whole demeanour (line 14)
   f) throws his body right about (line 15)
   g) his true character (line 16)
   h) all decent feeling (line 18)
2. Write one-word answers to these questions in your book.
   a) One word in the poem is not spelt as we would spell it now. Which word is it?
   b) Which word rhymes with **sand**?
   c) Which word rhymes with **asleep**?
   d) Which word rhymes with **change**?
   e) Which word rhymes with **appealing**?
3. Imagine that you were the shark in the poem. Tell the story in your own words, from the shark's point of view. Start when you are basking in the warmth of the sun, and suddenly you spot...
4. What would you say to your friends to encourage them to read this poem?

UNIT 8 Noisy Neighbours

Southborough Council
High Street Southborough

Environmental Health Department

Mr J Trigger
Flat 9
High Risings
Hornsey Lane
Southborough

1st October

Dear Sir

I fear that we have received yet another complaint from one of your neighbours concerning the noise emanating from your home. This is not the first occasion we have had cause to draw this matter to your attention; I refer to my letters of 29th July and 16th August.

On both previous occasions you assured me that the problem would cease forthwith, but those promises appear not to have been worth the paper they were written on.

The present complaint refers not only to the volume of the music which you, or other members of your family, are playing on your stereo from early morning until after midnight, but also to the sound of the dogs who it seems are tearing each other limb from limb, to the agonising sounds of the violin which one of your children is presumably learning, and to the electrical household appliances which I'm informed are in use incessantly.

This letter is our final warning before we shall be forced to take out a court injunction to restrain your total disregard for the welfare of your distraught neighbours!

Yours faithfully,

B Quiet

Mr B Quiet
Complaints Officer

Do you remember?

Write the correct answer to each question in your book.

1. Who is the letter from?
   a) The letter is from the Complaints Officer of Southborough Council.
   b) The letter is from Mr Trigger.
2. What is the Complaints Officer's name?
   a) The Complaints Officer is Mr L Noise.
   b) The Complaints Officer is Mr B Quiet.
3. When was the letter sent?
   a) The letter was sent on 1st October.
   b) The letter was sent on 1st December.
4. What is the letter about?
   a) It is about the noise coming from Mr Trigger's flat.
   b) It is about the smell coming from Mr Trigger's flat.
5. Is this the first letter sent to Mr Trigger about noise?
   a) Yes, this is the first letter.
   b) No, there have been other letters sent to him.
6. What happened when the last letter was sent?
   a) When the last letter was sent Mr Trigger made sure all the noise stopped.
   b) Nothing changed when the last letter was sent.
7. What will happen if this letter is ignored?
   a) The Council will take Mr Trigger to court if he ignores this letter.
   b) Nothing will happen if Mr Trigger ignores this letter.

More to think about

Write a sentence to answer each question.

1. How many letters has Mr Quiet sent to Mr Trigger?
2. How did Mr Quiet know a lot of noise was coming from Mr Trigger's flat?
3. Why is Mr Quiet particularly cross with Mr Trigger?
4. Does Mr Trigger live alone in the flat?
5. What are the main causes of the noise?
6. What will happen if the noise is not reduced?

Now try these

1. Copy these lists next to each other in your book. Draw a line between the words from the letter to the words or phrases that have a similar meaning. Use a dictionary if you need to. The first one has been done to help you.

Words in the letter	**Meanings**
emanating	promised
occasion	coming from
assured	constantly
cease	time
forthwith	awful
agonising	stop
incessantly	prevent
restrain	extremely agitated
disregard	lack of consideration
distraught	immediately

2. Write in your book a few sentences to answer each of these questions.
   a) It's a free country, so do you think people should be allowed to make as much noise as they want? Give reasons for your answer.
   b) Has anyone ever really annoyed you in some way? What was the reason, and how was it sorted out?
   c) What things should people be most aware of to prevent upsetting their neighbours?

UNIT 10 The Borrowers

The Borrowers are a race of tiny people living, hidden, in houses – or wherever they can find a safe, convenient place – who own nothing except what they borrow from 'human beans'.

"I've lost the crochet hook..."(they were making a bed-quilt – in woollen squares: there were thirty still to do), "I know where I put it," she went on hastily; "I put it on the bottom shelf of the book-case just beside my bed."
"On the bottom shelf?" repeated Mrs May, her own needle flicking steadily in the firelight. "Near the floor?"
"Yes," said Kate, "But I looked on the floor. Under the rug. Everywhere. The wool was still there though. Just where I'd left it."
"Oh dear," exclaimed Mrs May lightly, "don't say they're in this house too!"
"That what are?" asked Kate.
"The Borrowers," said Mrs May, and in the half light she seemed to smile.
Kate stared a little fearfully.
"Are there such things?" she asked after a moment.
"As what?"
Kate blinked her eyelids.
"As people, other people, living in a house who... borrow things?"

Mrs May laid down her work.
"What do you think?" she asked.
"I don't know," said Kate looking away and pulling hard at her shoe button. "There can't be. And yet" – she raised her head – "and yet sometimes I think there must be."
"Why do you think there must be?" asked Mrs May.
"Because of all the things that disappear. Safety-pins, for instance. Factories go on making safety-pins, and every day people go on buying safety-pins and yet,

somehow, there is never a safety-pin just when you want one. Where are they all? Now, at this minute? Where do they all go? Take needles," she went on. "All the needles my mother ever bought – there must be hundreds – can't just be lying around this house."

"Not lying about this house, no," agreed Mrs May. "And all the other things we keep on buying. Again and again and again. Like pencils and match-boxes and sealing wax and hair slides and drawing pins and thimbles –"

"And hatpins," put in Mrs May, "and blotting-paper."

"Yes, blotting-paper," agreed Kate, "but not hatpins."

"That's where you're wrong," said Mrs May, and she picked up her work again. "There was a reason for hatpins."

Kate stared. "A reason?" she repeated. "I mean – what kind of a reason?"

"Well, there are two reasons really. A hatpin is a very useful weapon and" – Mrs May laughed suddenly – "but it all sounds such nonsense and" – she hesitated – "it was so very long ago!"

"But tell me" said Kate, "tell me how you *know* about the hatpin. Did you ever see one?"

Mrs May threw her a startled glance. "Well, yes – " she began.

"Not a hatpin," exclaimed Kate impatiently, "a – what-ever-do-you-call-them, a Borrower?"

Mrs May drew a sharp breath. "No," she said quickly, "I never saw one."

"But someone else saw one," cried Kate, "and you know about it. I can see you do!"

"Hush," said Mrs May, "no need to shout!" She gazed downwards at the upturned face and then she smiled and her eyes slid away into the distance.

Mary Norton

Do you remember?

1. Write a sentence to answer each question.
   a) Who are the Borrowers?
   b) Where do they live?
   c) What were Mrs May and Kate making?
   d) What had Kate lost?
   e) Where did she think she had put the crochet hook?

2. Read these sentences about the story. Copy only the ones that are true.

   The crochet hook was missing, but the wool was still there.

   Kate told Mrs May about the Borrowers.

   Their name for people was 'human beans'.

   Kate wore lace-up shoes.

   The little people collected things like pencils, hair slides, drawing pins.

   According to Mrs May the Borrowers weren't interested in hatpins.

   Mrs May had seen the Borrowers on several occasions.

   Mrs May knew someone who had met the Borrowers.

More to think about

1. Write a sentence to answer each question.
   a) Why was the race of little people called the Borrowers?
   b) Why did the Borrowers call people 'human beans'?
   c) What time of the day, and at what time of the year, is the story probably taking place? How can you tell?
   d) How did Kate feel when Mrs May first mentioned the Borrowers?
   e) Why did Kate begin to feel impatient with Mrs May?
2. Make a list of the clues in the passage that tell us *The Borrowers* was written about 50 years ago.

Now try these

1. Whenever strange things happen people look for reasons. Do you think it is possible that there could be, or could ever have been, a race of tiny people like the Borrowers? Give your reasons.
2. Imagine that you were accidentally given a spoonful of medicine that had the unexpected effect of shrinking you. Write about some of the dangers, but also about some of the things you could do if you were tiny that you can't do at your usual size.
3. Does this passage from *The Borrowers* make you feel you would like to read the whole book? Give your reasons.

Progress Unit A
A Nasty Smile

The first person Wendy saw at school was Simon McTavish. He was roaring around the playground whirling his bag above his head. Wendy took a deep breath and walked into school hoping he wouldn't notice her.

"Now then children," Mrs Paterson began. "I've had an idea. And where do I always have my best ideas?"

"In the bath," they chorused.

"Quite right," she laughed. "Well now, I was in my bath last night and I was wondering what we should do for the Parents' Evening this Christmas. Year Three are doing the Nativity play this year. Year Four are cooking the mince pies and Year Five are decorating the hall. What shall we do? I know, I thought Year Six will put on an exhibition of 'Interesting Things' in the front hall, so that people will have something to look at while they're eating their mince pies. Well, what do you think?"

Simon McTavish pretended to yawn noisily, but she ignored him.

"Well then, why don't we all try to bring in something interesting, something from the past maybe, something from a far-off country, something amazing, something special."

Mrs Paterson did go on a bit, but Wendy liked her because she laughed a lot.

Sarah said she had a three-legged milking stool. Sharon had a telescope and Vince said he'd bring in a fox's tail.

"And how about you, Wendy?" she said.

There was only one thing Wendy could think of.

"We've got an old war helmet, Miss," she said. "It's my grandad's. He had it in the war. It's a bit rusty though."

"Like your grandad then," said Simon McTavish and everyone sniggered. Wendy felt the tears coming.

"A helmet will be just fine, Wendy," said Mrs Paterson quickly. Then she turned to Simon. "And Simon McTavish, you've got a brain like a soggy Weetabix."

Now they were all laughing at Simon instead, and Wendy suddenly felt a lot better. But for the rest of the day she kept finding Simon McTavish looking at her. There was a very nasty smile on his face.

Michael Morpurgo

Do you remember?

Think of sensible words from the passage to finish these sentences and write them in your book.

1. Wendy was afraid of....
2. Her teacher was....
3. Mrs Paterson had her best ideas....
4. She thought for Parents' Evening her class could hold an....
5. Wendy said she could bring....
6. When Simon McTavish was rude Wendy....

More to think about

Write a few sentences to answer each question.

1. What sort of person was Simon McTavish? Why do you think this?
2. How do we know that Wendy was afraid of him?
3. Why did Wendy like her teacher?
4. If you were Mrs Paterson, how would you have felt about Simon McTavish?

Now try these

1. What do you think happened in the end? Make up your own ending for this story.
2. If you were being threatened or bullied, write in your book what each of these people would say if you told them:
   a) your teacher b) your mum c) your grandad d) your best friend
3. Write in your book how you would feel, and what you would do, if:
   a) your younger brother or sister was being bullied
   b) your best friend was frightened of a gang in the playground.

UNIT 11 Around and Around it Goes

Water is a **liquid**; but it can also be a **solid** when it is very cold and turns to **ice**. It can also be a **gas**, when it evaporates and becomes **water vapour**.

The water cycle

Water is one of the most common substances, and without it life on Earth would be impossible. The oceans that cover three quarters of the Earth's surface can be thought of as our great water reservoirs. All the time, water is being evaporated from the ocean's surface by the warmth of the sun. High in the sky this moisture, or water vapour, turns into clouds which drift back over the land, often creating rainfall. As the rain falls, it seeps into the soil and eventually into rivers that flow back into the oceans, where it is ready to begin all over again!

Do you remember?

Write the correct answer to each question in your book.

1. What is water that has become solid?
   a) Water that has turned to a solid is ice.
   b) Water that has turned to a solid is water vapour.
2. How much of the Earth is covered by water?
   a) Three quarters of the Earth is covered by water.
   b) One quarter of the Earth is covered by water.
3. What happens when the sea is warmed by the sun?
   a) The sea begins to bubble.
   b) Some water turns into water vapour.
4. What happens to the water vapour?
   a) The water vapour turns into clouds and rain.
   b) The water vapour turns into blue gas.
5. Where does the most of the rain go?
   a) Most of the rain finds its way into rivers that flow back to the sea.
   b) Most of the rain turns into snow.

More to think about

1. These sentences about the water cycle have been muddled up. Write them in the correct order.

   Rain falls from the clouds.

   Warmed water turns into water vapour and rises into the sky.

   The rivers take the water back to the sea.

   The clouds drift over the land.

   The water seeps through the soil and back into rivers.

   As the water vapour cools it turns into clouds.

   Start with:

   Warmed water turns into water vapour and rises into the sky.

2. Write a sentence to answer each question.
   a) Why is this process called 'the water cycle'?
   b) Why is there usually more rain on the hills near the coast of large land areas than there is in their centres?
   c) Is there usually more rain if the wind is blowing towards the land or towards the sea?
   d) What would the weather be like on land if the wind was blowing the clouds away from the land and out to sea?
   e) What causes a river to flood?

Now try these

1. What do these weather words mean? Use a dictionary to help you.
   a) precipitation
   b) cyclone
   c) evaporation
   d) drought
   e) drizzle
   f) storm
2. Why would life on Earth be impossible without water?
3. Why are we sometimes short of water for our taps? What are the main problems for people when there is a shortage of water? What sorts of people suffer most?

Do you remember?

Copy these sentences. Fill in the missing words.

1. The only thing the chicken had known since she hatched had been other chickens and _______ _______.
2. Even being stung by fierce little cold _______ felt wonderful.
3. The noise the _______ made was deafening.
4. Being outside in the fresh _______ was great.
5. But the chicken had never realised how many different _______ go to make up fresh air.

More to think about

Write some sentences to answer each of these questions.

1. Why is the passage called 'I go chicken-dippy'?
2. Why did the chicken say she couldn't handle it at all?
3. The author has written mostly in short, sharp sentences. Why do you think this might be?
4. What things do you think the chicken was most pleased to have left behind?
5. What aspects of her new environment did the chicken find difficult to handle at first?
6. What message is the author trying to get across to her readers in this passage?

Now try these

1. Chickens are usually kept in huge flocks packed into sheds or in very small cages because farmers can produce eggs and chickens for food much more cheaply that way. Many people wouldn't be able to afford to buy eggs and chicken if they were all allowed to run free in fields. Also, more of the chickens would be killed by foxes if they were running free. How do you think chickens should be kept? Give reasons for your answer.

2. Imagine that you have had a serious accident and have been told you can't leave your bed for many months. What would you miss most? Think especially of some of the very ordinary things we usually take for granted. Make a list, and say why you will miss each thing.

3. This passage is from *The Chicken Gave It To Me* by Anne Fine. Do you feel that you would now like to read the rest of the book? Write a few sentences to explain why.

UNIT 15

Finding Your Way About

River is one of 12 books in a series called *Landshapes*. It is an excellent book about rivers, but if we are to be able to use it to find the information we need it is important that we can use the Contents page and the Index page.

The Contents (at the front of the book) tells us how the information is organised.

The Index (at the back) tells us where to find specific items of information.

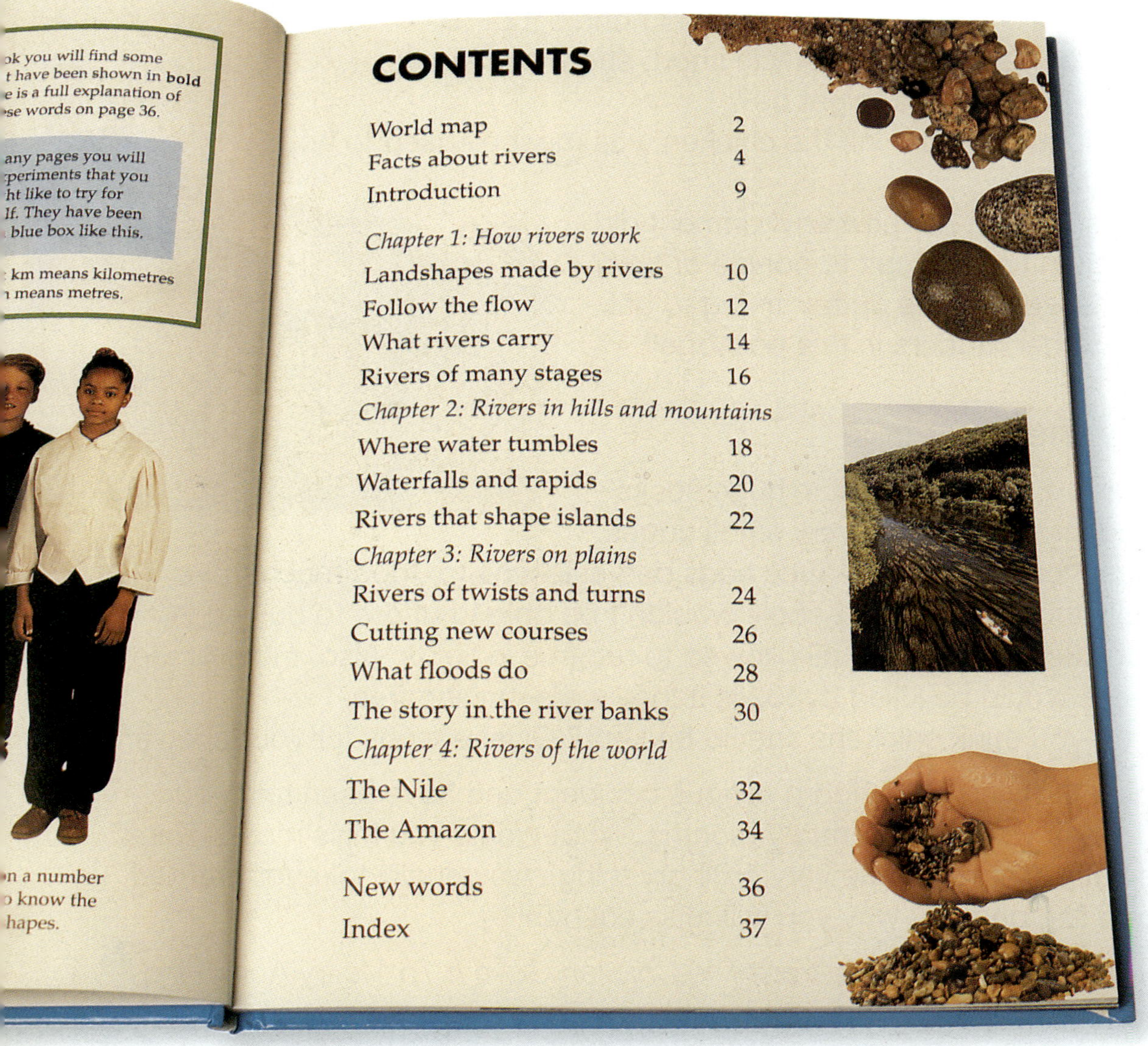

ok you will find some t have been shown in **bold** e is a full explanation of se words on page 36.

any pages you will periments that you ht like to try for lf. They have been blue box like this.

km means kilometres 1 means metres.

n a number o know the hapes.

CONTENTS